WHEN THE SHOOTING STOPPED

OSPREY
PUBLISHING

For Sally, who suggested it.

WHEN THE SHOOTING STOPPED

AUGUST
1945

BARRETT TILLMAN

OSPREY PUBLISHING
Bloomsbury Publishing Plc
Kemp House, Chawley Park, Cumnor Hill, Oxford OX2 9PH, UK
29 Earlsfort Terrace, Dublin 2, Ireland
1385 Broadway, 5th Floor, New York, NY 10018, USA
E-mail: info@ospreypublishing.com
www.ospreypublishing.com

OSPREY is a trademark of Osprey Publishing Ltd

First published in Great Britain in 2022

This paperback edition was first published in Great Britain in 2023 by Osprey Publishing.

For legal purposes the Acknowledgments on pp. 263–264 constitute an extension of this
copyright page.

ISBN: HB 978 1 4728 4898 7; PB 978 1 4728 4896 3; eBook 978 1 4728 4895 6;
ePDF 978 1 4728 4897 0; XML 978 1 4728 4899 4

23 24 25 26 27   10 9 8 7 6 5 4 3 2 1

Index by Alan Rutter

Typeset by Deanta Global Publishing Services, Chennai, India
Printed and bound in Great Britain by CPI (Group) UK Ltd, Croydon CR0 4YY

Osprey Publishing supports the Woodland Trust, the UK's leading woodland
conservation charity.

To find out more about our authors and books visit www.ospreypublishing.com. Here
you will find extracts, author interviews, details of forthcoming events and the option to
sign up for our newsletter.

Contents

Prologue

August 1945

"Bogies seven o'clock high!"

In the era of radio communication, the warning of unidentified aircraft above and behind the friendlies crackled with bone-chilling intensity. Instinctively, the young Americans – all aged between 19 and 26 – craned their necks over their left shoulders. The sharp-eyed ensign in the trailing Hellcat had saved an even worse surprise for his seven squadron mates. He was going to add more when his flight leader interrupted: "They're Japs!"

At that point none of the carrier aviators needed further instruction. They extended their left arms to full throttle, coordinating right hands with rudder feet in steeply banked turns to meet the threat.

In the cockpits of a dozen Imperial Navy Mitsubishi fighters – a mixture of nimbly elegant Zeros and potently ugly Jacks – aces and rookies alike savored the setup. Their controller had placed them in almost perfect position for a bounce on the intruders just over spume-tossed gray waves washing Honshu's eastern shore.[*]

The 20 contesting fighter pilots shared much besides Japanese airspace. Minutes earlier the U.S. Third Fleet had radioed a ceasefire, ordering the day's first strike mission to abort and

---

[*] Honshu is the largest and most populated island of Japan; the literal translation means "main province."

return to base because Tokyo had accepted surrender. With elevated pulses, the Hellcat pilots stuffed that joyous news under the manholes of their consciousness as they reordered their priorities. Job one now was survival. Nobody wanted to succumb to "the last man syndrome," to be the final casualty in a long, bitter, sanguinary war.

As the two American flights reversed into the diving Japanese dozen, gloved fingers curled around triggers in molded plastic stick grips. In that desperate maneuver the four-plane divisions lost cohesion as wingmen slid abeam of section leaders, breaking into fighting pairs. Any semblance of organization was lost as both formations shredded at the merge, hosing off .50-caliber machine gun ammunition in one direction and 20mm cannon rounds in the other.

Both sides scored hits; both sides took losses. One Hellcat caught a volley of explosive rounds and pitched upward, out of control. Another broke away, streaming smoke, seeking the sanctuary of the sea.

A Zeke lost a head-on encounter with six Browning .50s, gushed flame, and snap-rolled to destruction.

Then began the manic, unchoreographed dance that was dogfighting. If the war was seemingly over, the dying was not.

List of Illustrations

U.S. President Harry S. Truman, who as vice president succeeded Franklin D. Roosevelt in April 1945 and oversaw the rest of the war. (Naval History and Heritage Command))

British Prime Minister Winston S. Churchill inscribed a sentiment to the cruiser USS *Quincy* (CA-71) in Alexandria, Egypt, after the Yalta conference in February 1945. After four years he lost re-election in July, overlapping the Potsdam Conference. (Naval History and Heritage Command)

Nationalist China's leader Chiang Kai Shek fought the Japanese from 1937 onward. (Bettmann/Getty Images)

Chinese Communist leader Mao Tse-Tung, occasional ally and eventual victor over Chiang's nationalists. (Bettmann/Getty Images)

Admiral Lord Louis Mountbatten, Royal Navy, who held commands from destroyers in the Atlantic to the Southeast Asia Theater of Operations. (NARA)

Commanding Third Fleet's carrier striking arm was Vice Admiral John S. McCain, Sr., known for his low-key demeanor and his floppy hat without the grommet. (NARA)

Allies at sea. Admiral Sir Bruce Fraser, whose British Pacific Fleet operated alongside Fleet Admiral Chester Nimitz's U.S. Pacific Fleet. (Naval History and Heritage Command)

Admiral William F. Halsey, Third Fleet commander, consults a plotting table. To his immediate left is Rear Admiral C.H. McMorris, his chief of staff for the last two years of the war. (Naval History and Heritage Command.)

Sailors of the battleship USS *Pennsylvania* (BB-38) pump out water
 over her quarterdeck, after being torpedoed in Buckner Bay,
 Okinawa, on August 12. Note the hoses lead out through her
 aft 14-inch guns. (Naval History and Heritage Command)
Enthusiastic sailors mark up bombs on board USS *Shangri-La*
 (CV-38) during the final days of hostilities. (Naval History
 and Heritage Command)
Observing from a North American PBJ bomber, American-born
 Lieutenant Minoru Wada directs Marine Corps aircraft to
 a Japanese Army headquarters on the Philippine island of
 Mindanao, August 10.(Photo by Lt. David D. Duncan/
 FPG/Staff/Hulton Archive/Getty Images)
Major General Curtis E. LeMay directed the B-29 bombing
 campaigns from India, China, and the Marianas with
 increasing success. He also supported the atomic bomb
 missions that helped convince Emperor Hirohito to end
 the war. (USAF)
Colonel Paul W. Tibbets stands beside the Boeing B-29 *Enola
 Gay*, named for his mother, that he piloted on its historic
 atomic bombing mission over Hiroshima on August 6.
 (Bettmann/Getty Images)
A Japanese soldier walks through the atomic bomb-leveled
 city of Hiroshima, September 1945. Photographed by Lt.
 Wayne Miller, USNR. (NARA)
"Fat Man's" mushroom cloud over Nagasaki on August 9. (Courtesy
 of the National Archives/Newsmakers/Getty Images)
Soviet Premier Joseph Stalin, who ruled as head of government
 and head of state. (Photo by ullstein bild Dtl./ullstein bild
 via Getty Images)
Soviet Marshal Alexander Mikhailovich Vasilevsky, who
 commanded the triple-axis assault into Japanese-occupied
 Manchuria in August 1945. (Photo by TASS via Getty
 Images)
Russian sailors of the Red Banner Amur Flotilla are greeted by
 residents in the Chinese section of Harbin, Manchuria,
 August 1945. (Photo by: Sovfoto/Universal Images Group
 via Getty Images)

Engaged in Operation *August Storm*'s western prong, Red
Army automatic riflemen of the Trans-Baikal Front in the
streets of captured Hailar, Manchuria. (Photo by: Sovfoto/
Universal Images Group via Getty Images)

Last portrait of a warrior. The kamikaze master, Vice Admiral
Matome Ugaki, prepares to board a dive bomber at Oita on
August 15, prior to the last suicide mission. He holds a dagger
he had received from Admiral Isoroku Yamamoto. The
Yokosuka Judy crashed near Okinawa. (NARA)

Task Force 38 maneuvering off the coast of Japan on August 17,
two days after Japan agreed to surrender. The aircraft carrier
in lower right is USS *Wasp* (CV-18). Also present are five
other Essex-class carriers, four light carriers, at least three
battleships, plus several cruisers and destroyers. (US Navy/
NARA)

Allied troops brandishing fresh bread upon liberation from a
Japanese prisoner camp on Taiwan (Formosa). (Photo by
Keystone/Stringer/Getty Images)

August 29: with unrestrained emotion, Allied prisoners of war
at Aomori near Yokohama cheer wildly as approaching
rescuers of the U.S. Navy bring food, clothing and medical
supplies. The men are waving flags of the United States,
Great Britain, and Holland. (Photo by Keystone/Stringer/
Getty Images)

Consolidated B-32s at Yontan Airfield, Okinawa, in August
1945. A Dominator is refueled shortly after arrival from
the Philippines. B-32s on photo reconnaissance flights over
Japan were attacked after the Japanese peace acceptance on
August 17 and 18. Two planes were badly damaged with
one fatality. (NARA)

Imperial Navy ace Lt(jg) Saburo Sakai – veteran of China,
the South Pacific and Iwo Jima – was among those
who intercepted U.S. B-32 reconnaissance flights after
the Emperor's surrender announcement. (PJF Military
Collection / Alamy Stock Photo)

A Curtiss SB2C Helldiver over Tokyo on August 28.
Photographed from a USS *Shangri-La* (CV-38) plane by

Lt. G. D. Rogers. Note light traffic on the city streets, also burned out areas and damaged buildings. (NARA)

The iconic VJ Day image: *Life* Magazine photograph of a sailor kissing a "nurse" (dental assistant) in Times Square on August 14, 1945. (Alfred Eisenstaedt/The LIFE Picture Collection/Shutterstock)

Allied unity as women of Britain's Territorial Army Service link arms with U.S. soldiers during the VJ Day celebration in London's Piccadilly Circus. (Photo by Keystone/Stringer/ Getty Images)

American soldiers celebrate war's end with a flag-studded gathering in Paris, knowing they would not deploy to the Pacific. (Photo by Keystone/Stringer/Hulton Archive/ Getty Images)

Japanese delegates on Ie Shima, Okinawa, boarding General MacArthur's C-54 transport before flying to Manila on August 19. Approaching the top of ladder is the delegation head, Lieutenant General Torashiro Kawabe. Officer at left, behind the civilian envoy, is Rear Admiral Ichiro Yokoyama. (NARA)

Japanese Imperial Headquarters representative General Yoshijiro Umezu signing the Instrument of Surrender while General MacArthur (left) watches, aboard the USS *Missouri* (BB-63), Tokyo Bay on September 2. (Photo by Hulton Archive/Stringer/Getty Images)

U.S. Navy carrier planes fly in formation over USS *Missouri* (BB-63) during the surrender ceremonies, September 2. Photographed by Lt. Barrett Gallagher from atop the battleship's forward 16-inch gun turret. Aircraft types include F4U, TBM and SB2C. Ship in the right distance is USS *Ancon* (AGC-4), the 7th Fleet's amphibious flagship. (NARA)

General Douglas MacArthur with Japanese Emperor Hirohito during the U.S. occupation of Japan in 1945. MacArthur oversaw the nation's postwar transition to democratic government while rebuilding the economy. (Bettmann/ Getty Images)

Introduction

Seen from space, Earth's dominant feature is the Pacific Ocean. Its 62.5 million square miles cover more than one third of the planet's total surface. Nothing else comes close. For comparison, San Diego to Tokyo is 5,500 statute miles; even from Honolulu, Tokyo is over 3,800 miles, while in comparison the distance from New York to London is less than 3,500 miles. By August 1945, the wartime generation of Americans had received a concentrated course in geography, including the vast blue expanse of the Pacific in particular. Few had probably ever heard of Pearl Harbor in 1941, but four years later the large majority knew the significance of Guadalcanal, Saipan, Leyte Gulf, Iwo Jima, and Okinawa.

Indeed, in the 45 months between December 1941 and August 1945, the Pacific Theater of Operations absorbed the attention of the American nation and military longer than any other. Despite the Allied grand strategy of "Germany first," after the Japanese attack on Pearl Harbor, Hawaii, the U.S. was irrevocably committed to confronting Tokyo as a matter of urgent priority. American ground troops did not engage the Western Axis in North Africa until November 1942 and did not fight on the European mainland until almost a year later. But U.S. forces were immediately involved in the Pacific and would be until the war's end.

Allied forces were, of course, engaged elsewhere, most notably in the China-Burma-India (CBI) Theater. But the development of what British Prime Minister Winston Churchill called "triphibious operations" was necessarily perfected in the Pacific – a melding of land, sea, and air forces that took giant steps across 161 degrees of longitude from Honolulu to Tokyo. It was a long, bloody slog, averaging an advance of merely three miles per day. The human toll paid by American citizens on that road reached some 108,000 battle deaths, more than one third of the total U.S. wartime toll. In comparison, American combat losses in the Atlantic-European-Mediterranean theaters combined had reached some 185,900 by the time the fighting there ended with Victory-in-Europe Day on May 9, 1945.

By the summer of 1945 the nation was distressingly accustomed to mounting attrition. The first week in August alone added a further 7,489 dead, missing, or wounded, bringing the wartime total to 1,068,216 casualties. That meant 1,070 souls a day – the price of doing wartime business.

*   *   *

But there was hope – growing, even soaring hope. The stunning announcements of atomic bombs dropped on Hiroshima and Nagasaki on August 6 and 9 respectively seemed sure to force Tokyo over the tipping point. Employment of atomic bombs had followed the Allies' surrender demand issued from Potsdam, Germany, in July, two weeks before Hiroshima. Without actually indicating the use of nuclear weapons, the Allied declaration had stated, "We call upon the government of Japan to proclaim now the unconditional surrender of all Japanese armed forces, and to provide proper and adequate assurances of their good faith in such action. The alternative for Japan is prompt and utter destruction."[1]

To most Americans, the threat of "prompt and utter destruction" was justified, however it was delivered. To a war-weary population at home the immense devastation of conventional (and ultimately nuclear) bombing seemed only fitting, given revelations of Japanese atrocities from the Rape of Nanking in 1937 to the Bataan Death March in 1942, to attacks on Allied hospital ships in 1944 and 1945.

So too did they recall the apparent treachery of December 7, 1941 when two envoys were filmed visiting the U.S. State Department in Washington while bombs and torpedoes slaughtered U.S. ships, sailors, and soldiers in Hawaii.

America's boiling rage was fueled by the memory of Pearl Harbor over the subsequent four long years. Only much later did the true facts emerge: Tokyo *had* intended minimal notice of impending hostilities, but delays in decoding the complex secret messages in Washington had upset the schedule.

What few understand today is the vast gap – in fact more of a chasm – in the cultural ethos of East and West at that point in time. As the events of early to mid-August would show, the dropping of one, or indeed, two atomic bombs in no way guaranteed Japanese capitulation.

In the war zones, at home and abroad, people treaded a tenuous trail between continuing war and impending peace. When the peace finally came, it arrived at a heavy cost, not least of all the drawing of new battle lines in the forthcoming Cold War.

Indeed, the events of August 1945 influenced the world as nothing since, and their effects still reverberate today.

I

War or Peace?

August 1–14

Rumors wafted on global winds throughout the first half of August 1945: Tokyo was on the brink of surrendering; Tokyo was sure to fight to the bitter end. The thousands of sailors and airmen of the U.S. Pacific Fleet grew especially edgy; after all, they were most closely engaged against the Japanese Empire.

The geographic noose had been drawn taut around Imperial Japan's vulnerable neck in the preceding six months. In late March, U.S. Marines had seized Iwo Jima, 750 miles south of Tokyo. Securing that base put the Home Islands in range of land-based fighters to escort the Boeing B-29 firebirds from the Marianas that incinerated Japan's urban-industrial areas in the subsequent weeks and months.

In April more American amphibious troops had landed on Okinawa, less than 400 miles from Japan's southern island of Kyushu. Okinawa had been fully in Allied hands since June, with airfield construction proceeding throughout the Ryukyu chain of islands.

The empire had shrunk steadily since 1942 with worsening conditions at home. An island nation with a growing population, Japan had increasingly imported food since the turn of the century. As far back as 1901 Japan had imported 11.7 million yen of rice while exporting 6.9 million, a deficit of 4.8 million yen, or nearly 70 percent.[1]

At no point in the war had Japan been adequately prepared to deal with critical food shortages. Figures vary, but Japan began the war with approximately 6 million tons of merchant shipping. By early 1945 American submarines had choked off Tokyo's oceanic supply lines, and B-29 Superfortresses (often called Superforts) mined coastal waters in a program aptly called Operation *Starvation*. Thus, by August 1945, Japan's merchant marine possessed less than 2 million tons.[2]

Though facing almost certain destruction, in Tokyo the elected government was irrelevant. Left-wing and antiwar groups and political parties had been banned since 1940, with some prominent members arrested. Japan's only wartime election was held in April 1942, yielding a huge majority for the government-sponsored coalition of all permitted parties, the others being independents. The stated turnout was 83 percent; by comparison that November, American mid-term voters posted a mere 33 percent participation, well below the norm; Franklin Roosevelt remained enormously popular, and many Americans were unwilling to change leaders in wartime.

But elected officials who formed the Japanese parliament, the Diet, were largely administrative. In truth, Japan was run by just eight men: the six-member Wartime Supreme Council, the emperor, and his privy seal or chief advisor. By August 1945 the council was evenly divided between moderates favoring surrender and bitter-enders who vowed to die fighting. Without a majority decision and with the palace uncommitted, the stalemate remained and the war continued.

On the night of August 1–2, Major General Curtis LeMay's XXI Bomber Command in the Mariana Islands, 1,500 miles south of Tokyo, continued to display its strength. In the largest mission of the war to date, some 830 huge B-29 Superfortresses dropped 6,000 tons of bombs on five urban-industrial areas and added yet more mines to coastal waters, further limiting supply by sea. One bomber was shot down; ten of the 12-man crew were captured and ultimately survived the war.[3]

Meanwhile, the two-week Allied conference in recently conquered Potsdam, Germany, which had begun on July 17, finally concluded on August 2. Predominately focused on the immediate postwar situation in Europe, it also required Tokyo's unconditional surrender in a joint statement issued by the United States, Britain, China, and France. The Soviet Union, which participated in postwar planning, was at that juncture still officially at peace with Japan.

The leaders of the three major Allies had all attended the conference. President Harry S. Truman had only assumed office in April, following the death of Franklin D. Roosevelt. Four months later, almost to the day, Truman, as commander-in-chief of the world's greatest military power after the defeat of Nazi Germany, was determined to inflict a similar defeat on Imperial Japan.

At 61 years of age, Truman regarded the world from behind rimless glasses and a common-sense Midwest mindset. He had never graduated from college but had earned a varied living as an office worker, railroad agent, and farmer. A National Guardsman since 1905, he was activated for service in World War I, taking his artillery battery to France in 1918. He demonstrated leadership and professional competence in combat, laying a foundation for much greater responsibilities a quarter century later.

Discharged from the Army in 1919, Truman had returned to Missouri, married, and opened a clothing store partnership. The venture failed in 1921 and Truman sought other opportunities. He was elected an administrative county judge in 1922–24, then lost re-election and became a salesman before returning to politics. He resumed his judge position through two four-year election cycles, cementing his relations with the Kansas City Democrat machine. He oversaw various public works projects and became state director of the Federal Re-Employment Program in gratitude for the machine's support of Roosevelt's election in 1932. The position put Truman in close contact with FDR's aide Harry Hopkins.

Truman's political star rose due to Kansas City Democratic Party Chairman T.J. "Boss" Pendergast, a corrupt fixer who wielded enormous local power. Consequently, in 1934 Truman became an unlikely candidate for the U.S. Senate. In anachronistic terms, he was a networker, leveraging contacts with local and state politicians as well as his membership in the

American Legion and the Masons. He defeated the Republican incumbent, unknowingly setting himself on the road to 1600 Pennsylvania Avenue.

Truman's D.C. career proceeded by fits and starts, most notably in 1939 when "Boss" Pendergast went to prison for bribery and tax evasion. Nonetheless, in 1940 Truman won re-election to the Senate owing to an opposing split ticket. Subsequently he became known as a wartime reformer and pragmatist. In 1941 he stated that if either Germany or the Soviet Union seemed likely to defeat the other, the U.S. should support the underdog. Later he headed the Senate committee that bore his name, investigating wartime profiteering.

Approaching the 1944 presidential election, many Democrats sensed that Vice President Henry Wallace was more a liability than an asset, given his well-known left-wing philosophy. Roosevelt consented to a replacement, and Truman got the nod.

FDR was handily re-elected with an 81 percent sweep in the Electoral College. But following inauguration on January 20, 1945, Truman only met with Roosevelt twice, instead dividing his time between serving as President of the Senate and convivial poker games with cronies.

When Roosevelt died on April 12, 1945, Truman had an enormous gap to close. He knew nothing about the Manhattan Project and little about Allied grand strategy. Recognizing the deficit, he candidly told White House reporters, "Boys, if you ever pray for me, pray for me now." He added that he felt as if the moon, planets, and stars had fallen on him.[4]

Truman's wife Bess shared the sentiment. She confided to their daughter, "This is going to put a terrific load on Harry. Roosevelt has told him nothing."[5]

For the majority of the Potsdam Conference, Truman's British counterpart was Winston Spencer Churchill. Churchill was an anomaly. The product of an aristocratic father, whose once-brilliant political career had stalled and faltered, and a promiscuous American society beauty mother, he became one of the most significant figures of the 20th century. Graduating from Sandhurst Royal Military Academy in 1895, as a soldier and journalist he experienced a dizzying youth that included reporting from Cuba and riding in one of the last great cavalry charges, in the Sudan in 1898, and a heart-pounding escape from captivity in South Africa during the Anglo-Boer War (1899–1902). Between then and 1939 Churchill wrote nearly 20 books and pamphlets, most notably his gripping personal accounts of the Boer War.

Churchill's political career was marked by pragmatism as he gained parliamentary seats as a Conservative and Liberal. In 1911, after a succession of government ministries – still aged only 37 – he became First Sea Lord, bringing modern concepts to the Royal Navy including submarines and aircraft. However, during World War I his advocacy of the ultimately disastrous Dardanelles campaign forced him out of government for a time, and he returned to the Army, serving in France before ending the war as munitions minister. Subsequently, he published a four-volume history of World War I.

Over the next two decades Churchill was in and out of government but earned a comfortable living via his speeches and writing. He gained a wide readership: it was said that he used the English language as if he had invented it.

Balding and portly at 70, Churchill little resembled the dashing cavalier of the Sudan and South Africa of his earlier years, but he had killed in combat and retained an inner fierceness that sometimes belied his jowly exterior.

An outspoken opponent of prewar appeasement, Churchill returned to the Admiralty in 1939 ("Winston is back," gleefully declared the newspapers in delight) and rose to prime minister in May 1940 as France teetered on the verge of falling to Hitler's *Blitzkrieg*. More due to perception than reality, Churchill received wide credit for resisting Nazi conquest that summer during the Battle of Britain. The fact that the *Wehrmacht* lacked the capability for a successful amphibious landing on Shakespeare's "scepter'd isle" largely remains lost in wartime sentiment.

Churchill had forged a warm, enduring relationship with President Franklin Roosevelt, as they both had held civilian leadership roles in their respective admiralties. From 1941 onward the Anglo-American alliance was based on the "Germany first" doctrine, but America's crisis in the Pacific forced a delay. Meanwhile, Britain suffered massive losses to the Japanese, especially at Singapore, which Churchill called "the worst military defeat in British history." Nonetheless, the Anglo-Americans rebounded in the Mediterranean Theater, first with the invasion of French Morocco in late 1942, then Sicily and the Italian mainland in 1943.

Of course, the climax occurred in northern France in June 1944 with the successful D-Day landings in Normandy. Churchill could not stay away, going ashore six days later. He had already exhibited tremendous enthusiasm for the mechanics of Operation *Neptune-Overlord*, including mobile harbors and various "funny" versions of tanks and vehicles.

As a lifelong anticommunist, Churchill sought to limit Soviet advances in Europe, without much success. Nevertheless, he achieved an uneasy accommodation with Joseph Stalin during wartime conferences at Moscow in October 1944, Yalta in the Crimea in February 1945, and finally at Potsdam.

Yet amidst the power-brokering of the three major Allies following Germany's defeat in May came political change at home in Britain. A general election had been held on July 5. The Potsdam Conference had begun 12 days earlier, but the election results were not confirmed yet as additional time had to be allowed for counting the votes of servicemen and women. The entire English-speaking world, and not just the conference attendees, was stunned when Churchill lost. What appeared as staggering ingratitude by the British voters is probably better explained by the expected peace. Churchill was a warrior by instinct and preference; his countrymen recognized that fact and considered Labour's Clement Attlee far better suited to the fast-approaching era of peace.

A hard-working lawyer, financier, and politician, Attlee carved himself a career that largely defined Britain's Labour Party. However, during World War I he had yearned for military service and, though first refused at age 31, he had eventually succeeded in gaining an army commission. He survived the disastrous Gallipoli campaign – engineered by Churchill, whose strategic vision he admired – and was wounded fighting in Iraq. At war's end Attlee was a major on the Western Front.

In 1922 Attlee was elected to Parliament, leading to a role in the 1927 commission studying self-rule for India, a concept that eventually bore fruit after a 20-year gestation.

Attlee spent much of the postwar era refining his political philosophy, eventually moderating his earlier support of radical socialism. His relative youth favored him at a time when many of Labour's elder statesmen appeared uncomfortably accepting of trends in Germany, Italy, and Russia. However, Attlee also flatly stated that he preferred globalism over national sovereignty, and he largely opposed rearmament. But events in Europe forced a rethinking, and Attlee described Prime Minister Neville Chamberlain's approval of the 1938 Munich agreement as "one of the greatest diplomatic defeats that this country and France have ever sustained." Shortly afterward, Adolf Hitler's bloodless conquest of ethnic German territory in Czechoslovakia set Europe on the path to another conflagration.

In May 1940, with France on the verge of defeat, Attlee agreed to a coalition government of Labour and Churchill's Conservatives with the latter serving as prime minister. It was an unlikely alliance, but under growing wartime pressure it largely worked. In 1942 Attlee became deputy prime minister, with much of his time spent overseeing domestic matters. He earned admiration for reducing bureaucratic duplication and simplifying the mechanics of government administration.

Following Germany's surrender in May 1945, Churchill and Attlee advocated retaining the government status quo until Japan was defeated. However, hardline Labour politicians refused to continue the wartime political coalition, forcing an election.

Britain's war-weary population eagerly anticipated peacetime, presumably just months away, with strong support for a welfare state. The Conservatives' platform largely depended upon Churchill's wartime record and forceful personality, but lacked Labour's thorough philosophical approach. The July election result was an historic Labour victory, the first time the party had won a majority in Parliament.

Because the transition period overlapped with the final days of the Potsdam Conference, Attlee and Churchill both represented Great Britain. But Clement Attlee, the mild-mannered functionary, replaced the iconic bulldog whose face and voice had represented Britain for nearly the entire war. In 1950 Churchill published *The Grand Alliance,* the third book in his epic six-volume history of the war. Certainly it was an apt title, describing the enormously complex, multi-tiered transatlantic romance with America and the marriage of convenience with Russia. While the world largely saw the three heads of state, their military and civilian subordinates recognized not only differing wartime considerations, but the certainty of postwar disputes, global tension, and even potential conflict.

Meanwhile, halfway around the globe an entirely different kind of drama was playing out on the vast blue expanse of the Pacific Ocean.

INDIANAPOLIS RESCUE, AUGUST 2

Lieutenant (jg) Wilbur C. Gwinn was not looking for survivors of a major naval disaster. He had piloted his twin-engine Lockheed PV-2 Harpoon on a normal patrol, having lost his trailing antenna on the morning's first takeoff from Peleliu in the Palau Islands, 600 statute miles east of the Philippines. Later, flying at 4,000 feet almost 300 miles from base, Gwinn's crew unreeled the replacement antenna. It also snapped, requiring the combined efforts of the pilot and three crewmen to retrieve the whipping wire. As they pulled the line through a hatch, the fliers noticed an oil slick on the ocean.

Gwinn made a logical conclusion: the slick must be from a Japanese submarine since no friendly subs were known to be in the area. Preparing to attack ("This was our first contact and we wanted the sub"), the Harpoon opened its bomb bay.[6]

But on approaching the drop point, the fliers glimpsed men in the water. A quick count revealed dozens, identity unknown. Gwinn's radioman sent three messages, concluding, "One hundred fifty or more men in water. Circling for rescue planes to home in," adding the position by latitude and longitude.

The crew dropped everything of possible use, including rafts and a sonobuoy.

To the survivors of the cruiser USS *Indianapolis* (CA-35), the fat-bellied Lockheed was an angel of deliverance.

Indianapolis was a ship of historic record: she had been Admiral Raymond Spruance's Fifth Fleet flagship and had survived a bombing-suicide attack off Okinawa in March. Then, on July 16, she had delivered uranium and other components to Tinian in an 11-day dash from San Francisco. Those items went into the "Little Boy" atom bomb that would destroy Hiroshima on August 6.

On her return voyage from Tinian, shortly after midnight on July 30, the 12,000-ton cruiser was torpedoed by a Japanese submarine midway between Guam and Leyte. Of the 1,200 men aboard, nearly 900 went into the sea before she sank in just 12 minutes. Sailors forcibly swam through a growing clot of fuel oil that tired men out, choked their lungs, and blurred their vision. And that was the least of their problems.

What followed was a horrific experience amid a feeding frenzy of voracious sharks that lasted an agonizing three and a half days. Boatswain's Mate Eugene Morgan later recalled, "All the time the sharks never let up. We had a cargo net that had styrofoam attached to keep it afloat. There were about fifteen sailors on it, and suddenly ten sharks hit it and there was nothing left. This went on and on."[7]

The survivors were adrift almost literally in the middle of the Pacific Ocean, 600 miles west of Guam and 550 miles east of Leyte.

Nobody knew that "*Indy*" was lost – in the Philippines, naval communications and traffic-following protocols failed completely, with distress messages ignored and one officer reportedly drunk on duty. Meanwhile, seven groups of survivors drifted across a 30-mile expanse of the Philippine Sea, exposed to searing sun and frigid nights, with more men perishing from injuries, dehydration, and hypothermia than from sharks.

That morning of August 2, the sight and sound of an aircraft brought surging elation to survivors, some of whom had already accepted their fate. Marine Corporal Edgar Harrell said, "On that fourth day, I said, 'I hear a plane!' And we began to splash water, we began to yell, we began to pray – everything! And seemingly, when he got to a point that had he gone any further he would've gone over us, you know what he did? He made a dive."[8]

Gwinn was relieved on station by his skipper, Commander Richard Atteberry. Then Consolidated PBY Catalina amphibians arrived, the first flown by Lieutenant Robert Adrian Marks. The 28-year-old Indiana lawyer had considerable experience by 1945: having survived Pearl Harbor, he had gained wings of gold and served for the rest of the war.

Catalina pilots were discouraged from landing in heavy seas but Marks polled his crew, who voted to attempt it. Despite 10–12-foot waves, Marks put his ungainly "Cat" onto the water and taxied to the nearest group of survivors. His crew shoehorned an astonishing 56 sailors into the cramped interior or secured them to the wings. The PBY was unable to fly again but remained afloat until the first rescue ship reached the scene that night, Lieutenant Commander W. G. Claytor's destroyer escort *Cecil J. Doyle* (DE-368). Ten other vessels followed, in all saving 316 men in seven dispersed groups who were mostly reunited at Guam by August 8.

Among U.S. Navy single-event losses, *Indianapolis*'s toll of 879 appears second only to the battleship *Arizona*'s 1,177 at Pearl Harbor.

PREPARATIONS FOR ARMAGEDDON, AUGUST 5

On August 5, while burning 4.5 square miles of urban-industrial area, Major General Curtis LeMay's B-29s also dropped 720,000 leaflets over a dozen Japanese cities, advising people to evacuate before heavier bombing continued. In total more than 30 cities were bombarded with leaflets warning of impending destruction. The cautionary message was reinforced by broadcasts from Radio Saipan, the official station of the Office of War Information.

It was not an idle threat.[9]

The next day Armageddon descended.

The United States had invested enormous resources in two potentially war-winning weapon programs: the atom bomb and the Boeing B-29 Superfortress. Together they amounted to a cost of approximately $5 billion, or more than $70 billion today.

The Manhattan Project – the code name for the A-bomb program – originated with a letter that physicist Albert Einstein had written to President Roosevelt in 1939. The German-born genius – not yet a naturalized American citizen – had envisioned the atom as a source of endless power and an awesome weapon. Spurred by fears over a German bomb, in three years from 1942 the "Manhattan Engineering District" expanded into a nationwide project from Illinois to Tennessee to Washington State. Most of the design was conducted at a former boys' ranch at Los Alamos, New Mexico, with ultimate testing in a remote desert site called Trinity.

Coordinating the construction, research, and development staffs ultimately involving 130,000 people were two very different men. Major General Leslie Groves was the stout, driven, 49-year-old Army engineer who had overseen the construction of the Pentagon, at that point the world's largest building. His scientific opposite number, eight years younger, was the thin and often troubled physicist Dr. Robert Oppenheimer. Although an unlikely duo, together they worked tirelessly to beat Adolf Hitler to the atom bomb – a goal rendered unnecessary on VE Day – and instead delivered "the gadget" to the Pacific Air Forces.

The Superfortress was aptly named, the next-generation heavy bomber beyond Boeing's fabled B-17 Flying Fortress. In fact, the B-29 was far more than a generational leap because it incorporated so many innovations: pressurization of the cabin, remotely controlled gun turrets, high speed, and intercontinental range. After early engine problems were solved, it became a war-winning weapon and the only means of delivering a five-ton nuclear weapon. But it required exceptional expertise for maintenance and operations. From bases in the Marianas, 11-man crews routinely logged 15-hour missions – twice the norm in Europe – nearly all flown over the oceanic expanse to Japan. The risks were clear; only half of the fliers who went into the sea were recovered.

Selected to command the nuclear tactical unit was a former pre-med student, 30-year-old Colonel Paul Tibbets, a highly experienced bomber pilot known for his calm competence and leadership ability. Almost three years earlier to the day, he had flown the lead plane in the first American heavy bomber mission over occupied Europe. Now he was literally "the old man" to aircrews in the 509th Composite Group, as his chosen navigator, bombardier, and senior squadron commander were only 24 and 26 years of age.

Arriving at Tinian Island in the Marianas, Tibbets reported to Major General Curtis LeMay while maintaining extreme security. LeMay was known as a miracle worker among heavy bombers, having previously held commands in Britain and China before arriving in the Pacific.

Probably the most accomplished military airman of his generation and the least concerned with his public image, Curtis Emerson LeMay crammed three if not four careers into 35 years of service.

Earning his wings in 1929, LeMay drew "pursuits" but soon managed a transfer to "bombardment," as he reasoned that wars are won on offense, not defense. Already an expert pilot, as a junior officer in the mid to late 1930s he had helped bring the B-17 Flying Fortress to fruition, achieving an eye-watering reputation for long-range navigation in the pre-radar era. In one notable event he located his target – a single ocean liner – an astonishing 700 statute miles off the East Coast.

As a bombardment group and wing commander in 1942–43, LeMay had led the 305th Bomb Group, one of the most innovative units of the Eighth Air Force in England. There he had solidified his command philosophy: leading from the front and demanding accountability in an unyielding quest for excellence. He took his concept of lead crews – specialists in specific targets – from Britain to China and the Pacific, and established a series of remedial education and training courses. It was a philosophy he eventually expanded as postwar chief of the Strategic Air Command.

At 37 – the youngest major general since Ulysses S. Grant in 1862 – LeMay was partially responsible for saving the trouble-plagued B-29 program, both in India and the Marianas, and thereby perhaps assuring an independent U.S. Air Force. He reduced operational losses to little more than what would be expected of routine airline operations over oceanic distances. In March 1945 his decision to shift from conventional high-altitude bombing to lower-level incendiary missions burned out the heart of Japanese urban-industrial areas before he was finally tasked with overseeing and coordinating the proposed atomic bomb attack.

Later, LeMay was quoted as saying, "When you kill enough of them, they quit fighting." That blunt assessment was ultimately to be proven correct.

Despite their difference in ranks, the two accomplished airmen were on a first-name basis from long affiliation and mutual respect. LeMay gave Tibbets everything needed to deliver what the general called "the firecracker" to its destination.

The Manhattan Project's frantic rush to master the atoms had succeeded brilliantly, with a garish predawn flash in New Mexico on July 16. When the plutonium-fueled weapon burst with the power of 22,000 tons of TNT, it spawned the atomic age, and the world would never be the same.

But earlier that month – on July 4 – Hungarian-born physicist Leo Szilard had written an open letter to his Los Alamos colleagues urging them to join him in protesting any use of nuclear weapons.[10] On the 17th, the day after the successful New Mexico test, Szilard sent President Truman a letter questioning the morality of nuclear weapons, with 70 other signatures. The petition said in part:

> The war has to be brought speedily to a successful conclusion and attacks by atomic bombs may very well be an effective method of warfare. We feel, however, that such attacks on Japan could not be justified, at least not until the terms which will be imposed after the war on Japan were made public in detail and Japan were given an opportunity to surrender.[11]

Manhattan's dissenting scientists and engineers had set themselves an impossible goal, as they had no context for the A-bomb decision process. Top-secret information available to policy makers in Washington – notably Japan seeking Soviet assistance – would not be released for three decades. Furthermore, the extremely delicate maneuvering in the Allied camp, and especially in Tokyo, permitted no public discussion.*

Indeed, Allied analysts shared a distinctly contrary view, based on hard information. This was in part due to the enormously successful "Magic" radio intercept program that had yielded not just intelligence ore, but nuggets of gold. In those first days of August a Far East information summary of military and diplomatic traffic concluded, "Until the Japanese leaders realize that an invasion cannot be repelled, there is little likelihood that they will accept any peace terms satisfactory to the Allies."

The Magic transcripts proved revelatory to American snoopers. Only three or four messages held any reference to Tokyo's hope for a negotiated surrender, while a dozen or more clearly showed the continued dominance of Japan's bitter-enders within the Japanese war cabinet. Among the most conclusive intercepts was Foreign Minister Togo's admonition to Ambassador Sato in Moscow, "Please bear particularly in mind that we are not seeking the Russians' mediation for anything like an unconditional surrender."[12]

Given the evidence of Tokyo's intransigence, atoms would inevitably be split. Nonetheless, authorization for the first nuclear mission took a long, circuitous route. On July 25, General Carl Spaatz, commanding U.S. Strategic Air Forces, had first received approval from the Army Chief of Staff, General George C. Marshall, and Secretary of War Henry Stimson. But Marshall was in Potsdam with Truman, so the actual order went through Marshall's deputy, former artilleryman General Thomas T. Handy in the Pentagon. From there, the directive trickled downward, to Twentieth Air Force in D.C., and finally to LeMay in the Marianas. The four-paragraph directive stated in part, "The 509th Composite Group will deliver its first special bomb as soon as weather will permit visual bombing after about 3 August." The approved targets included Hiroshima, Kokura, Niigata, and Nagasaki.[13]

---

* See Chapter 3 for details of Japanese communications with the Soviet Union prior to surrender.

RAIN OF RUIN, AUGUST 6

Shortly after 2:00 a.m. on August 6, Paul Tibbets and his crew boarded the B-29, newly christened as the *Enola Gay* for the colonel's mother. In the Superfort's belly hung the 9,700-pound uranium-fueled weapon bound for the port city of Hiroshima. The Manhattan Project had already tested the "Fat Man" plutonium design three weeks before, but "Little Boy" was simple enough to deploy directly to combat without further testing. It was accompanied by a naval ordnance and radar officer, Captain William "Deak" Parsons, who would arm the bomb in flight.

Six hours outbound from Tinian, *Enola Gay* and the two support B-29s – *The Great Artiste* and *Necessary Evil* – crossed the Honshu coast. Minutes later, over Hiroshima, aboard *The Great Artiste*, Dr. Luis Alvarez from Los Alamos released instrument packages to gauge the weapon's yield. Looking upward, residents on city streets noted the "B-san," the nickname Japanese civilians had given to the frequently spotted B-29s, and two parachutes drifting down.

Then, from 31,000 feet, bombardier Major Thomas Ferebee dropped "Little Boy," *Enola Gay* lurching upward as it shed five tons. Immediately Tibbets and copilot Captain Robert Lewis wrestled the huge bomber into a 160-degree diving turn away from the target. Forty-three seconds later, the bomb erupted with the power of 15,000 tons of TNT.

A bright light shone through the plane, then two shock waves overtook *Enola Gay*, then nearly 12 miles from the detonation. Almost immediately a surging, roiling purple-gray mass arose over the target. Tail gunner Sergeant Robert Caron, with the best view, later remarked that there were too many fires on the ground to count.

The fliers were at once ecstatic and awestruck. Tibbets described Lewis pummeling his shoulder, exclaiming, "Look at that! Look at that! Look at that!" Some men tasted something like lead, fearful of radioactive contamination.

But once the emotional spike had passed, Lewis turned introspective, writing in his log, "My God, what have we done?"[14]

Hiroshima had been nearly destroyed. Among the thousands of stricken citizens was Dr. Fumio Shigeto of the Red Cross hospital.

Waiting to board a trolley barely a mile from the atomic flash, he witnessed an other-worldly sight: several passengers turned an eerie white bordering on invisibility. Instantly dropping to the pavement, Shigeto pressed his hands against his ears and tightly shut his eyes. Upon shoving himself from under a heavy beam, he noticed the sun obscured by swirling smoke with clouds of dust he feared was poison gas.

As a breeze cleared the smoke and dust, Shigeto beheld industrial-grade devastation with collapsed buildings, scorched and smoking bodies, and survivors screaming in pain as skin dangled from extended arms.[15]

Among the estimated 66,000 people immediately killed were at least a dozen Americans held as POWs, all previously shot down during July 1944 attacks on the Kure fleet anchorage, an ill-advised strike that had expended lives and aircraft against an already immobilized enemy fleet. The POWs included Army bomber crewmen and a dive bomber crew off USS *Ticonderoga* (CV-14). It is worth noting that postwar researchers have theorized that some of the men included in an original, longer list had been murdered previously.[16]

Forty minutes later, Japan's Soaring Wind Air Defense Division reported "a violent, large special-type bomb, giving the appearance of magnesium."[17]

Enola Gay, with *The Great Artiste* and *Necessary Evil*, returned to Tinian Island, mission accomplished.

At that point, many politicians and senior military commanders alike expected Japan to capitulate.

Nothing happened.

General Groves had predicted that it would take two bombs: one to demonstrate the weapon's astonishing power and another to convince Tokyo that the first was no fluke.[18] It seemed that he was about to be proved right.

Sixteen hours after "Little Boy" pulverized Hiroshima, President Truman issued a 1,100-word statement. He said in part:

We are now prepared to obliterate more rapidly and completely every productive enterprise the Japanese have above ground in any city. We shall destroy their docks, their factories, and their communications. Let there be no mistake; we shall completely destroy Japan's power to make war.

It was to spare the Japanese people from utter destruction that the ultimatum of July 26 was issued at Potsdam. Their leaders promptly rejected that ultimatum. If they do not now accept our terms they may expect a rain of ruin from the air, the like of which has never been seen on this earth. Behind this air attack will follow sea and land forces in such numbers and power as they have not yet seen and with the fighting skill of which they are already well aware.[19]

Japan had rejected Potsdam by officially ignoring it.

Tokyo's rulers, like most authoritarian regimes, placed its own agenda above its population. However, the government allotted a variety of support organizations to the stricken city, mainly from Kure Naval Base, lending assistance to a stunned, irradiated, surviving population. Meanwhile, following Truman's statement, Imperial General Headquarters dispatched a high-level team to confirm whether an atomic bomb had in fact been detonated. The crew was led by Lieutenant General Seizo Arisue, head of the army investigations section, and Dr. Yoshio Nishina of the Physical and Chemical Research Institute, who had studied physics in Britain, Germany, and Denmark. They were joined by seven others who had worked on Japan's own dead-end nuclear weapons program.

Delayed by mechanical problems, on the 8th the team's aircraft flew to Yoshijima Airfield, three miles out of Hiroshima. Before landing, the passengers crowded the windows, gaping at the rubbled urban landscape that had once been a city of some 350,000 people.

After surveying the damage and absorbing information from preliminary reports, the team held an army-navy meeting on August 10 – a day after the second nuclear mission – where they would conclude that Hiroshima had, in fact, been destroyed by an atom bomb. However, with insufficient information, the investigators underestimated the danger of radiation. Thousands would pay for their error.[20]

STALEMATE AND DOGFIGHTS, AUGUST 7–8

Despite the shattering event in Hiroshima, Japanese war aims proceeded the next day. One project in particular indicated Tokyo's commitment to greater military capabilities.

Japan's attempts to produce a jet aircraft spanned the world's oceans and months of erratic effort. Japanese military attachés to Berlin had seen trials of the Messerschmitt 262 jet interceptor in 1942 and had immediately recognized the potential. Subsequently, the Imperial Navy authorized design work on an aircraft based on the German model.[21]

In December 1943, Commander Kinashi Takakazu's submarine *I-29* had been dispatched on a globe-spanning mission from Singapore to Lorient, France, to exchange resources and information. A submariner since 1927, Takakazu was considered Japan's greatest skipper, in 1942 sinking the U.S. aircraft carrier *Wasp* (CV-7) and a destroyer while also damaging a battleship – all with only one spread of torpedoes.

Following *I-29*'s three-month transit, including two refueling rendezvous with German ships, in mid-April the submarine loaded passengers including German engineers with samples of jet and rocket engines plus production drawings. The largest included a disassembled Me 163 *Komet* rocket fighter.

After the nearly 13,000-statute-mile reverse trip around Africa, Takakazu finally returned to Japanese-occupied Singapore in mid-July. The passengers, including a naval technical officer, then proceeded to Japan by air, but the engines and *Komet* remained aboard *I-29* for later delivery.

Four days out of Singapore, bound for Kure, *I-29* entered Luzon Strait. There, on the afternoon of July 26, USS *Sawfish* (SS-276) spotted the enemy boat on the surface and destroyed it with three torpedoes. All hands were lost including Takakazu and, of course, the disassembled Me 163.[22]

However, the blueprints and other technical specifications arrived in Tokyo where the Nakajima company – normally an army client – began work on a naval jet named *Kikka*, or "Orange Blossom." The concept was a fast, short-ranged attack aircraft carrying up to 1,700 pounds of bombs. The folding wings led some observers to assume that the Imperial Navy envisioned a futuristic concept of jets from purpose-built carriers. But, in fact, the wings were intended to fit *Kikka*s into caves and other confined spaces.

Though designed by the same team that had produced Nakajima's *Gekko* ("Moonlight" or Irving) night fighter, by early August 1945 Japan's jet had been nearly a year in development, having commenced in September 1944.

Japanese engineers had faced serious obstacles throughout the development process, including metallurgy suitable for jet turbine blades. The early power plants were inadequate, and Nakajima's ultimate solution was influenced by the Me 262's Jumo turbojet. Time was so short that the three landing gear were borrowed from other aircraft. Production was limited by resources and the availability of a skilled labor force, but by August 1945 a prototype was ready for testing.

The *Kikka*'s performance was never empirically determined, though early estimates placed top speed as high as 430mph at altitude; however, that was a full 100mph less than the Messerschmitt 262. Sea-level top speed was reckoned at roughly 385mph, probably inadequate to outpace most Allied fighters.

But one advantage to the *Kikka* project was fuel. The World War II generation of jets often ran on kerosene, and the Japanese opted for "low-grade pine oil," regularly distilled from needles and twigs.[23]

The test pilot assigned to evaluate the *Kikka* was Lieutenant Commander Takaoka Susumu. At 33 he was a well-regarded officer and aviator from the academy class of 1932. He had risen to command carrier bomber units, and from 1941 had served mainly at the Naval Air Technical Arsenal.[*]

---

[*] When the Japanese Self-Defense Force was authorized in 1954, Susumu returned to the cockpit and tested the nation's first indigenous jet trainer. He retired as a brigadier general in 1962, then joined Mitsubishi Heavy Industries (information courtesy of Osamu Tagaya on J-Aircraft.com).

On August 7, a day after the atomic bomb explosion at Hiroshima, Susumu lifted the *Kikka* off Kisarazu Naval Base's short runway on the east shore of Tokyo Bay. He logged a successful flight of less than 20 minutes, leaving the wheels down the entire time – not unusual for a maiden flight – and never exceeded 170 knots (195mph).

Astonishingly, despite the rapidly worsening situation, development efforts continued. Concern about runway length led to rocket-assisted takeoff (RATO) pods on the prototype, ready for flight on the 11th. However, the rocket power jolted the aircraft into a tail-low profile, and upon RATO burnout the jets continued functioning, though the *Kikka* decelerated as the nose wheel returned to the ground, and the pilot chose to abort the effort. The plane overran the runway edge, ripping off the landing gear on a ditch near the bay. Clearly, the developmental jet fighter would not turn the tide of war.

Shortly thereafter work ended on the second *Kikka*. More than 20 others were partly completed before the war was finally concluded. The *Kikka* would never fly in combat. Indeed, the time and effort wasted on the nascent jet would have been better spent enhancing production of piston-engine fighters.

The United States Marine Corps' final aerial tally – by an Okinawa-based night fighter – fell in the early morning dawn of the 8th. Second Lieutenant William E. Jennings was vectored onto a bogey about 40 miles from the island's northeast tip. The controller put him within range of the Hellcat's radar, where he closed to firing distance. Shortly after 3:00 a.m. the Kawasaki Ki-61 Tony flamed beneath a full moon. It was Jennings' first victory and the 2,697th credited to Marine Corps aviators since the defense of Wake Island 44 months before.

Meanwhile, Army Air Force (AAF) fighters continued making their mark. The P-47N was the Pacific Thunderbolt, a far different machine than the original models first committed to combat in 1943. Longer ranged with more endurance, the N permitted one-way missions of more than 700 miles. Loping along at 235mph with external fuel tanks, consuming about 80 gallons per hour, the N model delivered exceptional reach. It even had an autopilot, probably unique among World War II fighters. By July 1945, three P-47N groups stretched their Pacific legs from Okinawa bases, reaching far afield.

On the 8th, nine Thunderbolt squadrons patrolled Kyushu airspace for two hours, mainly around the industrial city of Yawata. Leading the 413th Fighter Group was Colonel Harrison R. Thyng, a 27-year-old New Hampshire native. A low-key, popular leader, his pilots called him "the Hairy Thing," and his record was nearly unique. Flying American Spitfires in North Africa in 1942–43, he had downed five Axis aircraft. Now he flew a vastly different fighter, trading his three-and-a-half-ton Spitfire for an eight-ton Thunderbolt.

During a seven-minute dogfight with Nakajimas that morning, the 413th Group claimed five definite kills. Thyng put his experience to use by hammering an Oscar that dropped out of sight, credited as probably destroyed.

Like Thyng, Lieutenant Colonel Carl R. Payne had gained victories over German and Vichy planes in Africa, followed by a Nakajima at Yawata that day. They were two of only four American aces to score against three enemy powers.

That day Radio Tokyo gave its first full report on the Hiroshima bombing, concluding with the claim that the Americans had used methods which "have surpassed in hideous cruelty those of Genghis Khan."

More was to come, far sooner than many Japanese – or Americans – expected.[24]

VENGEANCE FOR PEARL HARBOR, AUGUST 9

Lacking a response from Tokyo, three days later another B-29 departed Tinian bearing an atomic bomb. This one was dubbed "Fat Man" and was of even greater power than "Little Boy." The primary target was the historic Japanese town of Kokura with a huge army arsenal; the secondary target was Nagasaki with, among other assets, a large harbor and shipyards.

Unlike Hiroshima, Nagasaki was known by Allied intelligence to contain a POW camp. However, so did the other potential atomic targets, requiring a hard-eyed calculus: risk killing scores of friendlies in order to end the war. Although General Carl Spaatz and Admiral Chester Nimitz, Commander-in-Chief Pacific Ocean Areas, opposed targeting Nagasaki for that reason, the city remained on the list. Postwar sources varied, but it is generally estimated that some 80 Allied personnel perished in and around Nagasaki.[25]

Major Charles Sweeney, the 25-year-old squadron commander, had piloted his plane, *The Great Artiste*, modified as a monitoring aircraft on the 6th. But on the 9th he flew Captain Fred Bock's bomber called *Bockscar*. However, mechanics discovered that the fuel system on board *Bockscar* trapped 600 gallons of unusable gasoline, a potential deficit of 3,600 pounds. Tibbets offered the option of scrubbing the mission but Sweeney preferred to continue, maintaining the momentum begun at Hiroshima and avoiding an expected weather delay.

At 3:45 a.m. on the morning of the 9th, Sweeney and his flight engineer firewalled their throttles, lifting off from Tinian for the briefed rendezvous with supporting B-29s. Among these was Fred Bock and his crew flying *The Great Artiste*, with observers and monitoring gear, accompanying their usual bomber.

About three hours out, a chilling development arose. The bomb's weaponeer, Navy Commander Frederick L. "Dick" Ashworth, sleeping beside "Fat Man," was awakened by his assistant, Army First Lieutenant Philip M. Barnes. As Ashworth told a friend, Barnes shouted, "Hey, Commander, Ashworth, Dick! We got something wrong here!"

Ashworth exclaimed, "Are you sure?" Then he took a look. He immediately saw the cause of Barnes's concern: the red light on "Fat Man's" casing flashed from a steady off-on pace to an accelerated tempo. "Oh my God!" His mind raced; the atom bomb might self-detonate if its radars mistakenly sensed a lower altitude. "Do you have the blueprints?"

The "ordies" removed a panel and began tracing wires compared to the blueprint. After what must have been ten dry-mouthed minutes they found the glitch – two switches had been incorrectly installed. Barnes reversed the settings and the manic flickering ceased.

Somehow, Ashworth was able to resume sleeping. Barnes remained seated beside the weapon, his vision welded to the indicator while acutely conscious that if *Bockscar* descended too low, oblivion awaited.[26]

Meanwhile, circling south of Kyushu, Sweeney waited in vain for his support plane with photo systems to confirm prevailing conditions, though weather recon crews had already reported acceptable conditions at both Kokura and Nagasaki. Running short of fuel, he proceeded to the primary target, Kokura, with its huge arsenal complex. However, the previous night's attack on nearby Yawata had produced heavy smoke over Kokura, and Sweeney made three runs without sighting the target. Out of options, he diverted 100 miles southwest to Nagasaki. Probably unknown at the time, one of Nagasaki's arsenals had produced the torpedoes that slew American battleships at Pearl Harbor.[27] Now a terrible vengeance was about to be inflicted.

The undercast was thinner at Nagasaki, allowing Captain Kermit Beahan to bomb visually, as ordered. On his 27th birthday, through a gap in the clouds, he drew a bead on the Mitsubishi Steel and Arms Works, two miles from the briefed aimpoint. Shortly before 11:00 a.m. the Texan released the plutonium-fueled "Fat Man," which detonated 1,600 feet above ground, apparently just 1,500 feet off target from a 29,000-foot altitude.

Bockscar shook under five shock waves, which Sweeney described as "being beaten by a telephone pole."[28]

Orbiting about 25 miles away, the 507th Fighter Group witnessed the attack on Nagasaki, a city already familiar to some Thunderbolt pilots. It had become a "bomb dump" for weather-aborted missions, as immobile ships in the harbor were an alternate target. Now it was largely destroyed.

One of the pilots flying from Ie Shima off Okinawa's west coast was First Lieutenant Raymond Tarte, a Minnesotan approaching his 25th birthday. As he later recalled:

We're tooling around out there, waiting for the B-29 that went in with the atomic bomb to come out so we can escort them back home, and all of a sudden one of our pilots shouted, "There she goes!" It would've been spectacular if the weather was clear and we could have seen the thing go off, but it didn't turn out that way. Anyway, it was an historic moment, and we all knew it.

The white mushroom cloud rose through the undercast, prompting several pilots to press their triggers to the halfway detent, shooting newly issued color film.[29]

The experience of one teenage girl spoke for many. Midori Nishida was a messenger at the Steel and Arms Works. With her hair on fire, she abandoned her position, seeking shelter in the street. There she entered an apocalyptic horror scape: the Urakami River crammed with corpses; walking skeletons, charred and naked, wandering aimlessly. No buildings remained erect in Nishida's area, the remains now flattened, smoking rubble.

Fires raged for more than 12 hours.[30]

Meanwhile, Sweeney's plane, *Bockscar*, lacked sufficient gasoline to reach Iwo Jima, let alone Tinian. Escorted by *The Great Artiste*, he turned toward Okinawa, milking every gallon and every foot of altitude. In a superb piece of flying and fuel economy, he nursed the struggling Boeing 450 miles to a squeaker of a landing at Yontan Airfield, using every foot of runway. One of his engines died from fuel exhaustion just before touchdown; the flight engineer estimated they had just seven gallons remaining.

The death toll for the two atom bombs remains speculative. Hiroshima fatalities are widely estimated at 90,000 to 120,000; Nagasaki at 60,000 to 80,000, with 70 percent of the industrial area destroyed. The figures are worth comparing to LeMay's massive Tokyo fire raid in March 1945, with approximately 85,000 dead.

Back home in the Marianas, Chuck Sweeney and his friends celebrated the certainty of Japan's surrender.

And again, nothing happened.

The next day, August 10, Lieutenant Ray Tarte's fighter squadron returned to Nagasaki.

We were stunned by the destruction. Everything was leveled. The sky around us was all different colors: pink, brown, you name it. And we were so dumb, we didn't know that was dust from the atomic bomb that could have been really radioactive. They didn't tell us any of that. So we're tooling around there 1,500 feet over Nagasaki... The dust from the day before was still in the air, and with the sun shining it made all these different colors. I could see no activity on the ground whatsoever. In fact, you could only see maybe half a brick building standing, or a wall or something. Otherwise it was completely gone.[31]

Paul Tibbets proceeded on the assumption that another bomb would be used. As he related in 2002:

The second bomb was dropped and again they [the Japanese] were silent for another couple of days. Then I got a phone call from General Curtis LeMay. He said, "You got another one of those damn things?" I said, "Yessir." He said, "Where is it?" I said, "Over in Utah." He said, "Get it out here. You and your crew are going to fly it." I said, "Yessir."

I sent word back and the crew loaded it on an airplane and we headed back to bring it right on out to Tinian.[32]

The most cited likely date for "the third shot" was August 19 and, perturbed by problems with the Nagasaki flight, Tibbets resolved to fly the next atomic mission himself. But the target remained speculative, including prospects of a night strike on Tokyo for greater visual effect. There were some concerns about the emperor's safety largely due to his perceived influence in achieving surrender, but such hopes were rapidly fading. If Emperor Hirohito could not rein in his war cabinet, he served little purpose for the Allied cause.

In Washington the War Department Targeting Committee and 20th Air Force Headquarters compiled separate lists. Between them they named nine cities, although Secretary of War Henry Stimson scratched Kyoto from the list. Thanks to his own prewar travels, he appreciated the city for its cultural value.[33]

On the 10th, Truman directed that a third bomb would only be used at his specific order. Project Manhattan continued producing atomic fuel for the next series of weapons.[34]

On the ground in Nagasaki, stunned in the radioactive rubble were perhaps as many as 70 people who had astonishingly survived both atomic blasts. However, the Japanese government formally recognized only one, Tsutomu Yamaguchi. A 29-year-old native of Nagasaki, he was a Mitsubishi Industries engineer who had been on an extended business trip in Hiroshima on August 6. Like many witnesses, he remembered an airplane at very high altitude, then two parachutes descending – *The Great Artiste*'s monitoring packages.

"Then there was a great flash in the sky and I was blown over."[35]

Later calculations placed Yamaguchi just two miles from Ground Zero, leaving him temporarily blind with ruptured eardrums and serious burns.

Upon return to Nagasaki after treatment for his injuries, Yamaguchi resumed work on the morning of the 9th. He later recalled that he was being scolded by a superior for his fanciful tale of Hiroshima when "Fat Man" detonated. Though a similar distance from the previous bomb, Yamaguchi escaped additional harm for the moment. But in the following days he began vomiting with a persistent fever – the effects of radiation poisoning. Eventually he recovered sufficiently to serve as an English interpreter for the Allied occupation forces.[36]

THE WAR AT SEA, AUGUST 7–12

While Allied and Japanese pilots were dogfighting in the skies above, the war continued at sea. Although the loss of Imperial Japanese Navy vessels was debilitating, the sinkings of nearly 50 merchantmen in the first two weeks of August truly decimated Japan's continued ability to wage war.

Particularly effective were XXI Bomber Command's B-29 mines, which accounted for one third of the merchant losses. The largest loss was *Kibitsu Maru*, a 9,500-ton army landing craft depot ship and lead vessel of her class from 1943. On August 7 she struck an air-dropped mine between Kobe and Yokohama. The captain put her aground, the second such event since she had developed a serious leak in April. She had resumed service three months later, but the American mine ensured it was a short-lived return.[37]

On the 8th the 5,500-ton *Rashin Maru* steamed in a convoy off northeast Korea – the nation having been absorbed into the Japanese Empire in 1910. Another accomplished voyager, she had been built in Quebec in 1919, known as *Canadian Seigneur* until sold to a Japanese firm in 1933. But unknown to the crew of the *Rashin Maru*, the American submarine USS *Pargo* (SS-264) had penetrated the minefields of Tsushima Strait between Japan and Korea, one of seven boats stalking the Sea of Japan. *Rashin Maru* was her ninth victim in eight patrols over the previous two years.

It had indeed proved to be happy hunting for the Pacific Fleet's submarines in the final year of the war. By August 1945 Admiral Nimitz's submarines would have claims totaling 4,000 Japanese ships and 10 million tons. However, the Joint Army-Navy Assessment Committee (JANAC) evaluating wartime claims revised the figure downwards to 1,314 ships (33 percent of the original figure) amounting to 5.3 million tons.

It was still a remarkable success story, particularly when one considers that the ten highest-scoring submarines typically sank 85 percent of the ships credited (191 versus 226) and two thirds of the presumed tonnage.[38] Clearly, greater success went hand-in-hand with greater experience.

Commander Joseph B. Icenhower, a West Virginian from the Annapolis class of 1936, had placed the submarine *Jallao* (SS-368) in commission 13 months before. During her maiden patrol he had earned a Navy Cross for sinking a Japanese cruiser in the battle of Leyte Gulf.

On July 31 Icenhower took *Jallao* on her fourth war patrol – his personal 11th. Gaining radar contact late on the 10th, Icenhower decided "to look him over." He conducted a five-hour surface stalk through the night, closing from eight miles to barely 1,500 yards, confirming, "a very long single-stacked ship low in the water. Since he was obviously a Jap and headed for a Jap port, proceeded to attack position ahead." He fired four torpedoes spaced from forward of the bow to aft of the stern; two struck meat.

However, the hardy merchantman, circling under power, "although listing, seemingly had no thought of sinking," so *Jallao* came hard about and shot two of her stern "fish," both misses.

Icenhower spent 20 minutes regaining position for another firing solution, expending his last two loaded bow tubes from 1,000 yards.

0214: Observed and heard one torpedo hit exactly amidships.
0218: Heard tremendous explosion.
0219: Ship sank.

Icenhower proceeded to his lifeguard station off Japan, en route to a post-retirement career as a fiction and nonfiction author.[39]

The victim was the 5,700-ton *Teihoku Maru*, formerly of French registry and seized by the Japanese in Saigon, carrying 3,000 tons of rice and other desperately needed supplies. She was also the last significant Japanese loss to American submarines in World War II.*

In total, more than 60 Japanese vessels were sunk during August, mostly by U.S. aircraft and air-dropped mines around the Home Islands and Korea. But two naval actions stand out because they coincided with the atomic bombs.

The same day as the A-bomb on Hiroshima, a Japanese Army light bomber caught the submarine USS *Bullhead* (SS-332) on the surface in the Java Sea. Deployed from Freemantle, Australia, she was on her fourth patrol, having been credited with four enemy vessels totaling 1,800 tons on her second outing. The single-engine Mitsubishi claimed hits with two depth charges, and the enemy fliers circled for about ten minutes, noting the sea roiled with spurting bubbles and fuel oil. *Bullhead*, only eight months old, took all 84 men to the bottom.[40]

* See "Red Star at Sea" (p. 109) in Chapter 2 for Soviet action at sea during this period.

Nimitz's headquarters, with more knowledge than Third Fleet, had waved off naval air operations over southern Japan on August 9. Consequently, Task Force 38 raised its sights several notches to the northern tip of Honshu.

As Third Fleet's striking arm, Task Force 38 was a stunning assembly of naval power, with more than 100 ships crewed by 90,000 men. Vice Admiral John S. McCain's command prepared to launch air attacks and patrols from 17 fast carriers deployed in four groups. In all, the 16 U.S. carriers deployed some 1,100 aircraft, including more than 850 Hellcat and Corsair fighters plus Helldiver bombers and Avenger torpedo planes.

In addition, four Royal Navy carriers – HMS *Indefatigable*, *Implacable*, *Formidable*, and *Victorious* – embarked about 250 Seafire fighters derived from the legendary Supermarine Spitfire, as well as Fairey Firefly two-seat fighter-bombers together with U.S.-built Corsairs and Avengers. The British flattops and escorts – separately dubbed Task Force 57 – were wedded with McCain's force as Task Group 38.5. However, the British carriers did rotate in and out of the fleet, depending on supplies and repairs.

Shortly before the Nagasaki bomb detonated, the British Pacific Fleet logged a notable mission. The carriers had launched offensive "ramrod" missions against shipping in Onagawa Bay on Honshu's northeast coast. Five Japanese escorts and auxiliaries were bottled up there, making them vulnerable to an aircraft attack.

One of HMS *Formidable*'s four-plane flights was led by Lieutenant Robert Hampton Gray, a 27-year-old Canadian art student who had first attacked Axis shipping in Norway 12 months before. Then, in late July, he had helped sink a 1,200-ton Japanese destroyer in the Inland Sea.

Leading his Corsairs low over the bay, "Hammy" Gray selected his target. He reckoned it was a destroyer but in fact it was the 870-ton sloop *Amakusa*.

Shore batteries and shipboard guns immediately opened fire on Gray. They were accurate – they shot one of his 500-pound bombs off the rack – but he pressed on with his slanting dive. Nearing the drop point, Gray's Corsair burst into flames from repeated hits. He might have aborted the attack to make a water landing, but that was not his way.

Trailing pilots saw Gray's remaining bomb arc from his wings onto the target. *Amakusa* erupted in a tremendous explosion. She capsized quickly, sinking with most of her crew, but Gray, too, disappeared in the smoke, spray, and debris.

Vice Admiral Sir Phillip Vian recommended Gray for "his brilliant fighting spirit and inspired leadership." Thus, Gray received the last Victoria Cross of the war, only the second awarded to a Fleet Air Arm pilot in six years of conflict. Two other ships in Onagawa Bay also were sunk.

On the afternoon of the 9th, USS *Essex* (CV-9) launched a strike against Ominatu Naval Base, targeting shipping in Montsu Bay, also located in northern Honshu. Lieutenant (jg) Vernon T. Coumbe attacked a transport, dropping his 500-pounder, and bent the throttle seaward. But an astute 25mm antiaircraft gun crew struck the Corsair, which began haemorrhaging oil. With the engine losing vital fluid, the propeller jerked to a halt.

The Illinois aviator ditched his F4U five miles south of the target, an unenviable location. But he had hope of rescue. Inflating his life raft, he spent several hours holding his position against the westerly wind trying to push him ashore into certain captivity.

With fading daylight, Coumbe realized he would remain afloat overnight. After perhaps 45 minutes' sleep, he awoke around 3:00 a.m., aware of a faint gray on the eastern horizon. He realized that he had drifted perhaps seven miles easterly and sat about one mile seaward from a small fishing village.

Surveying the Japanese shoreline, Coumbe discerned a beach north of the village with a wooded area just inland. It looked like a good hiding place until his friends came searching for him. He dragged his raft and emergency equipment into the oak, spruce, and pine underbrush, then dozed fitfully. Then, around 6:00, he heard an unmistakable sound – the patented purr of Pratt & Whitney engines. They belonged to his squadronmates' Corsairs, led by Lieutenant Jack H. Tripp. They had overflown Coumbe's ditching position, then expanded the search.

With surging optimism, Coumbe dug into his survival kit and raised a signal pistol, firing a star shell. On the narrow beach he waved his white scarf for good measure. With the blue fighter-bombers circling protectively, Coumbe launched his raft and reached 300 yards offshore where he began an endurance contest against the wind. Finally he was forced to return to the beach, but he was confident that a rescue would ensue.

He was right. Around noontime four *Essex* fighters appeared, led by Lieutenant T. Hamil Reidy, Coumbe's skipper, escorting two floatplanes from the battleship *North Carolina* (BB-55). One of the Corsairs descended dangerously low, either from exuberance or attempting to drop another raft. Whatever the reason, Lieutenant (jg) Clinton E. Wear, one of Coumbe's roommates, mushed out of a turn, caught a wingtip, and cartwheeled to destruction.

Nevertheless, Coumbe realized that his time had come. A good swimmer, he reckoned that he could make better progress without his raft and struck out, trying to swim against the surf. But the incoming tide was too heavy; he barely got off the beach. Therefore, the senior OS2U Kingfisher pilot, Lieutenant Ralph R. Jacobs, turned upwind in a landing approach. He set his floatplane down and taxied close, approaching Coumbe within perhaps 25 feet.

Without a back-seater, Lieutenant Jacobs stood in his seat with one leg on the wing, trying to toss a line to Coumbe. Then a heavy wave rocked the plane, knocking Jacobs off balance. He was pitched overboard, his left foot shoving the throttle as he fell. The empty Kingfisher set off, making its own course away from the scene as shells from Japanese guns exploded nearby.

Circling close by, Lieutenant Hamil Reidy could hardly believe it. To convince himself, he made two low passes confirming that nobody manned the Kingfisher. "I thought I was dreaming," he recalled. "The plane was taxiing in a straight course better than most pilots could do."

Then Japanese gunners caught on to the situation and began dropping shells near the two pilots in the water.

Reidy radioed the second floatplane pilot, Lieutenant (jg) Almon P. Oliver. He made a good landing in the surf, motored within 75 yards of shore, and held his Kingfisher steady while Coumbe and Jacobs tried climbing aboard.

Oliver recalled, "I soon had two very large and very wet people crammed into the back seat. How they managed to get into the cockpit, I'll never know, but the alternative was unacceptable at the moment."

Turning hard about, Oliver coaxed the overloaded floatplane through the tossing waves.

By then the enemy gunners had shifted their attention to the errant Kingfisher, firing at what appeared to be another fleeing American. Reidy decided to deny the plane to the Japanese and rolled into a strafing pass, leaving it sinking.

Oliver staggered into the air but realized he still had multiple problems.

Recognizing that I would have difficulty with navigation, weather, and fuel with the unbalanced load I was carrying, I intended to land at sea near the rescue sub. After some deliberate thought, however, I decided to try to make it back to some ship in the fleet. Fortunately we picked up the ZB [homing] signal and made it back to the *North Carolina* with *no* fuel left aboard. So on August 10, 1945, I picked up the first and only downed pilot from within Japan proper, not one but two.[41]

Vernon Coumbe was back aboard USS *Essex* the next morning "well suntanned, hale and hearty."[42]

The rescue mission was Oliver's last flight in an OS2U. But it was certainly noteworthy: his parents received 100 or more newspaper clippings of the feat, including two from Italy.

Meanwhile, individual Japanese pilots still flung themselves at American ships, especially the isolated radar pickets. On Tomcat Station Number One, 50 miles southwest of the task force center, the destroyer *Benner* (DD-807) and her three partners controlled two four-plane divisions of fighters to "delouse" returning U.S. strike missions, lest an enemy tried to tag along.

A large Gearing-class ship at 3,500 tons, *Benner* had reported on station on the 8th. *Benner* was new, only commissioned in February 1945 under Commander John Munholland, Annapolis class of 1932. She was teamed with the 2,200-ton Sumner-class ships *J. W. Weeks* (DD-701), *Hank* (DD-702), and *Borie* (DD-704), each commissioned the previous summer.

All four destroyers featured three turrets mounting twin five-inch dual-purpose guns, effective against surface or aerial targets. The "five-inch 38" barrel was 38 calibers long (nearly 16 feet), capable of blasting a 55-pound projectile downrange at approximately 2,600 feet per second. Equipped with the variable-time (VT) proximity fuse, the round could destroy an aircraft with a near miss at several miles. The turrets were controlled by wartime-developed optical or radar means, proving deadly effective in combat, claiming 35 percent of shipboard shootdowns.

The Gearings also boasted four 40mm mounts (twin and quadruple) and ten or more 20mm single mounts. Ironically, the latter two came from neutral countries. The powerful Bofors 40mm cannon was a prewar Swedish design that had impressed Britain early on. The U.S. Navy adopted the type for domestic production in early 1942.

Bofors twin mounts, the most common, were served by seven-man crews, including four loaders. Manually fed by four-round clips, the weapon threw a two-pound explosive projectile at nearly 2,900 feet per second, rated effective to 11,000 yards, although fuses typically detonated the round at half that distance to minimize friendly casualties. One or two hits often could destroy a single-engine aircraft, and Bofors became the most effective antiaircraft guns with nearly 40 percent of credited ships' kills.

Combined Navy and Army need was such that 40mm ammunition peaked at 12 million rounds per month in late 1944.[43]

The Swiss-designed 20mm Oerlikon was a ship's last-ditch defense. Gun crews considered it "unbelievably simple and almost trouble free," with a relatively fast reload for the 60-round drum and a quick-change barrel.

The gunner attached himself to the Oerlikon by stepping into the curved shoulder braces and snapping a belt around his waist. The gunner's problem was immensely simplified with a gyro-stabilized, lead-computing sight. The shooter placed the reticle on the target and tracked it inbound without indulging in ballistic mental gymnastics. When he depressed the firing handle, the gun spit out about 480 heavy rounds per minute.

A good loader could replace the empty 60-round ammunition drum with a fresh one in several seconds. Meanwhile, the spotter watched for new targets and checked for safety measures.[44]

By August 1945 the Pacific Fleet had a well-established doctrine for combat information centers (CICs). In the confined steel space of the CIC, heated electronics glowed with phosphors on screens. Typically, destroyers had a CIC watch officer, an intercept officer, four operators for a surface search and two air search radars, two plotters, a status board keeper, a dead-reckoning trace plotter, and a talk-between-ship recorder. "Radar plot" was crowded but comfortable, being one of the few air-conditioned compartments. Yet finessed tactics and doctrine, paired with the latest available technology, and with the war's conclusion surely just round the corner, still did not prevent Allied loss of life in those final days of the conflict.

On August 9 *Benner* and the three Sumner-class ships in their formation, Tomcat One, steamed in a three-mile circle, affording overlapping protection from their antiaircraft guns. Just before noon two Japanese aircraft probed the formation. The second – identified as either a twin-engine Kawasaki Nick or Mitsubishi Dinah – evaded at 27,000 feet and disappeared, apparently with the ships' location.

The action began just after 3:00 p.m. when *Hank*, controlling the newly arrived combat air patrol (CAP) about 140 miles offshore, got a 40-mile contact. But the Hellcats found the rare Aichi Grace naval bomber was too fast to catch in its dive. Valuable moments were lost when the radar officer held fire to avoid the possibility of hitting the friendlies.

The Japanese pressed the attack, emerging from clouds at about two miles. Flying a weaving course inbound, the Grace (also identified as a fixed-landing-gear Val) overflew *Benner*, while ships' guns winged the intruder. *Benner*'s SC surveillance radar failed during the action due to vibration from the heavy guns, but all ships continued shooting.

Passing between *Benner* and *Borie*, the Grace swerved toward *Hank* in a steep turn while 20mm or 40mm gunfire struck the Aichi. It dropped a bomb off *Borie*'s starboard bow, wiping out the forward guns by blast and shrapnel, including two five-inch turrets. Still drawing heavy fire in a shallow descent, the kamikaze pilot dived into the superstructure.

Borie's skipper, Annapolis graduate Commander Noah Adair, Jr., had spent 14 years preparing for this moment. He and his command team were driven off the bridge but he continued conning his stricken, burning ship; his calmness under the worst combat conditions would eventually result in Adair receiving the Silver Star.

The other three destroyers maneuvered to protect *Borie* while presenting themselves broadside to likely attackers, maximizing available firepower.

Soon *Weeks* got a blip at 25 miles, tracking it inbound for five minutes. The Kawanishi George's apparent target was *Hank* whose five-inch main batteries opened up at 7,500 yards (nearly four miles), blasting out 55-pound shells. As the bandit pressed in, at least two ships' 20mm guns chipped in, shooting off the port wing and contributing to the splash close aboard.

At 3:50 p.m. a pair of Zekes tried double-teaming Tomcat One. Amid bursting antiaircraft fire, they tracked their prey, with *Benner*'s five-inchers scoring repeated shrapnel hits until one Mitsubishi crashed near *Hank*.

Shortly thereafter the second Zeke turned in to attack, reaching Oerlikon range inside the ships' perimeter. Like its partner, the Zeke splashed close to *Hank*, only 50 feet off the starboard bow.

The last attack came around 4:20, about 90 minutes after the first. Identified as a stubby Mitsubishi Jack fighter, the bandit selected *Benner*, which turned to unmask her portside guns and all turrets. The result was devastating: streaming flames, the fighter still crossed into the formation as the devoted kamikaze sought to keep his dying plane airborne. During the final seconds, Commander Munholland ordered full left rudder to avoid the falling wreckage.

That night *Borie*'s team mates searched for her survivors. *Hank* saved three men from the sea, joyous news aboard the battered, stricken *Borie*. The crash and ensuing gasoline-fed fire had killed 48 men and wounded 66, about one third of the crew. The bridge lost steering control for a while, but damage control teams doused flames and she resumed steaming. The stricken destroyer shaped course for Saipan, bound for Pearl Harbor and points east.

The kamikazes kept coming. On the evening of the 12th the veteran, battered battleship *Pennsylvania* (BB-38) lay anchored alongside *Tennessee* (BB-43) in Buckner Bay on Okinawa's southeast coast.* Both were Pearl Harbor survivors but "*Pennsy's*" skipper, Captain William M. Moses, had only been in command since early June.

Pennsylvania had only just returned from a major overhaul completed between March and July. Among other concerns, after 11 invasions her main batteries "were worn out from shooting at Japs from Attu to Luzon."[45] At Hunter's Point Shipyard, San Francisco, she had received replacements for her much-used 14-inch barrels, some retrieved from the mud of Pearl Harbor.

Salvors removed five naval rifles from the capsized *Oklahoma* (BB-37) which were refurbished, and six more from *Nevada* (BB-36). One of "*Pennsy's*" own barrels had been repaired previously. This immense task was completed in an astonishing five days.[46]

Anchored nearby to the *Pennsylvania* and *Tennessee* was the 10,000-ton light cruiser *St. Louis* (CL-49), a blooded veteran of 11 Pacific campaigns. Her wartime career had begun at Pearl Harbor where she was among the first ships to get underway during the attack, and her gunners claimed three Japanese planes.

Manning "sky aft" was Ensign Doniphon Shelton, turret officer of one of the three-gun mounts with no relevant duty at the moment. He was an experienced seaman who had served aboard two prewar battleships before entering Annapolis. His class had graduated a year early to meet wartime needs, and Shelton had already seen action including Leyte and Okinawa. Near Leyte Gulf on November 27 "*Louie*" had survived a 40-minute kamikaze attack, sustaining serious damage from a Val that impacted with its bomb. The explosion had knocked Shelton off his feet, leaving 16 dead and 20-plus seriously wounded.

That evening Shelton described Buckner Bay as "smoke pot time, as the kamikazes were frequent but not scoring. But then

---

* In July 1945, Nakagusuku Bay had been renamed for Lieutenant General Simon Bolivar Buckner, Jr., the last American general killed in World War II.

I tally-hoed a torpedo headed our way! It passed ahead of our bow and hit the *Pennsylvania* anchored next to us."[47]

As *Pennsylvania*'s cruise book noted, "At 2045 a Jap torpedo plane somehow slipped in over Buckner Bay without any warning and launched its torpedo at the indistinct silhouette of a large warship." One of the crew of the *Pennsylvania* wrote home: "We didn't get the Jap plane, but we sure busted hell out of his torpedo!"

Actually the Japanese had launched four aircraft – Nakajima *Tenzans*, or Jills to the Americans. One aborted en route and one disappeared but the others skirted the harbor's smoke screen.

One Type 91 torpedo was well aimed, boiling through the bay's dark waters and slamming into the target at 40 knots. It hit well aft on the starboard side, and the warhead – at least 520 pounds of boosted TNT – inflicted extensive damage.[48]

The explosion tore a 20- by 30-foot hole, killing 20 men inboard of the site and injuring ten. Many compartments were flooded and the ship settled heavily by the stern. "But, by the Herculean efforts of the ship's repair parties and the prompt assistance of two salvage tugs and an LCS [landing craft support vessel], the flooding was brought under control."

With her propellers inoperable, the next day *"Pennsy"* was towed to shallower water for easier damage repair. She remained there for over two weeks while salvage operations continued, and a temporary patch was fitted over the gaping hole. Later, among others, Captain Moses commended Chief Shipfitter R.F. Smith for diving operations plus Lieutenant L.D. Williams and Chief Electrician Scharn for electrical damage control work.[49]

Then, on the 18th, *Pennsylvania* finally departed Okinawa towed by two tugs with a spare, "proceeding tortuously" to Guam 1,400 miles away. Lugging 31,000 tons of dead weight, for three weeks the vessels made as little as two knots when seas were heavy, and never more than seven. But her war was finally over.

Sailors and pilots on both sides were still dying even with a Japanese surrender so clearly on the cards. But while combat operations continued throughout the first half of August, a residual drama was played out far from the fighting.

OLYMPIC TRIALS, 1943-45

While naval air combat carried on unabated, groundwork continued for the ultimate objective, an invasion of Japan. The overall Allied invasion plan, aptly titled *Downfall*, originally had been discussed at the 1943 Casablanca Conference, calling for a two-phase assault: Operation *Olympic* against the southern island of Kyushu in November, and Operation *Coronet* on the main island of Honshu the following March. Both would be enormous undertakings: *Olympic* involved about 350,000 men in combat units plus a further 125,000 support personnel; *Coronet* more than half a million. In comparison, the initial D-Day landings in Normandy committed approximately 150,000 Allied troops.[50]

Building the force to invade Japan required a gargantuan combination of planning, coordination, and logistics. Previously, Admiral Ernest King, chief of naval operations, had reportedly quipped, "I don't know what the hell this 'logistics' is that General Marshall is always talking about, but I want some of it." In fact, the Navy was the essential factor in transferring troops from Europe and the United States. Nearly everything without wings had to go by sea, and so did many aircraft.[51]

By August 1945 at least four armored divisions were based in the continental United States, with two or more infantry divisions preparing to deploy west.

The Army also intended to redeploy more than 395,000 men directly from Europe, all between September and December. They included units dedicated to *Olympic* or *Coronet*, representing Army Ground Forces, Air Forces, and Service Forces.

At the same time planning proceeded for 477,000 soldiers and airmen to round out the *Coronet* order of battle, moving from Europe through "ConUS" to the Pacific between September 1945 and April 1946. That amounted to a total of nearly 875,000 personnel moving halfway around the world in eight months. And that did not count Army, Navy, and Marine Corps personnel already in the Pacific.

Nor did the redeployment figures include Doolittle's Eighth Air Force units transitioning to B-29s with 102,000 aircrew and maintainers, either from Europe or originating in the States. The transport burden was further increased by 75,000 European Theater hospital patients beginning in late 1944.

Despite the clear logistical nightmare of such an undertaking, there was one clear advantage to the Allies. Throughout the war they had consistently outperformed the Axis in the crucial realm of supply, which was far more than simply building "stuff." King's quip concealed the Anglo-American mastery of the logistical trilogy: planning, production, and distribution. British historian Richard Overy properly noted that the American "tooth to tail" ratio of warfighters to rear-echelon and support personnel ran 18 to one; Japan operated at a support to combat ratio of a mere one to one.[52]

Within the gigantic task of planning *Downfall*, model making played a crucial role. It was little heralded amid the scope of the global conflagration, but became a growth industry during the war. Tens of thousands of scale recognition ship and aircraft models were produced in the U.S. by model makers ranging from school children to military professionals. Perhaps at the upper end of the craft were those who manufactured terrain models from plaster and rubber.

Commander Burt Benton's Terrain Model Unit (TMU) had some 200 officers and artisans to produce extremely detailed 3-D terrain maps of Pacific Theater targets. In January 1945 the team moved from Washington to Pearl Harbor, joining the Joint Intelligence Center's model unit. Installed in an unused warehouse, the TMU merged with other organizations to avoid duplication of effort.

The unit's output was tremendous, reaching 75 three-by-five-foot panels daily. After curing in ovens, and depending upon scale, many details were hand painted or airbrushed for micro realism. Finished products then were made available to assault units preparing for Operation *Olympic*, the invasion of Kyushu in November, which was to precede Operation *Coronet* by four months.[53]

Some of the model unit's clients were already preparing to use the products. That summer newly promoted Marine Corps Major John D. Cooper was assigned to III Amphibious Corps staff.

A veteran of Guadalcanal and Saipan, and former commander of the battleship *Pennsylvania*'s Marine detachment, he recalled, "After work when the logistics and shipping and schedules were done, we would commiserate over drinks. A recurring question was: 'How do you kill 70 million people?' After civilian actions on Saipan and Okinawa, that's what we thought it might take."[54]

Cooper's was no flippant comment. Beyond the military, Japan had organized the Volunteer Fighting Corps composed of all healthy males between 15 and 60, and females aged 17 to 40 – it was truly a nation under arms.[55] Moreover, Tokyo accurately anticipated the likely *Olympic* landing sites and reinforced them accordingly. But despite updated intelligence of Japanese defenses, the in-theater Allied supreme commander insisted on discounting U.S. radio intercepts as deception. General Douglas MacArthur foresaw his destiny fulfilled in leading *Downfall*, the greatest invasion of all time.

*　　*　　*

General of the Army Douglas MacArthur became the most celebrated American soldier of World War II, excepting his erstwhile subordinate and future president Dwight D. Eisenhower.

MacArthur was heir to military glory, the son of a youthful Union officer who received the Medal of Honor during the Civil War. Born on an Arkansas Army post in 1880, MacArthur excelled at West Point, standing first in the class of 1903. Two years later he accompanied his father, then a major general, on a tour of the Far East, including Japan, which defeated Czarist Russia in 1905.

MacArthur was nominated for the Medal of Honor after a 1914 action in Mexico, then won a fighting reputation as a division chief of staff in World War I. He emerged from the Western Front with two Distinguished Service Crosses.

The stellar academy graduate returned to West Point as superintendent immediately after the Great War, rising to Army Chief of Staff in 1930.

In 1936, no longer chief of staff, MacArthur accepted a lucrative advisory post with the Philippines, becoming a foreign field marshal before officially leaving the U.S. Army. One of his aides was then-Major Eisenhower of whom MacArthur said, "This is the best officer in the Army," adding, "When the next war comes he should go right to the top."[56]

With war against Japan a growing prospect, MacArthur was recalled to active duty in 1941. However, from December onward his underfunded, poorly equipped U.S. and Philippine forces were a poor match for Imperial Japan's accomplished conquerors. The fact that MacArthur's air force was caught on the ground several hours after Pearl Harbor was seldom addressed, and his public image was little marred.

MacArthur evacuated his wife, son, and half a million dollars from the islands in mid-March, establishing headquarters in Australia. In a blatantly political and public relations move, Army Chief of Staff George C. Marshall (no admirer of MacArthur) pushed for the Medal of Honor, despite any remote relevance to the medal's criteria. For MacArthur it was "third time lucky," following his nominations in Mexico and France.

Over the next three years MacArthur led the Southwest Pacific Theater, advancing through New Guinea to the Philippines. Unlike his erstwhile subordinate Eisenhower, MacArthur proved a marginal coalition commander, often ignoring contributions of Australians and other allies.

MacArthur's command style remained consistent through most of his career, ranging from egotism to megalomania. His cultivated image ran to "Field Marshal Casual": a faded four-star general's hat, aviator sunglasses, and an absurdly large corncob pipe seemingly lifted from Mammy Yoakum in the *Li'l Abner* comic strip. He surrounded himself with sycophantic courtiers, most notably his abrasive chief of staff and a consistently inaccurate intelligence chief. However, the Southwest Command produced results, partly due to MacArthur's senior airman, Lieutenant General George C. Kenney.

*   *   *

In contrast, Admiral Chester Nimitz, Pacific Theater Commander, read the developing intelligence with growing concern. While he did not doubt that *Olympic* would succeed in ultimately conquering Kyushu, he feared the likely toll. That summer, with his finger on the intelligence pulse, he noted that an early estimate of 200,000 Kyushu defenders had leaped to 300,000 with additional army divisions deployed from Honshu. Not only would the latter number require more than 700,000 pairs of American boots on the ground, but it would also put the Navy in a situation all too similar to Okinawa, with a very real possibility of prohibitive losses to Japan's hoard of kamikaze suicide pilots.

Consequently, in June Nimitz had written to the irascible Chief of Naval Operations Ernest King, advocating cancelation of *Olympic* and proceeding directly to *Coronet* on Honshu. Scheduled for March 1946, *Coronet* offered the advantage of additional time for blockade and bombing further to reduce Japan's ability – and perhaps willingness – to resist.

Nimitz's concern was well founded. On August 2, U.S. intelligence now estimated some 534,000 troops on Kyushu – approximately 11 divisions with two more possibly on the way. On August 5, the estimate was revised to some 600,000 men in 14 divisions. In fact, postwar evaluation of Japanese documents indicated as many as 900,000 troops on Kyushu, a figure that may have omitted the large civilian militia.[57]

Nimitz's concerns were shared by his immediate subordinates, including Admiral Spruance of the Fifth Fleet. As Nimitz's biographer later noted, "During July Spruance was on Guam planning Operation *Olympic* with his and Nimitz's staffs. The more he studied the proposed invasion, the deeper became his foreboding that the losses in ships and men would be heavy."[58]

Additionally, radio intercepts dating back to June indicated that the Japanese had dispersed more than 900 suicide aircraft throughout Kyushu.

Based on the eight-month combat record of the kamikazes – between 12 and 20 percent success – perhaps 150 of those 900 planes were likely to hit an Allied vessel. How many ships might be sunk or scrapped depended on several variables, including how many victims required multiple hits.[59]

Against that chilling backdrop, on August 10 Admiral King issued a notice to Chester Nimitz: "This is a peace warning."[60]

Nimitz had justifiable concerns about the likelihood of peace. Indeed, as the events of the next few days would prove, nothing was guaranteed.

✳   ✳   ✳

If ever a major military commander came from far behind for the big win, it was Chester W. Nimitz.

Born in the Texas Hill Country in 1885, young Nimitz grew up working in the family hotel but was enthralled with his German grandfather's merchant marine sea stories. Though lacking a high school diploma, with extra tutoring Chester entered the Naval Academy at age 16, earning varsity letters in rowing. But he was also a standout scholar, standing seventh among the 114 in the class of 1905. His classmates described him as being "of cheerful yesterdays and confident tomorrows," and "possesses that calm and steady Dutch way that gets at the bottom of things." However, as he much enjoyed relating to future admirers, Nimitz in fact became seasick on his first naval deployment.[61]

Nimitz dodged a potentially fatal professional bullet in 1908 when he ran a destroyer aground in the Philippines. Found guilty at court-martial, he received a letter of reprimand and got on with his career.

With his family background, Nimitz was assigned to study diesel engines in Germany, overlapping his honeymoon. Thereafter, demonstrating a diesel in the Brooklyn Navy Yard, he lost part of his right ring finger in the new engine.

Subsequently, as a qualified submariner, Lieutenant Commander Nimitz spent most of World War I on the Atlantic Fleet staff. Later he established the first Naval Reserve Officers Training Corps unit, formed at the University of California.

Promoted to rear admiral in 1938, Nimitz hauled within range of retirement with 35 years' service. But instead, the next year he took command of the Bureau of Navigation – subsequently the Bureau of Naval Personnel – setting him on a collision course with history.

Following the Pearl Harbor debacle, President Roosevelt selected Nimitz to take over the Pacific Fleet from a longtime friend, Admiral Husband Kimmel. It was a stunning decision: "Chet" Nimitz was a two-star admiral elevated over numerous seniors. But he hastened from Washington to Hawaii, arriving by flying boat on Christmas Day. At month's end he became a full (four-star) admiral, having never worn a vice admiral's three stars.

With his battleships sunk or sidelined and his submarines largely ineffective from scandalous torpedo failures, Nimitz turned to his aviators. During the first months of 1942 he sent aircraft carriers on a widespread series of raids, hit-and-run operations intended to keep the Japanese off balance. The oceanic road back began in the Coral Sea that May, the first carrier duel in history, followed by the epic victory at Midway a month later. The Navy's quasi-official chronicler, Samuel Eliot Morison, observed that under Nimitz morale rose "several hundred percent."[62]

Early that year Nimitz assumed another role as Commander Pacific Ocean Areas (CinCPac). Thus he became a theater commander equal to General Douglas MacArthur's Southwest Pacific Area.

After the victorious bloodletting at Guadalcanal, of America's six front-line carriers in 1942, only two remained in mid-1943.[*] But new-generation ships and aircraft arrived in Hawaii that summer, spawning the power behind the Central Pacific offensive. Over the next two years CinCPac forces rolled back Japanese conquests throughout the Central Pacific, climaxing in the Philippines in late 1944.

Though possessing enormous responsibility, Nimitz allowed himself relatively few respites. But as a true Texan his daytime relaxation often involved his Colt target pistol and occasionally sipping bourbon in the evenings.

Keeping closer to the Pacific War's enormous geography, in January 1945 Nimitz moved his CinCPac headquarters to Guam. The relocation also allowed him to coordinate with Major General Curtis LeMay's XXI Bomber Command.

---

[*] U.S. carriers lost in the Guadalcanal campaign: *Saratoga* torpedoed in August; *Wasp* sunk in September; *Hornet* sunk in October. *Lexington* and *Yorktown* were lost at Coral Sea and Midway.

By August Nimitz's Pacific Fleet included more than 6,000 ships, nearly 15,000 aircraft, and about 2 million personnel, including all six Marine Corps divisions.

PEACE WARNINGS, AUGUST 10–13

From Nimitz's CinCPac Guam headquarters, on August 10 the word went out that Japan was going to sue for peace, prompting unlimited joy among the servicemen and women even if their commander was hesitant. First Lieutenant Al Wood of the 19th Bomb Group, stationed on Guam, wrote home:

> The (peace) offer was announced over the loudspeakers around 10 p.m. Shortly thereafter, a total repeat of the Fourth of July celebration broke loose with flares, tracer bullets and gunshots. The loudspeakers then repeatedly sounded the order "Cease firing, cease firing" in a most military fashion. This drew a response of several more rounds of firing. After things quieted down, the action moved to the officers club, which stayed open to 1:00 a.m.[63]

In fact, Japan had not made formal peace overtures, but back-channel approaches via neutral nations, notably Switzerland.

Much closer to the action, Admiral William F. Halsey's Third Fleet pondered what the "peace warning" actually meant. Riding his flagship, the 48,000-ton battleship *Missouri* (BB-63), "Bull" Halsey was the jut-jawed seadog whose 1904 Annapolis classmates had reportedly said, "He looks like a figurehead of Neptune." Naval aviation had needed senior officers between the wars, and Halsey was selected to qualify for carrier command. He received his golden wings in 1935 at age 52, and seven years later became America's favorite fighting admiral after Pearl Harbor.

Halsey possessed the seniority for fleet command though he had stumbled badly on two occasions. In October 1944 he had left the amphibious shipping in Leyte Gulf vulnerable to Japanese counterattack, and in December he had run Third Fleet through a tropical storm, later christened "Halsey's Typhoon," with significant losses on both occasions. Though Halsey's judgment in those incidents cost the U.S. Navy seven ships and nearly 1,500 sailors, by then he was politically bulletproof. Neither Chester Nimitz in the Pacific nor Ernest King in Washington was willing to hand the Army Air Forces a public relations victory in the coming battle for an independent U.S. Air Force.

Carrier aviators feared creation of a unified department of defense and a separate air force with good reason, as postwar events demonstrated. Harry Truman's army bias, dating from the Great War, led him to advocate disbanding the Marine Corps, slashing naval funding, and absorbing naval aviation into the Air Force, possibly excepting maritime patrol and antisubmarine operations.

But the serious political battles would not be joined until after VJ Day. Meanwhile, Halsey's subordinate was still Vice Admiral John S. McCain, Sr., commanding Task Force 38, Third Fleet's carrier striking arm. "Slew" McCain was no scholar – he had graduated in the bottom 30 percent of the Annapolis class of 1916 – but advanced steadily. "Real aviators" regarded him as another "Johnny Come Lately" because, like Halsey, he received his wings at age 52. A Task Force 38 staffer said, "I don't think he could fly an airplane to save his life but he filled the slot when it was needed."[64]

Among subordinates McCain was popular in some quarters. He cultivated a sloppy, even slovenly appearance by removing the grommet from his billed hat, leaving the material a shapeless khaki lump. He insisted on rolling his own cigarettes, carrying papers and Bull Durham tobacco in a shirt pocket. Occasionally flakes of tobacco dribbled onto his clothes. However, he had a first-class staff that covered for the boss when necessary.

Weather had scuttled Honshu carrier air strikes on the 8th, so the next day McCain had launched his tailhookers to scour Honshu airfields, returning with claims for nearly 400 aircraft strafed, bombed, and rocketed. Carrier planes had struck widely elsewhere, from the east coast of Japan to the west coast of Korea. The gloss-blue aircraft had sunk five auxiliaries, a tanker, and a merchant cargo ship, losing 26 planes, while a kamikaze had sunk the destroyer *Borie*.

Ever pugnacious, the "Bull" had jotted in his diary, "an excellent day."[65]

Third Fleet operations on the 9th had partly been the result of Army concern about several hundred Japanese planes on northern airfields. Most were within reach of Okinawa, especially for a one-way mission. It was not a rhetorical matter: in May the Japanese Army had launched 12 bombers bearing 168 suicide commandos against two U.S. air bases on Okinawa. Five planes reached Yontan Airfield, destroying or damaging 38 aircraft and 70,000 gallons of aviation fuel. A far larger operation was planned against the Marianas for late August.[66]

Meanwhile, the Far East Air Forces unloaded their full menu against Japanese naval and industrial targets: B-24 Liberator heavy bombers, B-25 Mitchell and A-26 Invader medium bombers, plus A-20 Havoc attack planes. Low-flying Army aircrews claimed eight vessels, mostly cargo ships, between Kyushu and Korea, leaving as many more damaged. Simultaneously, more than 200 Thunderbolt and Mustang fighters strafed and rocketed airfields, transport, and storage facilities.[67]

U.S. and British warships had bombarded Honshu and Hokkaido targets seven times between July 14 and August 9, involving seven American battleships and one British. The U.S. 16-inch naval rifle threw a 1,900-pound high-explosive shell as much as 23 miles. It arrived with authority, delivering a large bursting charge that leveled many structures. The big guns put some of Japan's remaining industry within range, assuming aerial observation, but the task group often shot from half that distance or less.

The bombardments began and ended with Kamaishi on northern Honshu, 60 miles north of Robert Hampton Gray's August 9 Victoria Cross action. Home to one of Japan's largest iron works, Kamaishi and its port were strategic targets.

Beside the potential damage to Japan's faltering steel plants, Third Fleet planners hoped to goad enemy aircraft into a response. But none appeared, to the disappointment of aggressive Hellcat and Corsair pilots circling overhead.

The bombardment unit was led by Rear Admiral John F. Shafroth, Jr., the 280-pound son of a Colorado governor. An all-round athlete, he had graduated from Annapolis in 1908 where his friends considered him to possess "more bovine characteristics than anyone else in the class. Good natured and light hearted." Now 58 years old, he had come up through destroyers and cruisers.[68]

The August 9 operation involved an Anglo-American surface force totaling three battleships, six cruisers, and 12 destroyers. The ships opened fire from about seven miles and shot off nearly 3,000 shells in almost two hours, making four passes along the shore, pounding the iron works and docks. It was fairly close range for the big ships' 16-inch guns.

In a rare media event, some of the bombardment was broadcast live from the battleship *Iowa* (BB-61) to Stateside radio. Listeners heard the powerful booms of major-caliber artillery but obviously had no concept of the immense concussive effect of a ton of steel blasting from 66-foot barrels at more than twice the speed of sound. Aboard destroyers and cruisers, the five-, six-, and eight-inch guns forced sailors to seek their own protection from the powerful eruptions sending shells arcing downrange in their ballistic trajectories.[69]

As many as 1,700 Japanese workers and residents were killed in the northern operations, as were dozens of Allied prisoners held in Kamaishi, unknown to Allied intelligence.

Postwar evaluation revealed that the bombardments reduced Kamaishi's pig iron and coking coal production by more than half.[70]

That evening, sitting in his wardroom aboard the *Missouri*, Halsey received King's tentative stand-down message. The chief of staff – bespectacled, studious Rear Admiral Robert "Mick" Carney – read it aloud: "Through the Swiss Government, Japan stated that she is willing to accept Allied surrender ultimatum issued at Potsdam, provided they can keep their emperor."

Lacking definite orders to cease fire, Third Fleet attacked airfields and coastal shipping on the 10th and refueled on the 11th, intending to strike Tokyo environs the next day. Aside from McCain's carriers, other warships needed more than ammunition and fuel oil – provisions were running so low that some crews were left with dehydrated carrot salad.

There followed "an avalanche" of amplifying messages, some contradictory. Then, after midnight, Carney interrupted his boss's restless sleep with an intercept from Army News Service: "The American Secretary of State, speaking for the Allied Powers, has accepted the surrender of Japan, provided that the Supreme Allied Commander rule Japan through the authority of the Emperor."

Thus, Third Fleet was befuddled by information and now also by the weather. A typhoon bearing down on Halsey's operating area forced itself into planning concerns, and the question remained whether to launch strikes as scheduled on the 13th. Halsey mulled over his options and decided to keep punching. He signaled McCain, "Attack Tokyo area tomorrow unless the Nips beat us to the punch by throwing in the sponge."

In turn, McCain advised his carrier commanders, "Keep alert for tricks and banzai attacks X The war is not over yet X The Nips may be laying their national game of judo, waiting until we are close and unwary."[71]

*   *   *

Army airpower had flexed its muscles on the 10th as nearly 200 heavy and medium bombers plus 220 P-38s and P-47s hammered the Kumamoto area 50 miles east of Nagasaki. A previous July mission had razed one fifth of the city's area, but Far East Air Forces still targeted the aircraft plant and other facilities.

On a sea sweep, nearly 40 B-25 Mitchells scoured the Sea of Japan between Kyushu and Korea. The targets were destroyers, cargo vessels, and small ships, many of which incurred damage, but proven results were minimal: no confirmed sinkings by Army planes though a small freighter was slain by unknown aircraft and two were thought victims of Army air-dropped mines.[72]

However, it was not entirely one-sided. On the 10th the Liberty ship *Jack Singer* (named for a war correspondent killed in the Pacific earlier in the war) was victim of an aerial torpedo off Okinawa with one injury reported. The freighter was further damaged by a typhoon and written off as a loss, too heavily damaged to repair.

Events in Tokyo compounded the confusion. Rival factions issued contradictory exhortations to keep fighting and to accept surrender. A hardline army officer, Lieutenant Colonel Masao Inaba in the Military Affairs Bureau, drafted a message he recommended for distribution by the war minister: "We are determined to fight resolutely, although we may have to chew grass, eat dirt and sleep in the fields. It is our belief that there is life in death."[73]

Meanwhile, diplomatic red tape indicating willingness to accept the Potsdam Declaration inched its way through the foreign ministry. But astute Japanese recognized the precious value of time – a third atom bomb might descend without warning, on Tokyo or another large city. Therefore, a courageous editor of Domei News Agency, Saiji Hasegawa, risked much by authorizing transmission of acceptance in the most secretive means available: by Morse Code in English. Hasegawa hoped that any military monitors would be delayed in translating the message, which could bring fatal consequences to him and his colleagues.

Hasegawa's text was sent at 8:00 p.m. in two messages aimed at the United States and Europe.

On the opposite side of the globe, Domei's broadcast was safely received. At 7:30 on the morning of the 10th, American communications stations heard the plain-language message and quickly notified Washington.

The Japanese foreign ministry then followed up the unauthorized Domei transmission. Prime Minister Kantaro Suzuki cabled his delegation in Geneva agreeing to the Potsdam terms, but insisting on one condition – that Emperor Hirohito be allowed to retain his sovereignty. While Suzuki awaited an official response, a rogue faction of the military, unable to accept what in their opinion was the emperor's shameful capitulation, began to mobilize a coup attempt. The palace drama would play out over the next few days.[*]

Meanwhile, Truman immediately convened his brain trust: Chief of Staff Admiral William Leahy, Secretary of War Henry Stimson, Secretary of the Navy James Forrestal, and newly appointed

---

[*] See "Tokyo Impasse, Paper Bombs, and Final Dogfights, August 9–15" (p. 71).

Secretary of State James Byrnes. It was an eclectic assembly: Truman and Stimson had been front-line artillery officers in World War I. Forrestal was a naval aviator and financier. Byrnes was a former congressman, senator, and Supreme Court justice. Leahy had run the Navy Bureau of Ordnance that produced the egregious crop of World War II torpedoes. Recalled to service after a 42-year career, he had famously insisted, "The atomic bomb will never go off, and I speak as an expert in explosives."[74]

Discussion focused on the crucial matter of whether Hirohito should remain on the throne. Throughout the day the five men argued back and forth, finally reaching a compromise: upon agreement to surrender, the emperor and a freely elected civil government would rule under direction of a Supreme Allied Commander.

With that crucial point settled, the Washington elite approved sending the draft to key allies. After a day of confusion and wild speculation, during which the president negotiated the terms with the British, Chinese, and Russians, a compromise was struck: the Supreme Allied Military Commander, almost certainly General Douglas MacArthur, would rule Japan through the authority of the emperor.

✳ ✳ ✳

Vice Admiral Matome Ugaki commanded the Fifth Air Fleet on Kyushu. On August 11 he journaled:

> Even though it becomes impossible for us to continue organized resistance after expending our strength, we must continue guerrilla warfare under the emperor and never give up the war. When this resolution is brought home, we can't be defeated. Instead, we can make the enemy finally give up the war after making it taste the bitterness of a prolonged conflict.[75]

Farther down the chain of command, a typical reaction was from a fighter ace of high standing in the Imperial Navy, Lieutenant (jg) Saburo Sakai. His combat career had begun in China in 1937, continuing through the Philippines, New Guinea, the Solomons, and Iwo Jima. Despite the loss of an eye in 1942 he continued flying, recalling, "The nation was being torn asunder, our cities lay prostrate and flaming as if trampled by a gigantic foot. There was no doubt in anyone's mind that the end was near, that soon the fighting would be transferred to our soil. There was no possibility of surrender. We would fight to the last man."[76]

The bitter-enders were not limited to those in imperial uniform. In his memoirs, Foreign Minister Mamoru Shigametsu wrote, "Day by day, Japan turned into a furnace from which the voice of a people searching for food rose in anguish. And yet the clarion call was accepted. If the Emperor ordained it, they would leap into the flames."[77]

Knowing the depth and determination of such entrenched Japanese attitudes, the Americans continued to consider their options. In Washington, Army Chief of Staff George C. Marshall had earlier discussed contingencies with Secretary of War Henry Stimson. Marshall was fully aware of Japan's "fanatical but hopeless defense methods," especially as American forces closed in. He understood that new tactics and weapons were needed and had therefore revealed, to Stimson's surprise, that during an invasion he and his planners were seriously considering gas – not the newest and most potent, but something that would sicken the enemy sufficiently to "take the fight out of them." It might be a form of mustard gas, which he correctly saw as more benign than phosphorous and flame throwers. Marshall added that such gas would not be used against civilians or dense populations but merely against those "last pockets of resistance which had to be wiped out but had no other military significance."[78]

Despite the likely adverse public and wider world reaction, some military commanders had argued that gas could have been a far more humane method on several islands. Peleliu, Iwo Jima, and Okinawa were honeycombed with caves and tunnels impossible to reach from the outside. Tear gas might have forced some Japanese holdouts to surrender rather than die by fire or explosives. Stronger variants, such as blister agents like mustard gas, certainly would have inflicted fatal or debilitating casualties on the defenders, but also would have reduced American losses.

However, Franklin Roosevelt had pledged no first use of chemical weapons, and his ghost influenced his successor despite Tokyo's own frequent use of gas in China.[79]

That had left the second option: blockade.

In the summer of 1945, the U.S. Pacific Fleet owned the waters surrounding the Home Islands. Okinawa, the last major island seized from Japan, had fallen in June. American submarines had choked off Tokyo's declining merchant marine, essential to importing vital supplies, while U.S. naval and army aircraft dominated imperial airspace.

Eventually a sea-air blockade would succeed. The enemy's willingness to resist was one thing; his physical ability to fight through starvation was another. But a blockade would require months, probably with millions of deaths from malnutrition and disease. And beyond Japan itself, as long as the war continued, perhaps 250,000 Asians perished from hunger, disease, and Japanese cruelty – every month.[80]

There was another factor, seldom referenced: some 400,000 American families had sacrificed a loved one to the war effort. Despite a generally unified wartime population, the U.S. eagerly anticipated enjoying the long-awaited peace. Race track attendance was up; some consumer goods began reappearing; and Detroit had begun planning postwar Fords and Chevrolets rather than Sherman tanks and Liberator bombers. A postwar life beckoned.

From Pearl Harbor to Japan was 3,850 statute miles. American forces had sailed, slogged, and flown that saltwater route in 44 months – a sanguinary average advance of just 20 miles per week. Soldiers and sailors wryly joked, "Golden Gate in '48." The nation was tired, worn down by unrelenting effort laced with grief while borne by grim determination. A peace warning would not suffice. Whatever the wishes of the hardliners, peace was desperately needed for the sake of ordinary Americans and ordinary Japanese.

*   *   *

Although the approaching typhoon three days before had veered away, still confusion persisted in Third Fleet. On the

13th, shortly after midnight, Nimitz ordered Halsey to cancel the scheduled strikes and steam off Tokyo "with caution." But almost immediately CinCPac rescinded that message, permitting resumption of offensive sorties following daybreak. The result was another big haul on the 13th, whatever the accuracy of the squadrons' claims: 400 planes thought destroyed or damaged and 19 splashed by patrolling fighters. In turn, the carriers lost 16 aircraft with half a dozen fliers.

As Halsey related, his radio operators' earphones stayed hot while monitoring a continuous stream of orders and advisories. The fleet was scheduled for underway replenishment on the 14th – the 43rd day at sea – with resumption of strikes on the 15th. McCain signaled his task force, "Our orders to strike indicate that the enemy may have dropped an unacceptable joker into the surrender terms X This war could last many months longer X We cannot afford to relax X Now is the time to pour it on X Show this to all pilots."

Rear Admiral Mick Carney was just as frustrated. That night he wrote in his order book, "Peace be damned! Back to Tokyo tomorrow!"[81]

The accelerating pace of events left many combatants in a lingering state of confusion, on both sides. On the afternoon of the 13th all officers at Oppama Air Base near Yokosuka on Tokyo Bay had been summoned to a closed meeting with "the commandant." To some of the fliers he appeared "pale and visibly shaken." Speaking faintly, leaning on his desk for support, the senior officer began, "What I am about to tell you is of the utmost importance and must be regarded as absolutely top secret. I rely upon your integrity as officers of the Imperial Navy to keep this information strictly to yourselves."

The officer paused, either gathering his thoughts or seeking the words. Finally he croaked, "Japan has decided to accept the enemy's terms. We will abide by the Potsdam Declaration."

With tears welling in his eyes, the captain added, "I want all officers to cooperate with me to the fullest. Order must be maintained at this base. There may be hotheads who will refuse to accept the decision to surrender. We cannot afford to have our men violate whatever conditions our country accepts. Remember – and never forget it – that His Majesty's orders come before anything else."[82]

Sakai did not identify the senior officer; it was most likely Rear Admiral Chiaki Matsuda who had served in the Japanese embassy in Washington during 1930–31 and had commanded the super battleship *Yamato* through 1943.[83]

The meeting broke up amid a mixture of stunned disbelief and galling anger. Sakai, the tough old dogfighter, noted some pilots wept.

TOKYO IMPASSE, PAPER BOMBS, AND FINAL DOGFIGHTS, AUGUST 9–15

Tokyo now faced an impasse: a divided Supreme Council with Hirohito facing a brutal reality – destruction or surrender. In late July, following the Allies' declaration from Potsdam, Foreign Minister Shigenori Togo had presented the details to Hirohito. The emperor asked if they were the "most reasonable to be expected." Togo said they were, prompting Hirohito to agree "in principle." However, three of the council ministers had resisted.

Late on August 9 the civilian government leadership had decided to accept the Potsdam Declaration, but the powerful "Big Six" council remained split. Some feared that surrender would mean an end to "the Japaneseness of spirit" in the nation. But Prime Minister Kantaro Suzuki and Navy Minister Mitsumasa Yonai had joined Togo in urging surrender.

Prior to this point the palace had been in turmoil for weeks. A major player working behind the curtain was the nobleman Marquis Koichi Kido, Keeper of the Privy Seal as the emperor's closest advisor.* Heir to a well-placed political family dating from the 1850s Meiji Restoration, Kido was 56, 12 years older than Hirohito. In 1941 Kido had supported General Hideki Tojo for prime minister owing to the perception that he would rein in army radicals bent on war. In view of eventual events, it was one of the most ironic moves in Japanese history.

---

* The title Marquis is the English translation for the equivalent aristocratic rank in Japan.

Subsequently, Kido quietly advocated for a negotiated peace, a potentially dangerous stance given the nation's history and tolerance of political assassination. On the 13th he secretly spoke with Prime Minister Suzuki. At length Kido wore down the aging former admiral with ultimate practicality: "If we bring about peace now, four or five of us may be assassinated but it would be worth it. Without wavering or hesitation, let us carry out the policy to accept the Potsdam Proclamation."

To Kido's enormous relief, Suzuki replied, "Let us do it!"[84]

Finally, Hirohito too decided to exert his authority. In a move unprecedented in his nation's history, on the 10th, following a midnight meeting of the Supreme Council in the palace air-raid shelter, he overrode the three hardliners. That startling news was transmitted to Japanese envoys in Switzerland and Sweden for distribution to the U.S., Britain, and other combatants.

Yet much remained to be done, complicated by communications, by time zones, and by events that would extend the uncertainty – and the fighting.

In America, around midnight on the 12th, the word began filtering out. Station KGEI in San Francisco relayed the Allied response, which indicated the emperor would become subordinate to the occupying powers. That prompted some confusion in Tokyo. Army hardliners interpreted the situation as violating the sacred *Kokutai* – Japanese self-identification and/or sovereignty.

From that point, events spiraled out of control.

Major Kenji Hatanaka, a relatively minor officer in the Imperial Guard, recruited superiors in resisting surrender. They included two lieutenant colonels (one being War Minister Korechika Anami's brother-in-law) and a full colonel. They pleaded with Anami to prevent formal acceptance of surrender, but he declined to respond. Recognizing the growing treason, he gathered other senior army officers to oppose the nascent coup. Half a dozen generals signed Anami's statement, asserting, "The Army will act in accordance with the Imperial Decision to the last."[85]

Late on the 14th, Hirohito recorded a statement for broadcast to his subjects the following day, couched in the best possible terms. In the Rescript on Termination of the War, he acknowledged that events had gone "not necessarily to Japan's advantage."* Without using the term "surrender" he accepted the Allies' Potsdam Declaration.[86]

Before midnight on the 14th, when Hatanaka and other zealous officers of the Imperial Guard learned of the emperor's recording, they proceeded with their desperate plans. However, simultaneously the last B-29 mission flew east of Tokyo, prompting air-raid sirens to wail in caution. Additionally, a wide blackout settled over the capital, complicating the plotters' efforts. From overhead, Superfortress crews marveled at the dark earth where Tokyo had to be hiding.

Captain Carl Schahrer, pilot of the 21st Group's *Boomerang*, said, "I recall flying over Tokyo only because the radar operator told us. We couldn't see anything, although it was a clear night. It was close to midnight."[87]

Meanwhile, the violent drama continued. War Minister Anami committed suicide, leaving a note of apology to the emperor, for what is unclear.

The conspirators had hoped to detain the emperor to prevent him proceeding with the announcement, but he remained concealed in a bunker.

However, in the early hours of the 15th, Hatanaka and an unnamed air force captain barged into the office of Lieutenant General Horishi Mori commanding the Imperial Guard Division. His support was essential to a successful coup, but he and his brother-in-law, Lieutenant Colonel Michinori Shiaishi, flatly refused. Hatanaka and his accomplice killed both officers and forged a letter directing the guard to support the plotters. Thus armed, the coup proceeded while the emperor remained safely out of sight.

The plotters disarmed the palace police and detained 18 people, including radio technicians who had recorded the emperor's speech. The voice disks remained well hidden but Japan's tentative surrender teetered on history's edge.

---

* See the section in Chapter 3 "Denial, Acceptance, and Atrocity" (p. 144) for details of the radio broadcast and the confusion it caused.

Other bitter-enders spread throughout Tokyo and Yokohama, hunting senior government officials for assassination. Forewarned, the intended victims fled or entered protective custody while their homes were burned by the rebels.

At length Hatanaka and his partners learned that forces of the Eastern District Army were en route to quash the rebellion. Hatanaka pleaded for ten minutes of radio time to explain himself to the nation but he was denied. An imperial regimental commander discerned that the supportive letter in General Shiaishi's name was a fake, and ordered Hatanaka and several cohorts out of the palace.

On the morning of the 15th, General Shizuichi Tanaka, commander of the Eastern District Army, drove to the palace and ordered the rebellious troops to disperse. He declared that the leaders' treachery could only be expunged by suicide. Hatanaka recognized the reality: he had committed treason against the emperor and the state, murdered his commanding general, and fomented confusion at the critical juncture in modern Japanese history. Shortly thereafter he and his acolytes shot or stabbed themselves to death on the palace grounds.

Despite his role in ending the revolt, General Tanaka also committed suicide nine days later, expressing regret at his inability to defend the capital against massive American airpower.

Assured that the emperor could remain a titular figure, Japan agreed to "bear the unbearable."

The world's greatest conflagration seemed headed toward a conclusion, but hostilities continued nonetheless.

✣   ✣   ✣

Meanwhile, on Guam a crash program began, printing millions of leaflets to be dropped on major Japanese cities warning of future atomic attacks. The pamphlets were augmented by Japanese language broadcasts from Radio Saipan. The "LeMay Leaflets" spoke directly to Japan's population:

> Read this carefully as it may save your life or the life of a relative or friend. In the next few days, some or all of the cities named

on the reverse side will be destroyed by American bombs. These cities contain military installations and workshops or factories which produce military goods. We are determined to destroy all of the tools of the military clique which they are using to prolong this useless war. But, unfortunately, bombs have no eyes. So, in accordance with America's humanitarian policies, the American Air Force, which does not wish to injure innocent people, now gives you warning to evacuate the cities named and save your lives. America is not fighting the Japanese people but is fighting the military clique which has enslaved the Japanese people. The peace which America will bring will free the people from the oppression of the military clique and mean the emergence of a new and better Japan. You can restore peace by demanding new and good leaders who will end the war. We cannot promise that only these cities will be among those attacked but some or all of them will be, so heed this warning and evacuate these cities immediately.[88]

Following unsettled weather patterns, conditions had improved enough on the 10th for the carriers to launch against enemy airfields. Halsey baldly stated, "We were hoping to fatten our score," optimistically claiming 175 grounded planes destroyed and 153 damaged against 18 carrier aircraft lost. There was more behind the numbers than was evident.[89]

Some of the Navy activity occurred in the dark aboard dedicated night-flying carriers such as USS *Bon Homme Richard* (CVN-31). With Japanese shipping constantly open to daylight air attack, coastal traffic increasingly moved at night. An air group commander described his innovative approach to low-level bombing, first developed in early 1944. Commander William I. Martin, the Navy's leading exponent of night bombing, recalled, "Our normal attack was at 250 feet and about 150 knots indicated (175mph) so we could maintain a steady altitude. When your target disappeared under your nose you'd count 'One alligator two,' punch the bomb release and you'd hit the waterline of a ship almost every time."[90]

Whether by day or night, since the ill-advised Kure strikes in July, costing about 100 pilots and aircrew to little benefit, the U.S.

Navy had been engaged in a numerical contest with the Army Air Forces. It was increasingly obvious that the airmen's cherished dream of an independent air arm would be decided by a postwar Congress, and a generation of admirals wanted a growing score to offset the nascent U.S. Air Force.

Far more concerned with the present, sailors and aircrews had marveled at the news of the two atom bombs, prompting speculation on whether Japan would capitulate or if the war would continue. At sea on August 11, in the carrier *Wasp* (CV-18), Lieutenant Commander Cleo Dobson, a Pearl Harbor survivor commanding a Hellcat squadron, confided to his diary:

> The atomic bombs the Army is dropping really must be the thing. I don't know why we are out here if they do as much damage as we are told. I think the Navy is a has-been now. I am ready for peace terms. We have word from Admiral Nimitz that the Jap air force may make one more big stand and to be ready. I wouldn't mind jumping about 10 to 12 of them.

Two days later, on the 13th, Dobson led his squadron in a low-level attack on an airfield 30 miles from Tokyo, claiming ten planes destroyed. "The Japs haven't quit because there was much AA today. I was over the Japs' mainland for an hour and seven minutes and didn't see one enemy plane in the air."[91]

Among Dobson's opponents was a dwindling number of Japanese aviators who had first entered combat in 1941. They included Lieutenant Commander Iyozoh Fujita, one of the Imperial Navy's senior fighter pilots with five years' experience and combat stretching from Pearl Harbor to Midway and the Western Pacific. Like his contemporaries who survived the war's Darwinian winnowing, he had reveled in the Mitsubishi Zero's early primacy. After a debut over China in 1940, the Type Zero Fighter (named for its sequence in the Japanese calendar year of 2600) became the standard by which naval aircraft were measured. Its exceptional range and performance were unlike anything the Allies possessed until 1943.

But American designers closed the gap, as Fujita later recalled:

During the early part of the war we felt that the weapons in our Zeroes (two 7.7mm and two 20mm guns) were adequate, but later on this was not enough. Our pilots wanted 13mm guns like the Grummans, but we were unable to have them and I don't know why. Our gunsights were adequate for the veterans, but I requested better ones like those used by the Americans. Again we never received them. I knew about the German Me 262 and their rocket fighters. We wanted them too but couldn't get them.[92]

That same day some 400 Army aircrews also swept over inland and coastal targets, concentrating on ports and airfields. Like most pilots, the fliers embraced low-level tactics, drawn by the raw thrill of flying fast and low, whether in medium bombers or fighters. The Fifth Air Force had long since perfected skip bombing, flying into the teeth of Japanese antiaircraft fire at high speed to minimize exposure to the defenses. Making 200–250mph masthead-height approaches, shooting their forward-mounted machine guns to suppress return fire, Mitchell and Invader pilots eyeballed the enemy ship growing in the windscreen, and perhaps 300 feet from the target they "pickled" two or four bombs that would skip along the water like tossed stones on a pond. The bombs, usually 500- and 1,000-pounders, had a four-second delay to prevent the aircraft from getting caught in its own ordnance blast.[93]

Increasingly, Army fighters attacked Japanese airfields. The standard strafing technique involved a squadron in close line astern formation, flying at 1,500 feet and 200mph. When the last four-plane flight leader came abreast of the field, he called for a 90-degree turn inbound. Each pilot then flew low across the field, shooting anything in front of him. At 200mph there was time for careful aiming, and the sheer volume of gunfire from 16 Mustangs often was enough to suppress flak. Reflected one squadron commander, "You could really put a lot of ammunition into a place."[94]

August on Ie Shima
That summer little Ie Shima represented an intersection of the Pacific War with the Fifth Air Force up from the Southwest Pacific Theater and the Seventh via the Central Pacific. By the

end of July its nine square miles and three runways hosted two bomb groups, three fighter groups, and two night fighter squadrons under the command of Lieutenant General James H. Doolittle. More aerial reinforcements were en route.

At age 48, Doolittle was arguably America's greatest airman. During the interwar years he had won every race worth entering, earned one of the first aeronautics doctorates, pioneered instrument flight, and midwifed high-octane gasoline between the Army and Shell Oil. In April 1942 he led the historic mission against Tokyo and other Japanese cities, boldly flying twin-engine bombers from the original aircraft carrier *Hornet* (CV-8). From there he commanded two air forces in the Mediterranean Theater before moving to Britain to lead "the mighty Eighth." With that mission completed, he again turned his attention to Japan.

Always leading from the front, on July 17 Doolittle had landed the first Eighth Air Force bomber on Okinawa. From briefings in Washington he had flown via Europe, stocking up on champagne for General of the Army Douglas MacArthur and a bottle of Napoleon brandy for Fleet Admiral Chester Nimitz. As he wrote, "I thought perhaps that might ease my way for me into their good graces."[95]

Two of Doolittle's five B-29 groups began arriving on Okinawa the first week in August, but his Pacific command was not slated to reach full strength until February 1946, anticipating the invasion of Honshu in March of that year. In the meantime the additional Superforts would pose another dagger at the imperial throat: from Kadena Airfield on Okinawa to Tokyo was a mere 950 miles, less than two thirds the distance from Guam to the Japanese capital.

That same month the command was expanded to include three P-47N Thunderbolt fighter groups on Ie Shima.

The long-ranged N model provided Army pilots with exceptional opportunities, as demonstrated by the 507th Fighter Group over Korea on August 13. The flight from Ie Shima was 740 miles one way, mostly over the East China Sea – just what the new Thunderbolt was designed to do.

During an eight-and-a-half-hour round-trip mission, the pilots were above Seoul for an hour. Thirty-eight Thunderbolts encountered as many as 50 airborne Japanese, claiming 18 victories. Five went to First Lieutenant Oscar F. Perdomo, a 26-year-old Texan who had never even seen an enemy aircraft in ten previous missions. In about five minutes he downed four Nakajima Oscars with his eight .50-caliber machine guns, and shredded a biplane trainer. He was the last American fighter ace of World War II.

But it was not all one-sided; it hardly ever was. One example might speak for others.

The 8th Fighter Group was one of the Pacific old timers. Beginning in early 1942 it had fought its way from Australia to New Guinea, the Philippines, and the East Indies flying P-40s, P-39s, and P-47s before converting wholly to P-38s. Landing at Ie Shima on August 6, the group immediately got down to business under the command of 26-year-old Colonel Emmett S. "Cyclone" Davis. The Pearl Harbor survivor had earned a fearsome reputation as a dogfighter based on the whirling vertical maneuver that inspired his nickname.

Leading a maximum-effort mission on the 10th, Davis's Lightnings attacked Kumamoto City on Kyushu, home of a major aircraft factory. The P-38s seared the area with napalm canisters, razing nearly one third of a city the size of Grand Rapids, Michigan. The results prompted a whimsical, "The two big bombs got their attention, and my sixty-two P-38s brought them to the table."[96]

Yet the attrition continued. Two days later, on the 12th, the group flew an afternoon glide-bombing mission against a railway bridge on Kyushu. One of the Lightnings took flak hits, and First Lieutenant Walter Sykes limped away on one engine, setting course for Ie Shima more than 400 miles distant. That was a huge advantage the twin-engine pilots enjoyed over other fighters.

Sykes made good progress, nursing his crippled Lockheed southwesterly for two and a half hours. Then the remaining Allison engine quit with little warning. Before Sykes could bail out, his plane stalled and dived into the sea. His friends circled in the waning daylight, unable to see him. A longer search the next day also failed to find him.

Several days later in Clark County, Washington, Sykes's family learned that he was presumed lost at sea, one of the last victims of World War II.[97]

Bombers Ascendant, August 13–14

On August 13, at Tinian's North Field, Major Earl Johnson of the 313th Bomb Wing briefed three new Eighth Air Force squadrons on a break-in mission, with 30 aircrews jotting notes on the target and defenses. Johnson recalled:

> About the middle of the briefing some guy came over from wing headquarters to get me to go see General (J.H.) Davies, which I did pronto. He said the mission had been canceled as "Peace was very close" so I went back and told the Eighth Air Force crews. They let out a big howl and moan, for I think many of them ended World War II without ever flying a combat mission.

That morning of the 13th on Guam, some quarters began hearing reports that an announcement from President Truman of the impending surrender was imminent. As the news spread throughout the island, giddy optimism took hold, tightened its grip, and held on.

That night "the word" continued to circulate that Tokyo was surrendering. A huge party kicked off and continued until dawn. Troops were restricted to their bases although the wing's band boarded trucks and circulated through four bomb group lodgments "to spread the joy."

Inevitably, the prospect of peace succumbed to officialdom. A radar officer, Lieutenant Al Wood, recalled, "Soon afterward we had our first barracks inspection with hats on and sleeves down. And a considerable interest in the point system for going home developed."[98]

Military members fervently counted points accumulated for length of service and any distinctions earned, sufficient points eventually leading to discharge. The "adjusted service rating score" allowed one point for each month served from September 1940; an additional point for each month overseas; and five points for medals and campaign stars.

Originally, enlisted soldiers needed 85 points in Europe but events led to a declining figure through year's end, with different standards for Army Ground Forces, Army Air Forces, and Women's Army Corps. No benefit accrued for age or marital status but dependent children under 18 provided a substantial bonus. Readers of the irreverent Sergeant Bill Mauldin's "Willie and Joe" comic strip understood the returning GI who extended his arms: "Come to daddy, you little twelve-point rascal!"[99]

That cartoon offered a heartfelt contrast to another Mauldin strip with Willie and Joe waiting at an embarkation port: "I don't remember any delays gettin' us over here."

The situation extended to the top, including Major General Curtis LeMay. Two letters to his wife Helen described the uncertainty:

Headquarters, USASTAF, Guam, August 13.

Things are certainly in an uproar out here pending the results of the negotiations with the Japs. I don't see how there can be any other answer than acceptance by the Japs of our terms. It has been a tremendous victory for Air Power. We licked them with our B-29, but whether we will ever get credit for it is something else again.

We all have our ears glued to the radio hoping for the good news. I imagine a lot of people will have to stay out here, but if the war is over, I think I have a good chance of coming home fairly soon.

The next day he wrote:

August 14.

Still no word from the Japs. It looks as though they have changed their minds and need a little more treatment.

I don't think much of the new office… it is hot and crowded compared to my other one. I have a WAC [Women's Army Corps] clerk… I don't know what she thinks of the setup as I'm not used to watching my language. Two hours out to investigate false rumor of peace.

This is worse than the war. I wish they would either give up and get it over, or say they are going to fight on so we can get down to business again. If we don't get back to routine and get some sleep, we will all be in a padded cell.

I'm going to try and go to bed tonight, but I don't expect to stay there very long.[100]

At sea, routine continued uninterrupted. Throughout the 13th, Navy day and night fighters from nine carriers claimed 19 kills, all offshore and some near the task force. Pilots debriefed in their ready rooms, while on flight and hangar decks, machinists and metalsmiths tended to engines and airframes. They expected another identical day to arrive with the sunrise.

Early on the 14th XXI Bomber Command continued its paper blitz, dropping thousands of pamphlets aimed at Japan's population. Circumventing government and military censors, the papers contained the revelation, "The Japanese government has offered to surrender, and every Japanese has a right to know the terms of that offer and the reply made to it by the United States Government on behalf of itself, the British, the Chinese, and the Russians. Your government now has a chance to end the war immediately."

LeMay's psychological warfare team enhanced the text by quoting Tokyo's conditional acceptance of the Potsdam Declaration as well as new Secretary of State James Byrnes's response on behalf of the Allied governments.

Providentially, some pamphlets fluttered from on high, landing on the Imperial Palace grounds. Kido fetched one and delivered it to the emperor's bunker, using the heaven-sent opportunity as a wedge between the moderates and the bitter-enders. He noted, correctly, that knowledge of negotiations likely would incite army units to revolt. Thus armed, Kido urged Hirohito to convene an immediate conference to discuss surrender.

Few papers in history have ever achieved their aim so quickly or so forcefully.

Following a short-notice session with his ministers, some in tears, Hirohito achieved his purpose. The cabinet agreed to acceptance of the modified Potsdam Declaration. Only one thing remained to be decided – how best to inform the nation.

The Information Board raised the prospect of an announcement over the radio. Otherwise some Japanese – especially the military – might doubt a published document's authenticity. Due to cultural sensibilities the cabinet decided upon a recording, as the imperial voice had never been heard by the population.

The meeting ended in agreement, with radio technicians quickly summoned to prepare the recording which, despite the attempted coup, was successfully broadcast on the 15th.[101]

Meanwhile, in sweeps over Japan, U.S. Army fighters notched 18 kills around airfields east of Tokyo. It was a last-minute opportunity for most of the Thunderbolt, Mustang, and Lightning pilots, as ten had never scored before. The Army's final credited victories occurred just after noon when 8th Fighter Group P-38s tied into a gaggle of speedy Nakajima Franks southeast of Hiroshima, claiming five. Belle of the brawl was Captain Raymond F. Meyer with two victories.

But attrition naturally continued on the Allied side as well. Throughout the month the Army Air Forces lost 144 aircraft operating against and over Japan, including two in the CBI Theater. On combat missions the Far East Air Forces wrote off 83 planes: 32 to antiaircraft fire; six to enemy aircraft; and 45 to other causes, mainly accidents and weather.

On those occasions when Japanese fighters intercepted Army missions, the enemy pilots downed four fighters and two medium bombers against AAF fighter claims of 84 kills.[102]

Also on the 14th, LeMay launched seven missions totaling more than 750 Superfortresses against army and navy arsenals, industrial areas, and rail centers. More than 400 Boeings bombed three targets in daylight. Additionally, of 160 fighters from Iwo Jima, just one was lost attacking an airfield near Nagoya. The young pilot flew too close to his leader and got tagged by antiaircraft gunners shooting at the first target. The wingman limped offshore and bailed out to be rescued by a submarine.

The "night shift" left for work late that afternoon: four bomb wings with 350 Boeings departing Guam for a nocturnal time over targets. Three wings with 174 Superforts were briefed for fire raids against two railroad towns northwest of Tokyo: Kumagaya (burning 45 percent of the urban area), and Isezaki (17 percent destruction). Meanwhile, nearly 40 Boeings dropped mines in coastal waters, further bottling up Japanese shipping.[103]

The main effort was to come from some 140 planes of Brigadier General Frank Armstrong's recently arrived 315th Bomb Wing. Since June his four B-29 groups had logged 14 previous missions against Japan's shrinking petroleum supply system. The 11 priority targets stretched the length of Honshu, an area the fliers called "Gasoline Alley."

Mostly flying at night, the wing's B-29s were optimized for blind bombing with the new Eagle radar. Whereas previous radars were best used for navigation, Eagle was precise enough for targeting through clouds. Eagle was able to place most of a typical bomb pattern within the perimeter of most oil refineries – exceptional accuracy for the time.

But now the 315th faced its greatest test. Armstrong had already told his crews, "War is hell but it is double hell in the skies."[104]

At Guam's Northwest Field, Armstrong's combat crews reported to their group headquarters for a mission briefing at noon on the 14th. Sitting on benches, the fliers watched intelligence officers reveal the crews' impending fate. It was another maximum effort, though the 315th Wing hardly ever flew any other type. When the drapes were drawn with the flight path pinned in ribbon, an audible gasp skittered through each Quonset hut. It was the longest nonstop mission of the war: a 3,650-mile round trip from Guam to the northwest coast of Honshu.

Navigators consulted their maps while bombardiers checked target folders. The Nippon Oil Company's Tsuchizaki refinery near Akita sat 300 miles north of Tokyo, which was bad enough. Moreover, Akita fronted on the Sea of Japan. Lying so far from Guam, Tsuchizaki was a virgin target, never previously attacked.

Despite the enormous distance, the bombers possessed a safety margin, expected to retain more than 1,300 gallons of 130-octane gasoline. Under most conditions that was almost two hours' reserve.

The 315th Wing included Colonel Boyd Hubbard's 501st Group. His plane was warming up on the runway when a jeep screeched to a halt and a staffer jumped out, giving the "cut engines" signal: "Admiral Nimitz says the war is over."

No sooner had Hubbard's props stopped turning than another messenger arrived. "Get going!" he shouted. "LeMay hasn't received word that the war is over!"[105]

Despite the risk, some men were determined to fly what seemed to be the war's last mission. Nearby, the 502nd Group's flight line officer, Lieutenant Nevada Lee, dealt with a bomber that had suffered a "ground abort." The pilot, Captain Daniel Robert Trask, declined an honorable exemption from the flight and insisted that the mechanics do what they could.

Meanwhile, at the head of the 315th Wing's departing line, Brigadier General Frank Armstrong sat fidgeting in *Fluffy Fuzz III*, his personal Superfortress bearing the pet names for his wife and son. Facing XXI Bomber Command's longest mission, Armstrong was concerned that a ceasefire order might come through while the wing was airborne. Therefore, he sent an officer to check with headquarters, ensuring that no message had been received. The courier quickly returned. As Colonel Hubbard had just learned, the war was indeed still on.

Armstrong stood on the brakes, ran up the four throttles monitored by his flight engineer, released the toe brakes, and accelerated down the runway bearing 50 tons of airplane, fuel, bombs, and living flesh. One hundred thirty-nine other Boeings followed.

Then, belatedly, came another. Lieutenant Lee's crew had fixed the problem with Captain Trask's plane, *The Uninvited*. The burdened bomber left the ground at 6:58 p.m., well behind the others.

Several hours outbound from Guam, Frank Armstrong's crews noticed the residual effects of three previous wings that had bombed eight to ten hours before. Captain John B. McPherson, a former Arizona cavalryman, wrote:

As we flew en route to our target off the east coast of Japan, it appeared that all of Honshu Island was ablaze from Nagoya to Osaka to Tokyo. The other wings bombed with a combination of general-purpose bombs to break up Japanese buildings and other structures, and incendiary bombs to set them afire. The 315th bombed only with 250-pound general purpose bombs against the oil refineries.[106]

Thus, the Superfortresses were caught in an airborne time warp. Most of them had bombed before midnight on the 14th while others were inbound with a briefed target time after midnight, the 15th – the day that Tokyo's long-awaited surrender was finally expected.

Final Mail Call

The attitude was no different at sea.

The 14th was a refueling day as Task Force 38 withdrew 300 miles offshore, affording carrier airmen a brief interval of rest tinged with uncertainty. But even routine operations came at a cost: three Hellcats and a Corsair.

Meanwhile, the first order of business was underway replenishment on a scale and competence unmatched anywhere on the world's oceans. As time permitted, some ships also conducted gunnery practice or familiarization with new types of ammunition.

However, the priority was fleet oilers and supply ships steaming alongside the carriers, passing bunker fuel, aviation gasoline, food, and ordnance, prompting some fliers topside to watch the evolution. Service Force Pacific, or ServForPac, was essential to maintaining carriers and their escorts at sea for weeks at a time, and underway replenishment was fascinating. The supply ships approached the carriers in a slight overtake, and when abeam, the "unreps" slowed to establish a compatible speed with the recipient vessels. Normally steaming about 150 feet apart at 12 knots, the provisioners required a fine degree of seamanship to keep an even strain on the connecting lines and fuel hoses between a laden 25,000-ton oiler and a 2,000-ton destroyer or a 27,000-ton carrier.

But most welcome of all – perhaps even most important – was receipt of backlogged mail.

Mail call had enormous implications for morale. For those who received letters – often bundled in batches – spirits peaked for a while. A familiar feminine script had the power to spike a man's pulse. Most recipients arranged them in order according to the postmarks, and some rationed them for hours or even days. Others, avid consumers of news from home, tore open the envelopes and absorbed everything at once.

Millions of service members lived in dread of the notorious "Dear John" letter – a girlfriend or fiancée writing to break off the relationship.

Then the ships came about, heading westward again.

That evening, strikes were announced to resume the next morning, and many aviators became more ill-tempered or edgy. Wrote one USS *Cowpens* pilot about a notoriously well defended target:

No flying, but briefing for the Tokyo-Shibaura Electric Plant again. We'll all get knocked off yet if they keep this up. Nobody can eat or sleep, we are so excited. Bets are being made everywhere on or against the surrender. U.S. State Department announced agreement by Allies to let emperor stay. Now if the Japs will only agree to the rest. Maybe they'll call off our electric plant hop. I feel sure they will.[107]

It was the same on every carrier, especially in squadron ready rooms. Without quite defining it, hundreds of aviators wrestled with the unthinkable. Nobody wanted to risk the ultimate irony – the final casualty in a war perhaps already won.

2

August Storm

U.S.S.R., August 9–31

No good news arrives in the dark.

An hour before midnight on August 8, Soviet Foreign Minister Vyacheslav Molotov summoned Japanese ambassador Naotake Sato to the Kremlin. During the 15-minute drive, Sato must have known what was coming. The adopted son of a diplomat, he was vastly experienced, a 62-year-old professional with previous postings in Manchuria, Poland, Britain, Belgium, and France, and a stint as a prewar foreign minister. As his limousine passed through the floodlit 15th-century walls with red-brick edifices and golden-topped minarets, he probably barely noticed the Kremlin's five palaces and four churches or cathedrals.

It was a meeting of two very different men representing two very different types of despotism. Molotov was an unlikely diplomat, the 55-year-old son of a butter churner. Becoming minister of foreign affairs in 1939, Molotov had crafted the stunning neutrality pact with Nazi Germany in the August of that same year. To Americans it was as if J. Edgar Hoover had suddenly started playing poker with Al Capone. The next month Germany launched World War II.

When Hitler invaded Russia in June 1941, Molotov's influence only expanded. He had accompanied Stalin to every major wartime conference, the most recent being Potsdam in July where the Allies repeated their demand for Japan's unconditional surrender.[1]

Undoubtedly that night Sato recalled a conversation with the Russian less than three months previously. In late May, Molotov had said, "We have had our fill of war in Europe, and our only desire is to obtain a guarantee of future peace." Yet all the while, the Trans-Siberian Railroad had kept shipping munitions and men eastbound at maximum capacity.[2]

Now, in their brief meeting shortly before midnight, Molotov informed Sato that Moscow had declared war on Japan, effective the next day – essentially within an hour. The reason was bluntly obvious: in August 1945 Japan still owned southern Manchuria. Stalin wanted it.

In a career that had spanned youthful revolutionary to undisputed ruler of the Soviet Union, Joseph Stalin (born Joseph Vissarionovich Dzhugashvili in Georgia in 1879) combined ambition, ability, and utter ruthlessness.

As a teenage Bolshevik, Stalin patiently rode the crest of the Communist wave from 1898 that finally toppled Russia's monarchy in 1917. He was fortunate in suffering only imprisonment under czarist rule, emerging to sit on the Politburo. Following bitter infighting after Vladimir Lenin's death in 1924, Stalin slowly solidified his grip, finally consolidating his role as head of both party and state. He became General Secretary of the Communist Party in 1922 and Chairman of the Council of Ministers in 1941.

Stalin's path to power was steeped in blood and terror. His policy of enforced agricultural collectivization worsened the 1932–33 famine that particularly ravaged Ukraine, resulting in at least 3 million deaths and perhaps more than twice that number. Historians and demographers variously estimate the U.S.S.R.'s internal death toll to between 8 and 20 million during the Stalin era, with nearly 800,000 in judicial executions alone.[3]

Prior to World War II, international fellow travelers had minimized or excused Moscow's actions, most notably the *New York Times'* Walter Duranty who received a Pulitzer Prize for his heavily biased accounts. Partly based on such coverage, President Franklin Roosevelt withdrew U.S. recognition of Ukraine as an independent state and officially recognized the Soviet Union.

Meanwhile, Western journalists who attempted to report the facts were denied further entry to the U.S.S.R.

Beginning in 1937, Stalin killed or purged about one third of the Red Army officer corps, including 27 of the 31 most senior officers. Like many despots, he was wary of competent subordinates who might pose a future threat. Russia paid dearly for this once war broke out, sustaining terrible losses against Finland in 1939–40, and especially following Germany's invasion in June 1941. Nonetheless, Stalin retained his steely grip and finally oversaw the avalanche that swamped Adolf Hitler in the Great Patriotic War.

Like Hitler, Stalin possessed an exceptional memory, a grasp of details, and absolute confidence in himself. A born opportunist, Stalin always seized any chance to expand Soviet territory regardless of political philosophy. His two-year alliance with his bitter enemy Hitler had benefited Russia in Poland between 1939 and 1941.* That his judgment occasionally failed him was best ignored by anyone in his orbit.[4]

✳   ✳   ✳

Northeastern China's historic division included Russian-dominated Outer (northern) Manchuria dating from the 1850s and China's Inner (southern) Manchuria. At first glance the rugged, often barren Asian landscape appears to offer little. But the region was rich in arable land, lumber, iron ore, and coal, with hydroelectric potential on the Yalu River bordering Korea.

Japan and Russia also had a long, bitter history. In 1905 Tokyo had emerged as a player on the world stage by soundly defeating Czarist Russia on both land and sea, the first time an Asian nation had defeated a European power on even terms.

After its 1931 conquest of Inner Manchuria, Tokyo established the oppressive Manchukuo puppet state under Imperial Army control.

---

* But beyond the 1945 Manchurian offensive, he also proposed to Truman that Soviet forces seize not merely the Kuril Islands but Hokkaido and part of northern Honshu. Truman declined in two days, and Moscow backed down.

Therefore, Japan gained a buffer against Soviet southern expansion and further increased its influence, with some 800,000 immigrants who often displaced Manchu landowners. The Manchukuo regime has been described as "one of the most brutally run regions in the world with a systematic campaign of terror and intimidation."[5]

Then, in 1939, the much stronger Soviet forces won a brief campaign on territory variously occupied by Manchukuo and Moscow's own Mongolian puppet regime. The dispute had centered on a ten-mile stretch of land east of the Khalkhin Gol River. Largely directed by then-Lieutenant General Gregory Zhukov, soon of World War II fame, the Red Army soundly defeated the Japanese in four months. Thus, with his flank secure, Joseph Stalin immediately joined Adolf Hitler in dismembering Poland at the start of World War II in Europe.

But with the European war finally concluded, Stalin could turn once again to Soviet interests in Manchuria. For so vital an area, surprisingly little information was available. A prewar geography article stated, "The exact size of Manchuria is not known. Between the maximum and minimum estimates there is a difference of 119,822 square miles."[6]

Actually, Manchukuo covered 460,000 square miles, only slightly less than California, Nevada, Arizona, and New Mexico combined. To conquer an area the size of the American Southwest, Moscow wasted no time on preliminaries. In fact, *Stavka*, the Soviet supreme command, began planning its Far East offensive before the Hammer and Sickle was raised over the Berlin *Reichstag* in May. Redeployment from the west had begun in April – a prodigious effort spanning 6,000 miles across the Eurasian landmass.

Logistics depended upon railroads, as far as they went. And the need was enormous: a dozen trains were required to transport a rifle or cavalry division; three or four to move a tank brigade. But some rail heads were as much as 400 miles from the nascent battle fronts.[7]

On poor quality or dirt roads, supply columns averaged perhaps 70 miles per day – a snail's pace in that vast expanse. Therefore, Moscow dispatched dozens of construction battalions and regiments to the three offensive fronts preparing for the envelopment of Manchukuo. The workers' priority was improved roads, the arteries bearing the conquering lifeblood of supplies.

Largely unappreciated by Russia's allies – and seldom acknowledged by the Soviets for decades – was the war-winning contribution of American trucks. Most notable was the four- or six-axle Studebaker-designed cargo hauler. Rated to carry 5,000 pounds of supplies, the "deuce and a half" was produced in prodigious numbers by two primary manufacturers – eventually totaling approximately 215,000 vehicles – with more than 150,000 shipped to Russia, mostly via Iran. Russians considered the "Studer" probably the most important item that America provided the U.S.S.R. with during the Great Patriotic War.[8]

For decades Soviet propagandists consistently denied that Moscow benefited significantly from Lend-Lease. But subsequently both Marshal Gregory Zhukov and Premier Nikita Krushchev stated that Lend-Lease had been vital to Russia's victory. In 1963 Zhukov spoke with typical bluntness: "Today some say the Allies didn't really help us... But listen, one cannot deny that the Americans shipped over to us material without which we could not have equipped our armies held in reserve or been able to continue the war."[9]

In Manchuria, from west to east, the fighting fronts spanned more than 2,700 miles across a landscape as varied as the Inner Mongolian desert and the beaches of the Sea of Japan. Manchuria often provided its own defense in the form of varied terrain, with deserts, marshes, and mountains, as well as numerous rivers. It was a domain that often resisted motorized transport but favored horses. Therefore, the Soviet order of battle included cavalry, especially useful for reconnaissance, while four of Moscow's Outer Mongolian divisions were mounted on hardy little ponies bred especially for the role.

Since June 1945 – a month before Potsdam – Tokyo moderates had entertained the growing but doomed hope of Soviet representation on their behalf for better terms. Foreign Minister Shigenori Togo (in office April to August) directed Ambassador Sato in Moscow to seek Soviet influence with the Western Allies in diminishing their demands, particularly preservation of the throne and – completely unrealistically – the militaristic nature of the government. Sato, the realist on the ground, recognized the futility but proceeded as directed.

Tokyo in fact went so far as to propose a military alliance with Moscow. It was an absurd notion, especially given the time and place – the first June meeting between diplomat Koki Hirota and Soviet Ambassador Jacob Malik had to be moved from the bombed-out rubble of Tokyo to a remote mountain resort.[10] As already noted, American intelligence was well aware of such overtures, and it was one of the deciding factors in ensuring that the first atomic bombing ultimately took place.

SOVIET BLITZKRIEG, AUGUST 8

Between one and ten minutes after Molotov's pronouncement to Sato, Marshal Aleksandr Vasilevsky's forces attacked Manchukuo on three fronts with the launch of what would postwar be known as Operation *August Storm*. From the west, north, and east, more than 1.5 million Soviet troops began the last offensive of World War II.

Vasilevsky's plan launched the western and eastern arms in a huge double envelopment, with Marshal R.Y. Malinovsky's Transbaikal Front from the west intended to meet Marshal K.A. Meretskov's First Far East Front in the east near Changchun in south-central Manchuria.

Malinovsky was a 46-year-old veteran of World War I and the prolonged campaigns at Kharkov, Stalingrad, and Ukraine. A corps commander when the war began, like all senior Soviet officers, he was a long-standing member of the Communist Party. Unlike many of his contemporaries, he had managed to avoid a date with Stalin's firing squads.

Kiril Meretskov, aged 48, was a true believer, having joined the Party in 1917. But his early devotion earned him no advantage, as he was arrested shortly after the German invasion in June 1941. The reason is uncertain because his file was destroyed after the war, but some theorize that he committed the sin of being proven right during the humiliating 1939–40 war against Finland. Nonetheless, despite imprisonment and torture, he was rehabilitated and given an army command, proving himself a capable leader. His victory at Leningrad in late 1941 enhanced his reputation.

Leading the northern attack on the Second Far East Front was General M.A. Purkayev, supporting Malinovsky and Meretskov. Bespectacled and studious looking, he turned 51 during the campaign. He had an unusually varied career. From czarist draftee in World War I he rose steadily in prominence, including a posting as Moscow's military attaché to Berlin. He served in senior staff positions until assuming command of the Kalinin Front in 1942. Sent to the Far East the next year, he probably knew the theater better than his contemporaries.

Commanding Japan's Kwantung Army in Korea and Manchuria was General Otozo Yamada, a 63-year-old former cavalryman who had seen action in the war with Czarist Russia 40 years before. During World War II he commanded two area armies and three independent armies, including those in Korea, Sakhalin Island, and the Kurils. In the summer of 1945 he possessed fewer than 800,000 troops – about half Vasilevsky's number – in 25 divisions, plus six independent brigades. Though he did have two armored divisions, Japanese light tanks were little more than pop-up targets for Russia's modern, battle-tested T-34s and heavier models. The Manchukuo puppet regime's 40,000 men, hastily conscripted, were poorly trained and lightly equipped.

At 2:00 a.m. on August 9, Kwantung Army headquarters at Hsinking issued a general alert: "The enemy on the eastern front has launched an attack. All area armies, armies, and units under direct command of Kwantung Army will immediately check the enemy advance in the border areas, and will prepare for war in all other areas."

Two hours passed before the Japanese Army monitored a Moscow radio broadcast confirming the state of war.[11]

In 1973 Marshal of Artillery K.P. Kazakov reflected, "Had the Japanese command studied more attentively our many offensive operations on the Western Front, it could have learned the simple verity: once the Red Army attacks, it strikes a deadsure and mortal blow."[12]

Prior to the start of the offensive, the Soviet Union's neutrality had ensured that Vasilevsky's staff officers were limited in their early intelligence-gathering options. Overflights of Japanese territory would have been a dead giveaway, as would snooping on the ground. Consequently, planning had proceeded mainly by relying on direct observation and signals intercepts. However, limited air reconnaissance had occasionally been conducted to 25 miles behind the border.

Vasilevsky delegated enormous importance to security. It included emphasis on stringent limitations upon the number of people involved in planning at the army and front level, and the tightest security on all documentation, often rendered in longhand, presumably in case the Japanese had cracked any Soviet codes.

In a move perhaps previously unknown, officers of the theater high command assumed false names and ranks, even signing documents with their new aliases.

The Russians integrated this approach and unit movements with a variety of training exercises, knowing the Japanese monitored such activity. By continuing previous routines on the borders, the Soviets presented their potential opponents with a "situation normal" impression on the ground. Intelligence professionals term the process "desensitizing" the enemy. Largely, it succeeded, despite reconnaissance in force by forward-deployed battalions that scouted their assigned terrain.

Perhaps most significantly, no radio traffic was permitted for newly arrived units, lest the Japanese monitor the force buildup.

Soviet preparations also included extensive use of camouflage and night operations to achieve tactical surprise within the strategic context. Largely the Russians were successful, noting, "Despite the fact that the Kwantung Army had intelligence on intensive Soviet troop movements, the Soviets succeeded in achieving surprise due greatly to 'brilliantly executed troop deployment and positioning at the borders.'"[13]

Planning for the offensive had been typically thorough and complex, and Vasilevsky's large staff had ample experience to draw upon. Soviet offensives in the west had been based on well-established doctrine, including but certainly not limited to stockpiling supplies in massive quantities while arranging for timely distribution to combat forces. A staff summary noted, "Heightened need for mobility because of depth of rear." Additionally, fuel supplies were carefully calculated to avoid running short when needed the most.

The planners also looked ahead to possible use of Japanese transport nets, particularly railroads. "In the Far East, importance of enemy railgoods: spare these; air landings should bring in railroad troop officers."

Arranging reliable communication between various echelons' headquarters and their operational counterparts was also critical. Telephone was preferred, as it was largely immune to interception, but rapid advances usually negated the option, forcing more reliance upon radio.

In all, the Russians committed 71 infantry and motorized rifle divisions, with five armor, cavalry, and airborne divisions plus independent tank and artillery formations totaling 1,650,000 men.[14] "The most serious difficulties were encountered in the Mongolian desert areas and with transport on the maritime rail line along the border. Suspicions had also been aroused by aerial reconnaissance along the border."[15]

Despite the Soviets' meticulous efforts at concealment and desensitization, they were not entirely successful. Subsequently, they learned that the Japanese and Kwantung armies had known of the substantial force buildup and identified some of the attacking units.

FIGHTING IN THE DARK, AUGUST 9

Within minutes of midnight, the three-pronged Soviet attack began under a moonless sky. Exploiting the Manchurian darkness without artillery support, lead elements of each prong crept forward, scouting the terrain, probing the seams between Japanese units. Any gaps could benefit the attackers, allowing the Russians to penetrate the defenses and identify positions that could be bypassed, surrounded, and cut off.

Battalion commanders issued detailed orders: vocal noise discipline; gear insulated or secured to prevent metallic sounds; automatic weapons well forward at likely points of contact. Any encounters probably would occur at close range, so many attackers carried extra hand grenades. Frequently grenades were the preferred weapon for blackout conditions, because unlike firearms, the source could not easily be determined.

Four and a half hours later the main force units stepped off, trailing the paths scouted by the lead attackers.

The Soviets' major barrier was the Amur River, one of the world's longest, separating Russia's far east from northeastern China. Broad in places and forested on both banks, it posed a significant natural barrier to invasion.

However, the Russian army had help. Naval forces were heavily committed to the Far East offensive, with the Pacific Fleet contributing nearly 100,000 sailors from infantry and amphibious units. They were instrumental in supporting the army with river crossings, especially where the retreating Japanese had destroyed bridges. The Amur Red Banner Flotilla's 12,500 sailors included an amphibious force of 200 riverine and landing craft plus monitors with 130mm guns, providing fire support for river crossings and amphibious landings.

Throughout the war, interservice rivalries plagued most combatant nations, especially Japan where the army-navy rift approached a full-contact sport. Certainly American generals and admirals feuded, but generally the Red Army and Red Navy got along, if only to avoid Stalin's chilly displeasure. Russian soldiers had long appreciated the hard-fighting sailors, distinctive in their round, tasseled caps with blue-and-white-striped undershirts, which were also a mark of naval infantry – the Soviet Marines.[16]

Meanwhile, across the barren terrain, the Soviets made astonishing progress. At sunset on the 9th, advance elements of Malinovsky's western forces were 55 miles from their start lines. They had encountered little opposition – mainly Inner Mongolian cavalry. His tankers had things almost entirely their own way. Despite challenging terrain, Colonel General A.G. Kravchenko's Sixth Guards Tank Army (with a tank corps and two mechanized infantry corps) clanked across more than 200 miles in merely three days. Thereafter, Soviet armored forces were limited mainly by what the logistic tail provided in terms of fuel and supplies.[17]

The Russians deployed over 5,500 tanks – nearly half being the latest T-34s with 85mm guns – and self-propelled guns, while Japan had 1,100, including four-ton "tankettes" of almost no combat value. Japan's heaviest tank was the 15-ton Type 97, with a 45mm or 57mm main gun. Neither could compete with the standard Russian 76mm weapon, let alone the newer high-velocity 85mm gun.

Though Russia produced some 65,000 tanks during the Great Patriotic War, attrition was horrific. Consequently, 4,100 American-built M4 Shermans or *Emcha*s became an important component of Russian tank formations, including the 46th Brigade of the 9th Mechanized Corps on the western Transbaikal Front. One of the officers was 23-year-old Captain Dimitry Loza, veteran of two years of armored combat, who oversaw much of his unit's transport from Czechoslovakia to Mongolia in June.

A veteran tanker commanding a veteran unit, Loza led a battalion of 21 Shermans, which he greeted as valued friends. "I walked up to the tank designated for me and patted it on the armor. 'Greetings, *Emcha*! Here we meet again!'"[18]

Some terrain favored the defenders, especially in the west where Malinovsky's forces faced the 4,000-foot Greater Khingan Mountains. But the Japanese were hampered by poor communications through most of the short campaign, leaving some units largely on their own. Nevertheless, many fought with all the fierce tenacity that imperial soldiers demonstrated throughout the war. For instance, at Hailar in the west, hard on the river of the same name, with a prewar population of 20,000, the garrison of 3,800 was besieged from August 11. The Japanese made good use of prepared defenses including trenches and concrete pillboxes. The Russians eventually seized the city on the 18th, reportedly inflicting a massacre upon POWs and civilians alike.[19]

As Captain Loza recalled, the region's thick, loamy soil became the tankers' "enemy number one... In the flat expanses of Manchuria, the Sherman literally swam across limitless bodies of water. Tropical August downpours, to which were added the contents of reservoirs emptied by the Japanese, had turned the ground into an immense sea. The tanks were forced to move hundreds of kilometers along railroad track embankments on the cross ties."[20]

Navigation in the mostly featureless terrain was little easier than at sea. Some commanders reported their maps being no more than 70 percent accurate, sometimes showing nonexistent roads. Yet the armored thrust drove southward, making up for lost time. As Loza recalled, "At midday on 10 August the main body of the 46th Guards Tank Brigade had reached the western slopes of the Grand Khingan Range. Our combat mission was accomplished a day earlier than specified." Thus encouraged, Malinovsky accelerated the schedule to reach the Lubeya-Tusyuan line by evening two days hence.

Sherman drivers shifted into low gear and gunned their Detroit-built engines to clank up the region's steep slopes, finally reaching the crest of Korobonlin Pass, 4,000 feet above sea level.

Even in the end game, logistics were strained due to road conditions and weather. Supply convoys lagged as much as 180 miles behind advance units, including the all-important fuel trucks. After outrunning most of their supply train, tankers often relied on more help made in America: twin-engine Douglas transport planes delivering fuel, ammunition, and supplies. Based on the prewar DC-3 airliner, the C-47 and its Russian-built Lisunov knockoffs maintained an air bridge to the front. Thus, for almost two weeks the Douglases helped sustain the armored advance.

On the brink of Tokyo's surrender, the Soviet steamroller maintained its momentum, on track to arrive bang on schedule.

EASTERN SLUGFEST, AUGUST 12–22

One of the few set-piece battles was waged at Mutanchiang on the Soviet eastern front under Meretskov. A five-day slugfest, launched on August 12, pitted perhaps 55,000 Japanese against five times as many attackers, who had breached the passes north and east of the city. Japanese antitank guns exacted a toll on Soviet armor, but that was not all. Fanatically devoted imperial soldiers strapped explosives to their backs, each determined to trade his life for an enemy tank. Russian soldiers guarded the armor's flanks, and the tanks sprayed lethal machine gun fire. Nonetheless, some Japanese survived to roll beneath Russian tanks and pull the lanyard that detonated their pack.

Though generally ineffective against Soviet armor, the Japanese suicide soldiers scored occasional upsets. One Russian tank brigade was nearly exterminated, losing all but seven of its original 65 tracks.[21]

Meanwhile, seasonal rains slowed the Russian advance.

Consequently, three Japanese divisions fought a rearguard action, permitting most of the imperial forces in the area to withdraw. With the advantage of higher terrain, often Tokyo's warriors required their enemy to take each defended hill the hard way – direct assault. However, nobody deployed as much artillery as the Soviet Union, and in some instances observers stood agape as tops of hills simply disappeared in a surging, boiling cloud of high explosives, destroying the defenders in place.

Nonetheless, the unexpectedly stiff resistance prompted Meretskov to change plans in midstream. He directed his Fifth Army to bypass Mutanchiang, requiring the First Red Banner Army to complete the task.

The final assault on the 16th resulted in an Asian Stalingrad beneath an avalanche of artillery and rockets. However, the individual qualities of the Japanese soldier were seldom better illustrated, with dirty, stunned survivors fighting not only house to house but room to room. Small groups of men hunted each other through the dust-covered rubble, relying on grenades and close-range gunfire to settle each dispute.

Early that afternoon all but the final doom-laden holdouts had been killed or routed, thus securing the Russian rear while the Fifth Army raced to victory.

However, Soviet triumph was stained with atrocity. Most prominent was the massacre at Gegenmiao (present-day

Gegenmiao zhen) in the southern part of the western front. Some 1,800 refugees had sought shelter in a Tibetan lamasery which was then overrun by Russian armored troops. Reportedly more than 1,000 civilians were killed, and scores of women raped in a two-hour period on August 14.

A survivor, then a seven-year-old girl, later recalled, "Over one thousand people were slaughtered. The tanks came after 11:00 in the morning, attacking as we fled from the fighting around Kou'angai. It was a crazy mix of sound from the tank engines and machine guns. Everyone was screaming as they ran to get away. Some people fell hit by bullets; others were crushed by tanks."[22]

Other witnesses said they saw parents kill their children before committing suicide rather than face the conquerors.[23]

A final act in the Manchurian drama occurred at Hutou, a strategic city on high ground at the confluence of the Ussuri and Sungacha rivers. Hutou was one of two "special fortresses" in the region, with concrete walls nine feet thick in some places. Originally defended by four infantry battalions and an artillery regiment, the garrison was steadily transferred away, until it was reduced to 1,400 men.

The fortress held out from the first day of the offensive until the last. The Soviets had seized the town on August 10 but the fortress defenders persisted in their samurai ethic. Beneath the cover of aircraft and artillery, the attackers unleashed explosives and flame throwers with raw gasoline poured into firing ports.

The Russians secured a key strongpoint – the central observation post – on the morning of the 14th but the defenders fiercely continued their resistance. The fortress lacked radio communication and, in an effort to convince Hutou's defenders to surrender, on the 15th the Russians sent a delegation of five captured Japanese bearing a white flag and news of Tokyo's capitulation. They met with a junior officer who, either disbelieving or uncaring, announced that they would never surrender. Then he swiftly drew his sword and severed the head of one spokesman.

The Russians immediately resumed the attack with artillery and air support, bouncing the remaining rubble while infantry proceeded with its grim task. Organized resistance collapsed on the 19th but mop-up operations against die-hard Japanese continued until the 22nd.[24]

*   *   *

Despite the success of the Soviet Far East offensive, the Japanese Army Air Force retained a presence in the region. On the afternoon of August 19, Captain Dimitry Loza's tank battalion came under air attack – a rarity in the campaign, given Russia's air supremacy. Six planes circled the lodgment where Loza's Shermans surrounded a solitary building. After years of operating under skies dominated by the Luftwaffe, Soviet tankers were experienced antiaircraft gunners. But the new enemy unveiled new tactics. In succession, each plane selected a target and dived on it, to destruction. Two attacked the building, one struck a Sherman, and the others selected trucks. None of the Japanese survived, though inspection revealed women in two of the wrecks, presumably wives or fiancées of the pilots.

Despite this attack, Loza's battalion reached its ultimate objective on the 21st. A Japanese officer, speaking perfect Russian, asked the conquerors how he should deploy his men and equipment.

The final acts of the offensive also came in the air. On the afternoon of August 15, 27 Petlyakov Pe-2s of the 55th *Bombardirovanny Aviatsy Polk* (Bombing Regiment) dive-bombed the railroad station at Ranan (now Nanam). Two Japanese fighters, described by the Soviets as Mitsubishi J2Ms, nicknamed "Jacks," tried to attack the Peshkas, but were bounced by an escorting Yak-9 of the 19th Fighter Regiment, one Jack being shot down and the other escaping.

Later that day, 34 Pe-2s of the 32nd Bomber Regiment struck the railroad station at Funei (now Nuren). A single J2M tried to intervene, but was shot down by Lieutenant Grib of the 19th Regiment.[25]

America's Lend-Lease assistance to the Soviet Union had also involved thousands of aircraft. They included nearly 2,500 Bell

P-63 King Cobras, upgrades of the P-39 Airacobra. The King Cobras had only arrived in May, equipping two regiments in the Far East.

On August 15 a P-63 of the 17th Fighter Regiment scored the type's only air-to-air victory. Junior Lieutenant I.F. Miroshnichenko was wingman to Captain Vyacheslav F. Sirotin, a 26-victory ace in the P-39. They observed two Japanese fighters, variously identified as Nakajima Ki-43 Oscars or older Ki-27 Nates, attacking Soviet transport aircraft. Miroshnichenko shot down one of the Japanese and forced the other to flee at treetop level.[26]

ISLAND WARS, AUGUST 11–SEPTEMBER 4

The Soviet Far East Military District was not limited to the Asian mainland. Russia already owned the northern half of Sakhalin Island dating from an agreement 40 years earlier. Unsurprisingly, then, on August 11, the 16th Army's 100,000 soldiers stormed across the border into Japanese territory. It was a prerequisite to conquest of the Kuril island chain between Russia's Kamchatka Peninsula on the mainland and Japan itself.

The Russians outnumbered the Japanese by three to one, in keeping with Soviet military mathematics and doctrine. But the defenders were typically stubborn, with several days of hard fighting from 17 bunkers and dozens of artillery and mortar positions. On the 15th came the emperor's broadcast with orders from Tokyo to cease offensive operations, thereby leaving some latitude for continued defense. Lieutenant General Kiichiro Higuchi's Fifth Area Army radioed instructions to the resident 88th Division who continued fighting to the last man. However, the Soviets eventually overcame stiff resistance to capture 18,000 Japanese defenders, setting the stage for the final act, the conquest of the Kurils.

Since 1939 Russia had observed Navy Day on the last Sunday in July, commemorating the czarist victory over Sweden in 1714. But in 1945, August 18 might have been termed "navy day," with three landings taking place in northern Korea, one in South Sakhalin, and another in the Kurils.*

In the Kurils, 60 Russian ships and craft, ranging from patrol boats and trawlers to transports, delivered a reinforced rifle corps of some 15,000 troops supported by an air division of perhaps 75 planes. Soviet forces completed their occupation of the islands on September 4 at a cost of some 2,000 casualties. Japan's garrison of about 20,000 sustained relatively light losses totaling barely 1,000, with more than 50,000 military and civilians surrendering.

On August 19 the Kwantung Army had broadcast a surrender order. Due to a mixture of confusion and opportunism, the Soviets regarded the ceasefire as incomplete, sending forward mobile detachments supported by airborne reinforcements in key cities.[27]

However, despite the seemingly impressive feat of conducting three amphibious landings in three separate locations, there was a distinct advantage to conducting such operations at the tail end of the war against a fatally weakened enemy. Postwar assessment noted that often the navy "Lacked timely orders for assault landings; unprepared; lacked craft and equipment. The Kurile landings involved many mishaps."[28]

Yet despite the lapses, *August Storm* was a smashing victory for Soviet arms. But, coming at the end of a four-year two-front struggle of titanic proportions against the Axis, it left many survivors more numb than elated.

Soviet personal accounts in English are scarce, but tanker Dimitry Loza probably spoke for many:

Victory over Japan Day occurred on 3 September. To us it was almost like any other day. It did not evoke that torrent of joy we felt on 9 May in the West. That victory had been eagerly anticipated for 1,418 days and nights. This one took less than

---

* In 1910, Korea had been annexed by Japan and was part of the Japanese Empire until August 1945.

a month. Here, in the Far East, "soldiers' salutes" with every kind of weapon, as were fired in honor of the victory over Germany, did not break the quiet of the night. It was nothing like that.[29]

END GAME IN THE KURILS, AUGUST 18–23

At the far end of the Kuril Islands, Shumshu was low-hanging fruit for the Soviets. It lay within 20 miles of the south coast of mainland Kamchatka and was little more than a long-range rifle shot – less than two miles – across a narrow channel from the large island of Paramushir, the main Japanese base.

Joseph Stalin was flexible in his views of international law. But in August he insisted that legality was on his side, as he chose to read the Yalta Conference as granting Moscow the Kuriles, extending southwest from Kamchatka.* Japan had accepted the Allied surrender terms on the 15th, but three days later, supported by 60 or more vessels, including U.S.-built landing craft, some 8,800 Soviet army and navy troops landed on Shumshu, last of the archipelago. From Moscow's perspective, it was a safe bet, as the Japanese seemed unlikely to resist. However, speed was still important and reputedly the operation was planned and launched in a mere 48 hours.

Shumshu itself posed a challenge to invaders. Its coast varied between sheer, unscalable rock and broad, sweeping beaches. The August temperatures ran in the low to mid-50s Fahrenheit, but the moist North Pacific air generated thick mist.

Caught amid the process of disarming, the 8,500-strong Japanese garrison scrambled to respond. Lieutenant General Tsutsumi Fusaki believed his command was justified in defending Japanese territory. The result was a rarity – a clash of armor between Russian and Japanese forces.

---

* The Yalta Conference took place in February 1945 between Churchill, Roosevelt, and Stalin and agreed the conditions for Russia entering the war against Japan.

The Russians landed on the northeast coast well before dawn. Both sides deployed aircraft, which were largely irrelevant in the weather, though a single kamikaze sank a Russian minesweeper.[30]

Advancing through an advantageous fog, about 40 Japanese Type 95 and Type 97 tanks clanked to the beachhead. Though possessing no heavy tanks beyond prototypes, the Imperial Army regarded the 15-ton 97 as a medium, but they were certainly nothing comparable to Soviet T-34s (29 tons), American Shermans (33 tons), or German Panzer IVs (27 tons). But lacking their own armor ashore, the Russians were hard pressed to repel these "medium" tanks. Later the defenders claimed to have killed some 100 Russians in the initial clash, but the Soviets rushed antitank guns to the point of contact. A close-range engagement in reduced visibility ended with half the Japanese vehicles destroyed or abandoned.

With a clear path, the Soviet amphibious force pressed inland. That night the soldiers and sailors rolled up Fusaki's coastal artillery positions. Subsequently, on the morning of the 19th, the Japanese managed to communicate to the Soviets that Tokyo had ordered a ceasefire, effective that afternoon.

Another three days passed before the defenders formally surrendered, concluding the last ground battle of World War II.

However, the Japanese certainly gave better than they got, inflicting some 1,500 casualties – 50 percent more than their own. It was probably the only occasion when Soviet losses exceeded Japanese.

The Soviets, masters of brute force, also recognized the advantages of political manipulation. On August 22 they arrested Manchukuo's 39-year-old puppet ruler Puyi. Emperor of the region since 1934 and officially the last emperor of China, he entered plush exile in Siberia, attended by his servants. He returned to China in 1950 after having undergone conversion to Communism.

DEBRIEF

The Far East blitz represented the acme of Russian military operations in the Great Patriotic War. An American historian properly described the Manchurian offensive as "a post graduate exercise for Soviet forces, the culmination of a rigorous quality education in combat begun in Western Russia in June 1941."[31]

Red Army losses in the 25-day campaign were 35,000 overall with 11,000 killed, while naval components added 1,400 casualties. In the Kremlin's hard-eyed accounting, it was nearly a bloodless conquest of an immense, productive area.[32]

Overall in the Far East, the Soviets captured 594,000 Japanese troops, including 143 generals and 20,000 wounded. Almost certainly the astonishing bag of general officers would not have occurred a month before, suicide being the preference.[33]

Postwar Western figures placed Japanese losses at 674,000 including 84,000 dead. American intelligence estimated that the Soviets captured 2.7 million Japanese, two thirds of them civilians. Eventually some 2.3 million were repatriated to Japan, with 254,000 known dead and 93,000 presumed dead.

Of some 220,000 Japanese farmers established in Manchuria, about 70 percent reportedly perished, including perhaps 80,000 in the severe winter of 1945–46. More than 10,000 were thought killed by outraged Chinese, or had committed suicide. Presumably the surviving 140,000 eventually returned to Japan.[34]

The Russians dismantled much of Manchuria's industrial plant within three weeks of the war's end, ceding the territory to the Communist Chinese. Thus, without realizing it, Moscow had set the stage for the next war, only five years downstream.

*   *   *

In the vacuum attending Japan's defeat, Soviet forces entered Korea in mid-August, advancing southward to the designated 38th Parallel that would mark the boundary between Soviet and American occupation zones. The Russians lost little time exploiting their control over the area, especially since many Koreans welcomed an end to 40 years of Japanese rule.

In the north, Korea already possessed two military organizations: Kim Il-sung's guerrilla force and the Korean

Volunteer Army headquartered in China. The Soviets established headquarters at Pyongyang and almost immediately founded an air force academy.

Meanwhile, the Americans – thin on the ground in the south – planned to retain many Japanese for continuity of government. The reaction among South Koreans was stridently vocal, leading to a quick reversal by the U.S. administrators. However, frequently they consulted their Japanese counterparts, who naturally recommended Koreans who had cooperated with Tokyo.[35] Two distinct Koreas were emerging and battle lines, however unwittingly, were already drawn for the coming Cold War.

RED STAR AT SEA

The Red Navy was active throughout the month of August. Among other Japanese ships, the globe-trotting, 6,000-ton *Kasato Maru* went to a lingering death. Originally British built as the cargo-passenger liner *Potosi*, she was purchased by Czarist Russian donations to become the troop transport *Kazan*. But she was scuttled by the Russians in the 1905 surrender of Port Arthur. She was refloated by the Imperial Navy, who claimed her as a war prize.

In her 45-year career, *Kasato Maru* had delivered Japanese emigrants to Hawaii, Mexico, Peru, and Brazil. She had then been absorbed into the navy in 1942.

On the 8th the old vessel sustained a three-hour attack by ungainly Beriev MBR-2 flying boats, a 1930s design with a rear-facing engine mounted over the wing. Capable of packing 300 kilos of ordnance, the naval bombers caught the ship off the mouth of Kichik River. Set afire, she sank in shallow water two days later.

The next day Russia's motor torpedo boats (MTBs) pulled off a daring success against Tokyo's depleted merchant marine.

From late 1943 Japan had rushed to mass-produce cargo vessels on something approaching the scale of U.S. Victory Ships – a case of "mission impossible." Some 80 of the 2A class were completed but more than 50 were sunk or crippled. Two featured in a Russian surface attack that scored significant success at Rajin Port, hard on the Russian border in northern Korea. Three Japanese merchantmen, the 6,870-ton sisters *Edamitsu Maru* and *Enpo Maru,* plus the 3,000-ton *Tensho Maru,* were too lucrative to pass up. Although they had been damaged by Soviet aircraft, the vessels remained afloat minus crews.

The Red Navy deployed some of its best torpedo boats against Rajin. Super sleek, more resembling a submarine than a surface craft, the G-5 class embarked a six-man crew with two torpedoes, boasting a claimed 53 knots. Two Russian MTBs, TK-549 and -550, launched four torpedoes at the immobile targets and claimed hitting all three. Several hours later, six more boats roared into the harbor, sinking Edamitsu Maru and Tensho Maru – a total day's haul of more than 16,000 tons.

The U.S., specifically the Joint Army-Navy Assessment Committee, credited *Edamitsu Maru* as "probably sunk" by American carrier aircraft but the Soviets certainly finished her off. Whatever the cause – singly or collaboratively – she was lost to the Empire of the Sun just as the emperor's sun was setting.

Russian submarines never approached the importance of their U.S., Japanese, or German counterparts, but still the Red Navy's boats played a role in the war in the Far East. On August 23 – officially Moscow and Tokyo still remained at war – the *L-19* attacked two Japanese ships on Hokkaido's west coast. Commanded by Captain Third Rank Anatoly Kononenko, the five-year-old submarine torpedoed a large auxiliary gunboat, inflicting severe damage with perhaps as many as 400 fatalities. Shortly thereafter *L-19* sank the 1,400-ton cargo vessel *Tetsugo Maru.*

The next day *L-19* and her 53 men disappeared in the area of La Parousse Strait between Sakhalin Island and Hokkaido, possibly victims of a mine.

✻   ✻   ✻

Although the Kurils were the swansong of Russian military operations in World War II, the region also featured in a U.S.

Navy postscript. On August 12 the distinction of probably the last shore bombardment of the war fell to the veteran light cruiser *Concord* (CL-10), a "four-stacker" product of parsimonious prewar naval budgets. Authorized in 1916, she was not completed until 1923, emerging as a 9,000-tonner with six-inch guns. She headed Task Force 92, which had pummeled Kurils targets since the previous year. Now, among three "prowling patrols," she was one of two light cruisers and 12 destroyers to clear northern waters of Japanese vessels. *Concord* encountered a convoy of six trawlers and sank each in turn, then steamed to join her team mates at the appointed hour to shell three islands.

Concord reached her assigned target an hour late, just as the other ships completed their mission. According to the ship's action report, "*Concord* blazed away with more than 50 rounds of six-inch shells to help set nine fires, visible far at sea, at Suribachi Bay (on Paramushiru), an important military, fishing and cannery center." The duty officer noted the ceasefire order at 8:06 p.m. on the 12th.

"About a minute later," sailor Fred Lumb recalled, "Lieutenant Commander Daniel Brand, the gunnery officer, high aloft in forward fire control, saw to it that one more round was fired by the *Concord*. Probably few who heard that shot really believed it to be a hang fire, but none doubted that it was the last round of the bombardment."[36]

3

The Day the Shooting Stopped

August 15

The most-awaited communication of the 20th century zipped across the nation by news wires.

> FLASH!
>
> Washington, Tuesday, Aug. 14 (AP) – The Federal Communications Commission monitored today a Tokyo radio broadcast saying "the text of an imperial message accepting the Potsdam proclamations will be forthcoming soon."
>
> This broadcast was received at 1:49 A.M. (Eastern war time) and more than an hour later the "imperial message" still was not forthcoming.[1]

Nevertheless, the news flash was too joyous to await developments.

Six hours west of Washington and 3,849 miles east of the war, a spontaneous celebration erupted in downtown Honolulu. Crowds of military men – Army and Marine khaki mixed with Navy white – paraded, rode, and congregated with shouting, waving civilians.

Formal and impromptu events overlapped. An Army marching band was swamped by a surging crowd on Ala Moana Boulevard while improvised confetti showered down from office buildings on either side of the street.

Military and private vehicles formed a cavalcade of overburdened cars and trucks, many with Stars and Stripes affixed. Others dragged garbage cans, cardboard boxes, and a few improvised rising sun flags. Celebrants crowded around Iolani Palace, adding to the din. Three dozen P-47 Thunderbolts overflew the celebrants, maintaining good formation.

On Waikiki Beach and elsewhere servicemen and women established themselves apart from the crowds, some of the more daring ladies with bare midriffs and two-piece bathing suits. In one surviving film clip a shirtless senior officer is warmly received when he arrives bearing five bottles of beer. Two of his hosts, still in uniform, display orange orchids. In another a uniformed Navy woman stands on a rocky shoal, pointing west, delivering heartfelt sentiments to those still beyond the horizon.[2]

OVER THE HORIZON

But beyond the horizon, the flying, fighting, killing, and dying continued – victims of Planet Earth's time zones.

General LeMay's enormously powerful bomber command in the Marianas lofted seven missions against urban-industrial targets throughout the 14th (Western Pacific date, 13th in the U.S.). All 735 would return to their island roosts, as LeMay had perfected B-29 operations to the point of airline routine: 3,000-mile round trips over an oceanic expanse, sometimes without loss of a single Superfortress. The huge bombers droned through the night beneath a first-quarter moon, trailing victory in their slipstreams.

The 313th Bombardment Wing had become LeMay's designated unit for sowing mines. Under boyish Brigadier General J.H. "Skippy" Davies, the wing's four groups had begun their role in Operation Starvation in April. He was an old Pacific hand, dating from the Philippines in 1941 when he led "maximum efforts" of a mere three planes.[3]

Early in the morning blackness of the 15th, Davies' Superfortresses each dropped six tons of 1,000- and 2,000-pound mines at ports on Honshu's north coast and Shimonoseki, the narrow strait between Honshu and Kyushu. It was the most vital choke point in the Home Islands, and repeatedly mined. Ironically, the mining included Miyazu, famously declared an open port for trade with the U.S. and Britain in 1899.

Post-mission analysis showed 35 planes laid their weapons where intended, flying between 8,000 and 13,000 feet in the two and a half hours beginning at 12:42 a.m.

Forty-two enemy aircraft made nine attacks on various B-29 formations – an unusually high number of night fighter encounters but indicative of the importance Tokyo attached to the mining operation. Only two bombers were hit by fighters' gunfire while the heaviest flak was at Shimonoseki, supported by perhaps 70 searchlights. One returning bomber was forced to land at Iwo Jima.

Among the other B-29s airborne after midnight were more than 130 led by LeMay's senior wing commander, Brigadier General Frank Armstrong. En route to the remote Nippon Oil Refinery at Tsuchizaki, the sky was full of B-29s. Approaching the Japanese coast, the 315th Wing saw hundreds of homeward-bound B-29s. Colonel Boyd Hubbard of the 501st Group and other aircraft commanders turned on their landing lights to avoid collisions in "the traffic jam above Honshu Island."[4]

Nine of Armstrong's planes aborted the mission, but 134 approached the plant within minutes of Davies' mine layers starting to work in Honshu waters. The 315th Wing carried 954 tons of 250-pound bombs, briefed to attack from 10,000 to 12,000 feet.

Participating in the wing's longest mission was Lieutenant Robert F. Griffin, a bombardier in the 331st Group. After narrowly avoiding a midair collision during the approach to the target, his crew caught sight of the refinery shortly after midnight. Flying at 11,000 feet, barely one minute from the target, the fliers gaped at "a huge thunderhead" topping perhaps 5,000 feet above. Griffin recalled the mission:

A few seconds from bomb release and we were almost touching the plane next to us. The captain advised that as soon as the bombs are released he will swing to the right and climb about a thousand feet.

"Bombs Away!" The captain took the plane off the bombsight, turned to the right and began to pull up. I stood up, somewhat straddling the bombsight, and leaned far forward so that I might see the bomb impacts. The large black cloud was just ahead.

We touched the cloud and Whoosh, the plane jerked violently upward. I was thrown up into the air and then dropped unceremoniously with my feet pointed upward, my backside where my feet should be and my head leaning back upon my seat. As I lay there looking upward at the plexiglass and the edges of the aluminum ribs of the plane's nose, it seemed that they were alive with fire. Sparks jumped all over. I thought, "This is it, the end of the line."

Then, as suddenly as it started, it stopped. We were out of the cloud. Ahead, slightly above us and to our right, was the plane that had gone down the bomb run with us. In spite of our turn and climb, he had crossed over and climbed higher while we were in the cloud. At this point, he was so close that I could see the tail gunner's face.

The thunderhead wasn't a rain cloud. It was a violent thermal cloud of smoke and debris that was drawn thousands of feet into the air by the heat of the huge fires and explosions from the bombing on the refinery. The sparking that I had seen on the plexiglass was akin to St. Elmo's fire that sailors see in the rigging of ships in a storm, but it was electrical discharges from all the charged particles thrown up into the cloud from the explosions on the ground.[5]

Captain Dan Task's *Uninvited* crew, last to take off, was also the last to return, having dropped the U.S. Army's final bombs on Japan's Home Islands at 3:39 a.m. Post-strike photography revealed no portion of the refinery left undamaged. "The three refining units were a tangled mess of wreckage, the main power plant still standing but seriously hit. More than 66 percent of the tank capacity was destroyed."[6]

A few hours after bombs away, outbound from the Japanese coast, radiomen tuned to the 50,000-watt station on Saipan. As one flier recounted, "We heard the announcement that Japan had accepted surrender terms and the war was over. The relief felt by all of us on the B-29 was followed by a glance at the four engines with the thought that they'd surely keep turning to get us back to Guam, and they did."[7]

Armstrong, the complete aerial warrior who had led America's first strategic bombing mission in Europe and the last in Asia, was quietly reflective:

> Every man aboard our aircraft was outwardly jubilant, but each experienced mixed emotions. We wanted no more of war, but it was difficult not to think of those who had not lived to see the dawn of this day. These thoughts brought waves of sadness, irony and gratitude. Too, there was a sudden surge of awe. Some of us had been in the business of killing for nearly four years. How would we adapt to a peaceful existence, and how much would we regret the havoc we had wrought, even though it had been absolutely necessary?[8]

One of the fliers was First Lieutenant Harold F. Adkins, navigator of the 501st Group's B-29 *Liberty Bell*. He recalled, "While returning from Akita the crews received the news that the war was over. They flew from the war they had been waging into the morning dawn that meant Peace. When we returned to Guam, liquor flowed freely. Those who drink, got drunk; those who didn't, stood by and took care of those of us who did."[9]

Meanwhile, the war continued at sea.

THIRD FLEET

The sun tinted the eastern horizon of the Pacific Ocean, greeted by heavy clouds and rain squalls over the Japanese mainland. Some 150 miles off the Honshu coast, men and ships of the U.S. Third Fleet prepared for another day at war – the 1,348th since the Japanese attack on Hawaii on December 7, 1941. It was Wednesday, August 15, and rumors made the rounds as they had for most of the month. The Army Air Force had dropped two city-shattering atomic bombs on Japan in the past two weeks, and many Allied sailors earnestly "wished they'd drop more" to hasten the end.

Some sailors and Marines expected the war to last another 18 months – and had no idea that some Japanese leaders prior to the atomic bombs had anticipated another three years. One persistent rumor was that Tokyo was hoarding 10,000 kamikazes to repel the expected invasion. In truth, Japan had nearly 14,000 aircraft for some 8,000 trained pilots.

Kamikazes, or the "Divine Wind," offered Japan the most bang for the yen. Marginally trained pilots sworn to dive airplanes into Anglo-American ships were far more effective than Japan's conventional bombers who had proven to be largely ineffective against U.S. and British naval forces. The Allies' sophisticated integration of radar, radio, and high-performance fighter aircraft had all but blunted the empire's "sea eagles" flying normal attack missions. But since the Divine Wind first blew in the Philippines the previous October, suicide pilots had sunk and damaged hundreds of ships. The crisis peaked off Okinawa in April and May 1945, with as many as 20 vessels struck daily. In the ten months since their debut, 1,200 kamikazes had sunk 34 ships and damaged 288, some never returning to service.

In Halsey's Third Fleet there was a tangible nervous tension. Despite missions interrupted by weather or at-sea refueling, by the 15th some men hadn't slept in three nights.

While many carrier pilots hankered for air combat, the hunting had thinned out. During July, Halsey's aviators only claimed 58 kills and just 32 through August 14.

Still, scheduled operations proceeded apace. Ships prepared hot meals before crews went to general quarters, with another serving after securing in the evening. Boxed K rations (lunch meat, cheese, biscuits, and powdered fruit drink) were stacked for distribution at midday although squadron ready rooms often had sandwiches and coffee.

That morning Vice Admiral John S. McCain's command prepared to launch air attacks and patrols from 17 fast carriers deployed in four groups. In all, the 16 U.S. carriers deployed some 1,300 aircraft, including more than 850 Hellcat and Corsair fighters plus Helldiver bombers and Avenger torpedo planes. Three Royal Navy carriers had turned for Australia, leaving only *Indefatigable* with her Seafires, Fireflies, and Avengers.

Rule Britannia

Integrating Anglo-American naval forces had posed a significant challenge, but it had unquestionably proved to be worth the logistical headaches as the Allies progressed from victory to victory. The British Pacific Fleet (BPF), scheduled to depart Third Fleet after August 10, needed time to refit and prepare for its role in the planned Kyushu invasion in early November. Its six large and four light carriers dispersed on various missions from the Philippines, the Solomons, and Australia to the China coast, repatriating prisoners of war and supporting operations to reclaim lost territory from the Japanese. The exception was HMS *Illustrious*, which returned to the Home Fleet for training in Britain.

Illustrious was the most in need of major work. Her prop shafts had never been quite right after the battering she had taken from Luftwaffe Stukas in the Mediterranean during 1941. *Formidable* also had residual bomb damage issues.

Indefatigable and her consorts operated as Task Group 38.5 including the four-year-old battleship *King George V*, two cruisers, and nine destroyers. The Royal Navy, facing the end of a six-year global war, understandably wanted a presence if Japan suddenly capitulated. Admiral Sir Bruce Fraser, commander of the British Pacific Fleet, asked to remain for a day or so to await events and Halsey agreed.[10]

For all its proud tradition and glorious record, in the 20th century the Royal Navy badly lagged in a vital area – at-sea replenishment. Historically the Royal Navy operated near fleet bases, whether Scapa Flow in the north, Plymouth on the Channel coast, or Gibraltar, Malta, Alexandria, Aden, Singapore, and Hong Kong during the peaceful interim years. The immense distances of the Pacific forced a belated rethinking in the Admiralty, only entirely corrected postwar. Sustained operations in the expanse of the world's greatest ocean had seldom figured in British planning until establishment of the British Pacific Fleet.

Nor were the British only limited geographically. Technical and organizational factors imposed problems that the U.S. and Japanese navies had long dispensed with. Admiral Sir Bruce Fraser perhaps wore more hats and dealt with more command levels than any Allied leader. The Admiralty in London issued general directives as to BPF strategic goals. Australia maintained most of his dockyards, air stations, supplies, and living facilities. Australia, New Zealand, South Africa, and Canada provided many of his ships and crews. All the while Fraser was subordinate to Chester Nimitz who oversaw operations throughout the Pacific Theater.

At 59, a full admiral, Fraser was too senior for seagoing and remained at his headquarters in Sydney. His senior officer afloat was Vice Admiral Bernard Rawlings. A year younger than Fraser but highly experienced, Rawlings had 41 years of service in fleet and diplomatic posts. He had previously commanded a destroyer, two cruisers, and a battleship.

Fraser conceded:

> At sea I had two distinguished and experienced admirals, Rawlings and Vian, and on shore looking after our supplies Admiral Daniel in Melbourne and Admiral Fisher at Manus (in the Admiralties, some 2,500 miles from Kyushu) responsible for the fleet train, the only means of keeping our fleet supplied at sea.
>
> The latter was perhaps our greatest headache. With the shortage of shipping it comprised an odd assortment of modern and elderly ships involving many nationalities but all doing their best. And then Admiral Nimitz turning his blind eye to Washington would always help us out in emergencies.[11]

The BPF lacked sufficient organic replenishment ships operating with task forces, relying on the civilian-staffed Royal Fleet Auxiliary as well as chartered British and Dutch vessels.

Additionally, until near the end of the war most fuel transfer was accomplished by the laborious, time-consuming stern to bow arrangement. The Americans' smoothly efficient side-by-side "unrep" was a revelation to some Britons.

The Pride of Task Force 38

Task Force 38 boasted not only a high level of competence, but experience. Seven of the carriers had been in the Pacific since 1943 and six had a year's combat behind them. Additionally, five of the ships' air groups – each with three or four squadrons – were embarked on their second combat tours.

But some individuals harked back even farther than their ships. Leading Fighter Squadron 86 in USS *Wasp* was Lieutenant Commander Cleo J. Dobson, survivor of *Enterprise*'s unwelcome greeting over Pearl Harbor on December 7, 1941.

Another "Big E" veteran was Commander Raymond Davis, commanding Air Group 16 in *Randolph* (CV-15), who had led dive bombers in the Guadalcanal campaign. Similarly, Lieutenant Commander Cecil H. Mester of *Lexington*'s Bombing Squadron 94 had flown at "The Canal" in 1942.

The first two carrier battles – Coral Sea and Midway – were represented by a handful of Pacific veterans, including Lieutenant Commander Walter A. Haas in *Ticonderoga*. Formerly of the original *Yorktown* (CV-5) sunk at Midway in June 1942, now he ran Bombing-Fighting Squadron 87. *Wasp*'s torpedo skipper was Lieutenant Commander Lawrence F. Steffenhagen who had flown outmoded Devastator torpedo planes at Coral Sea.

Among other Pacific warriors now squadron leaders were Commander Stockton B. Strong of *Shangri-La*'s (CV-38) fighter-bomber outfit – among the finest attack pilots the U.S. Navy had ever produced.

Additionally, the fleet air operations officer was Captain John S. "Jimmy" Thach, the Navy's outstanding fighter tactician, who in fact ran much of the task force for McCain.

Task Force 38's leadership recognized an essential fact: at rock bottom, aviators are supreme egotists; they take their lives in their hands each time they go to work. But whatever their technical abilities, there is always something more, something deeper.

Pride.

It was expressed in the fervent prayer, "Please, Lord, don't let me foul up." To "foul" up before one's friends was too bitter for most to consider. As generations of pilots quipped, "Better to die than look bad."

CAPs Continue

Meanwhile, combat air patrols remained constant throughout August. Night fighters were returning to their roosts as the first CAP prepared to launch from each task group. In the black predawn of 3:45 a.m. on August 15, the first fighter sweep's pilots groped their way topside from ready rooms, finding their assigned aircraft on the flight deck. Laden with parachute harness, Mae West, and survival gear, pilots handed their plotting boards to the plane captains, climbed to the high cockpits, and settled in. Then, as much by feel as by sight, they started engines, letting the Pratt & Whitneys settle into their throaty patented purr. The temperature gauges had barely risen toward the green zone when the air boss on each carrier passed the word: shut down. Some aviators began allowing themselves to think they might be spared another mission.

Minutes later that dream ended. Flight deck loudspeakers blared the order to launch, and Sweep One rolled down the wood decks at 4:30, exhausts glowing orange-red in the darkness.

In an atmosphere of uncertainty and disappointment, Strike Charlie was briefed and ready to man planes at 4:45 as scheduled. Aircrews on Charlie experienced the same uncertainty as the sweep. The decision was delayed at 5:15, prompting *Hancock's* Air Group Six to record, "To strike or not to strike! War or peace! But no canceling order came and pilots took off, uncertain whether this would be the last strike of the war."[12]

The reprieve was short lived: carriers remained bows into the wind and commenced launch at 5:32. Strike One Able went on schedule as hydraulic catapults slammed 103 bomb-laden aircraft off carrier decks. Strike Baker's 73 shortly followed, assembling over the spume-tossed blue-gray waves.

First contact was made by bent-wing Corsairs off *Essex* (CV-9). At 5:40 a.m. Lieutenant Commander T.H. Reidy, the newly promoted leader of Bombing-Fighting 83, led a CAP flight. Five days earlier he had led the rescue of Lieutenant (jg) Coumbe. Receiving a radar vector, Reidy latched onto a long, lean "bogey" near the task group. He closed in, identified the intruder as a speedy Nakajima Myrt reconnaissance bird, and dropped it into the wave-tossed gray ocean. It was Hamil Reidy's tenth kill, making him the last U.S. Navy double ace.

Rear Admiral Thomas Sprague's Task Group 38.1 was one of the most potent naval units afloat, with three Essex-class heavyweights and two Independence-class light carriers. That morning he launched a combined strike against targets on Honshu with squadrons from *Hancock* (CV-19), *Bennington* (CV-20), *Lexington* (CV-16), *San Jacinto* (CVL-30), and *Belleau Wood* (CVL-24) bound for the Shibaura Electric Company plant in Tokyo. Mission planners had laid out a dogleg ingress with a "back door" approach to the target, hoping to avoid the worst of the flak.

Bennington lofted a dozen Corsairs and two photo Hellcats against Hyakurigahara Airfield in central Honshu. They were led by Lieutenant Robert P. Ross, an experienced pilot with multiple kills as a *Belleau Wood* Hellcat pilot in 1943–44. Reconnaissance had found a lucrative batch of aircraft, and the information was so precise that the VBF-1 aviators concentrated their attention on the northeast corner, where 26 aircraft had been photographed two days earlier. One plane was ignited by strafing and rockets while ten were assessed as damaged.

The defenders put up light and medium antiaircraft fire that the attackers described as "intense and accurate." New weapons had been moved into the area since the attack of the 13th, and one gunner put a 25mm shell into Ross's F4U just behind the cockpit. Later the Corsair was jettisoned as unsalvageable.

Meanwhile, from a previous mission Lieutenant Ross recalled seeing parked aircraft at a base two miles west. The Americans spotted four planes stashed in some trees to the west and left them burning.

On the way back other pilots saw a 15-car train heading toward a tunnel. The fighters with remaining rockets fired them into the tunnel, collapsing the entrance.

Shortly thereafter, about 6:45 a.m., Ross's flight was ordered to jettison remaining ordnance and return to *Bennington*. The Japanese had agreed to surrender.[13]

✳   ✳   ✳

Earlier, at 4:15 a.m., *Hancock* had launched a dozen Corsairs under VBF-6's skipper, Lieutenant Commander LaVell M. Bigelow, plus four Hellcats of the ship's photo section, bound for Nagana Airfield in western Honshu. All carried rockets while the F4Us each had a 500-pound bomb. Four fighter-bombers became separated in clouds while the others continued.

Within sight of the target, passing over an active volcano, the flight heard an order to jettison ordnance. Lieutenant Herschel Pahl later admitted, "After going that far it's rather hard to keep from disobeying orders and going ahead with the attack."

The reason for the order was Japan's capitulation. But the radio frequency was blocked by extraneous calls from excited pilots "yelling and whistling and celebrating."

A repeat order from the air group commander, "99 Jamboree," clarified things: the war was over. At least officially.[14]

Leading *Hancock*'s second, 41-plane flight was Commander Henry L. Miller, a native Alaskan and an old hand from the Annapolis class of 1934. He had taught the Doolittle Raiders how to take off from a carrier in an army bomber and led a previous air group in 1943–44. Approaching the coast at 6:45, the air group commander monitored communications. Today he was target coordinator for all five air groups and received the call from "Christopher," Rear Admiral Sprague. "All Able and Charlie planes jettison bombs and return to base. I repeat…"

The mission report frankly stated, "Radio discipline and silence went to hell all over the Tokyo District as pilots cut loose on the air. 'The war is over – hooray!' Somebody sang, 'When the war is over we will all go USN [regular navy].' Two fighter pilots pulled out of formation and did slow rolls within sight of the Honshu coast."[15]

Without a radio relay flight, Sweep Able was beyond reach of the ship's VHF transmission 120 miles inland across Honshu, near the Sea of Japan. Therefore, Miller flew on to Sagami Nada, broadcasting the joyous news until Sweep Able One acknowledged. "Bombs were jettisoned at sea… and the last strike launched against Japan landed aboard *Hancock* at 0822."

The return course took eight remaining *"Hanna"* aviators within ten miles of the sacred mountain Fujiyama, en route to Sagami Bay leading to Tokyo Bay. "Then the trouble started."

Approaching Sagami Wan at 13,000 feet, abeam of the Corsairs, the Hellcats sighted two fighters identified as army Franks at 12 o'clock low – meat on the table. But as Herschel Pahl lamented, "We were ordered by Commander Task Group 38.1 not to attack except in self-defense. We just watched them."[16]

However, moments later the *Hancock* pilots realized that the Franks were decoys for at least five bandits stalking the Hellcats from below and behind. The Japanese were closing fast, threatening the last two F6Fs. The flight leader, Lieutenant Commander Bigelow, called for an immediate response.

Pahl saw the first three Navy Zekes closing on Lieutenant Corwin Wickham's section, the lead Japanese firing from long range. "I swung over sharply and fired on the Zeke closest to them with my wingman, Ensign D.C. Grant alongside me. Then the fight was on."

Pahl was an expert shooter: from full deflection he got immediate hits, noting glass and metal shedding. The Mitsubishi entered a tight turn that developed into a graveyard spiral, streaming flames. Pahl disengaged at 8,000 feet and zoom-climbed to rejoin the fight as his victim splashed into the Pacific.

Pahl joined the end of an aerial daisy chain: a smoking Jack pursued by a Hellcat pursued by a Frank. Pahl missed a Corsair "by inches" and drove the Frank into "a screaming dive," smoking as it entered the cloud deck. Moments later, regaining some altitude, Pahl got off a snapshot at a Frank diving vertically "with terrific speed."[17]

Lieutenant Wickham selected the last in a group of five Jacks. He hit in a deflection shot, drawing smoke as the propeller stopped. Passing close aboard, Wickham saw the pilot slumped forward, then the Mitsubishi flipped inverted into the water.

Wickham's wingman, Ensign Ray Killian, latched onto a Jack. He put a long burst into the stubby interceptor, which entered a slow roll. Killian fired again while it was inverted, drawing smoke and fire from its engine. He watched it spin into the ocean.

Meanwhile, Bigelow's Corsairs maintained a watchful overlook, alert to additional Japanese who might be lurking around. But no others appeared. The fighter squadron reported:

> After landing on deck about 0845 the flight learned that they had been recalled because official word had been received that the war was over, and hostilities had ceased. These divisions may have been the last divisions to see action against the Japs over Japanese territory. It was a fitting ending for Air Group Six, which was the first (as *Enterprise* Air Group) to see action in the war at Pearl Harbor on December 7, 1941.[18]

If the war was over, it was not apparent to other *Hancock* aviators. About 40 minutes after launch at 10:40, on the morning's third CAP, Lieutenant Marshall O. Lloyd's VBF-6 division was climbing to 30,000 feet when alerted to a lone bogey near the Royal Navy task group.

From 18,000 feet Lloyd called out the "meatball" 4,000 feet below and led the bounce. However, the Nakajima Kate – bearing a torpedo – sighted the Corsairs and turned into the threat. With the speed gained in the rapid descent, Lloyd and two others badly overshot the target as the Kate turned toward HMS *Indefatigable*.

Lieutenant (jg) Robert S. Farnsworth was positioned to press the attack. He split-essed into a near vertical dive, placing the Japanese in his gunsight. His first two short bursts went wide. Then, with a firm sight picture, he closed the distance and held the trigger down. The Kate gushed flames and exploded in midair, crashing about 100 yards from the British flattop. It was Bob Farnsworth's second kill after a Judy three weeks before. "Indefat" sent a thank-you message to Rear Admiral Sprague's Task Group 38.1.

As with other squadrons that day, the victors thought they had scored an historic triumph. "It is believed that this was the last enemy plane to be shot down over the Third Fleet. No later killing has been reported."[19]

The task group had also launched a two-part fighter mission with four each from light carriers *Belleau Wood* and *San Jacinto*.

The primary mission for both flights was photography with attacks on several airfields, time and fuel permitting. *Belleau Wood*'s contribution was led by Lieutenant James H. Parker, Jr. His section leader was Lieutenant (jg) Edward W. Toaspern, a 21-year-old New Yorker, already an ace from the squadron's previous deployment.

The Hellcats sighted land about 6:00 a.m., 25 miles off Inubosaki, a familiar coastal landmark. They began a climb for their runs at assigned targets. About 150 miles from base – roughly 65 from Tokyo – two VF-31 pilots called a tally-ho to the right at approximately 12,000 feet. Parker's *Belleau Wood* division split into two pairs, clawing for altitude to 8,000 feet. The strangers – single-engine fighters – were unidentified at first but the Americans planned to intervene if the bogeys threatened British Avengers and Fireflies about three miles distant.

With the bogeys identified as hostile, an aerial traffic jam ensued. The Hellcats broke off their initial runs to avoid Seafires diving through the formation to engage the Zekes. In the next few minutes four *Belleau Wood* Hellcats splashed six single-engine fighters, two by pilots who had never scored before. The VF-31 report describes the action:

> As it worked out, after the Jap fighters had peeled off one by one to make overheads on the TBMs (Avengers), the Jap fighters were no longer a group and in their pullouts they became vulnerable to the fire of the F6Fs. They seemed to have one attack in mind to be followed by rapid retirement into clouds. The clouds were 5/10 thick and in the pursuit it was possible to keep them spotted.[20]

Parker and Toaspern each claimed two Zekes, while wingmen Ensigns Francis R. Clifford and Robert A. Karp gunned single bandits. Karp identified his victim as an Oscar, probably a mistaken identity as there would be little reason for three army pilots to fly with a navy squadron.

In the brief fight the F6F pilots found their Hellcats were not only faster than the opposition but could outclimb and outdive them. And surprisingly, the Grummans were able to out-turn the Zekes and Oscars (if they were such), evidence of declining Japanese pilot skill. The Americans noted the enemy's only superiority was evading in a split-ess inverted dive. As the VF-31 report later concluded, "The Japs did not stick together, and the superior fire power of our fighters were the main contributions to a 100% successful mission." In exchange for six kills, one Hellcat was lightly damaged by machine gun fire.[21]

Meanwhile, the *San Jacinto* Hellcats maintained cover on the starboard beam roughly 1,000 feet above the *Belleau Wood* flight.

San Jacinto, *Belleau Wood*'s team mate in 38.1, prided herself as "flagship of the Texas Navy" and sometimes hoisted the lone star flag. Three VF-49 Hellcats each carried two 500-pound bombs while the fourth was a photo plane to scout future targets on Honshu's northern plain, 45 miles north-northeast of Tokyo. The mission represented all too rare an opportunity, as the squadron had only claimed seven shootdowns since May.

Still offshore, the *San Jacinto* aviators sighted an estimated 20 Japanese. The Hellcat pilots jettisoned their bombs, advanced throttles, and climbed to investigate likely hostiles. The situation quickly resolved itself, numerous Japanese fighters with a 3,000-foot altitude advantage threatening nearby British-piloted Avengers.

Lieutenant Allen W. Lindsay's pilots began a defensive weave by pairs, each wingman coordinating with his section leader. "Jap planes came from every section of the sky and it soon became a very mixed fight... The enemy fighters were very aggressive and abandoned their attacks on the torpedo bombers and began to make uncoordinated runs on our fighters."

Lieutenant Jack A. Gibson scored the first kill, shooting a Zeke off Lindsay's Hellcat. Gibson's .50 calibers went into the target's wing root, igniting a fuel tank. Gibson then tracked two more bandits, firing at wide angle with hits on both, but they seemed to survive. Soon another Japanese popped up from below Gibson's Hellcat, presenting him a low-deflection shot that proved fatal.

Lindsay in turn had his hands full, avoiding a Japanese who began an overhead run on him, closely followed by a second Zeke. He evaded the attacks, turned to seek opportunities, and latched

U.S. President Harry S. Truman, who as vice president succeeded Franklin D. Roosevelt in April 1945 and oversaw the rest of the war. (Naval History and Heritage Command))

British Prime Minister Winston S. Churchill inscribed a sentiment to the cruiser USS *Quincy* (CA-71) in Alexandria, Egypt, after the Yalta conference in February 1945. After four years he lost re-election in July, overlapping the Potsdam Conference. (Naval History and Heritage Command)

Nationalist China's leader Chiang Kai Shek fought the Japanese from 1937 onward. (Bettmann/Getty Images)

Chinese Communist leader Mao Tse-Tung, occasional ally and eventual victor over Chiang's nationalists. (Bettmann/Getty Images)

Admiral Lord Louis Mountbatten, Royal Navy, who held commands from destroyers in the Atlantic to the Southeast Asia Theater of Operations. (NARA)

Commanding Third Fleet's carrier striking arm was Vice Admiral John S. McCain, Sr., known for his low-key demeanor and his floppy hat without the grommet. (NARA)

Allies at sea. Admiral Sir Bruce Fraser, whose British Pacific Fleet operated alongside Fleet Admiral Chester Nimitz's U.S. Pacific Fleet. (Naval History and Heritage Command)

Admiral William F. Halsey, Third Fleet commander, consults a plotting table. To his immediate left is Rear Admiral C.H. McMorris, his chief of staff for the last two years of the war. (Naval History and Heritage Command.)

Sailors of the battleship USS *Pennsylvania* (BB-38) pump out water over her quarterdeck, after being torpedoed in Buckner Bay, Okinawa, on August 12. Note the hoses lead out through her aft 14-inch guns. (Naval History and Heritage Command)

Enthusiastic sailors mark up bombs on board USS *Shangri-La* (CV-38) during the final days of hostilities. (Naval History and Heritage Command)

Observing from a North American PBJ bomber, American-born Lieutenant Minoru Wada directs Marine Corps aircraft to a Japanese Army headquarters on the Philippine island of Mindanao, August 10.(Photo by Lt. David D. Duncan/FPG/Staff/ Hulton Archive/Getty Images)

Major General Curtis E. LeMay directed the B-29 bombing campaigns from India, China, and the Marianas with increasing success. He also supported the atomic bomb missions that helped convince Emperor Hirohito to end the war. (USAF)

Colonel Paul W. Tibbets stands beside the Boeing B-29 *Enola Gay*, named for his mother, that he piloted on its historic atomic bombing mission over Hiroshima on August 6. (Bettmann/Getty Images)

A Japanese soldier walks through the atomic bomb-leveled city of Hiroshima, September 1945. Photographed by Lt. Wayne Miller, USNR. (NARA)

"Fat Man's" mushroom cloud over Nagasaki on August 9. (Courtesy of the National Archives/Newsmakers/ Getty Images)

Soviet Premier Joseph Stalin, who ruled as head of government and head of state. (Photo by ullstein bild Dtl./ullstein bild via Getty Images)

Soviet Marshal Alexander Mikhailovich Vasilevsky, who commanded the triple-axis assault into Japanese-occupied Manchuria in August 1945. (Photo by TASS via Getty Images)

Russian sailors of the Red Banner Amur Flotilla are greeted by residents in the Chinese section of Harbin, Manchuria, August 1945. (Photo by: Sovfoto/Universal Images Group via Getty Images)

Engaged in Operation *August Storm*'s western prong, Red Army automatic riflemen of the Trans-Baikal Front in the streets of captured Hailar, Manchuria. (Photo by: Sovfoto/Universal Images Group via Getty Images)

Last portrait of a warrior. The kamikaze master, Vice Admiral Matome Ugaki, prepares to board a dive bomber at Oita on August 15, prior to the last suicide mission. He holds a dagger he had received from Admiral Isoroku Yamamoto. The Yokosuka Judy crashed near Okinawa. (NARA)

Task Force 38 maneuvering off the coast of Japan on August 17, two days after Japan agreed to surrender. The aircraft carrier in lower right is USS *Wasp* (CV-18). Also present are five other Essex-class carriers, four light carriers, at least three battleships, plus several cruisers and destroyers. (US Navy/NARA)

Allied troops brandishing fresh bread upon liberation from a Japanese prisoner camp on Taiwan (Formosa). (Photo by Keystone/Stringer/Getty Images)

August 29: with unrestrained emotion, Allied prisoners of war at Aomori near Yokohama cheer wildly as approaching rescuers of the U.S. Navy bring food, clothing and medical supplies. The men are waving flags of the United States, Great Britain, and Holland.
(Photo by Keystone/Stringer/Getty Images)

Consolidated B-32s at Yontan Airfield, Okinawa, in August 1945. A Dominator is refueled shortly after arrival from the Philippines. B-32s on photo reconnaissance flights over Japan were attacked after the Japanese peace acceptance on August 17 and 18. Two planes were badly damaged with one fatality. (NARA)

Imperial Navy ace Lt(jg) Saburo Sakai – veteran of China, the South Pacific and Iwo Jima – was among those who intercepted U.S. B-32 reconnaissance flights after the Emperor's surrender announcement. (PJF Military Collection / Alamy Stock Photo)

A Curtiss SB2C Helldiver over Tokyo on August 28. Photographed from a USS *Shangri-La* (CV-38) plane by Lt. G. D. Rogers. Note light traffic on the city streets, also burned out areas and damaged buildings. (NARA)

The iconic VJ Day image: *Life* Magazine photograph of a sailor kissing a "nurse" (dental assistant) in Times Square on August 14, 1945. (Alfred Eisenstaedt/The LIFE Picture Collection/Shutterstock)

Allied unity as women of Britain's Territorial Army Service link arms with U.S. soldiers during the VJ Day celebration in London's Piccadilly Circus. (Photo by Keystone/ Stringer/Getty Images)

American soldiers celebrate war's end with a flag-studded gathering in Paris, knowing they would not deploy to the Pacific. (Photo by Keystone/Stringer/Hulton Archive/Getty Images)

Japanese delegates on Ie Shima, Okinawa, boarding General MacArthur's C-54 transport before flying to Manila on August 19. Approaching the top of ladder is the delegation head, Lieutenant General Torashiro Kawabe. Officer at left, behind the civilian envoy, is Rear Admiral Ichiro Yokoyama. (NARA)

Japanese Imperial Headquarters representative General Yoshijiro Umezu signing the Instrument of Surrender while General MacArthur (left) watches, aboard the USS *Missouri* (BB-63), Tokyo Bay on September 2. (Photo by Hulton Archive/Stringer/Getty Images)

U.S. Navy carrier planes fly in formation over USS *Missouri* (BB-63) during the surrender ceremonies, September 2. Photographed by Lt. Barrett Gallagher from atop the battleship's forward 16-inch gun turret. Aircraft types include F4U, TBM and SB2C. Ship in the right distance is USS *Ancon* (AGC-4), the 7th Fleet's amphibious flagship. (NARA)

General Douglas MacArthur with Japanese Emperor Hirohito during the U.S. occupation of Japan in 1945. MacArthur oversaw the nation's postwar transition to democratic government while rebuilding the economy. (Bettmann/Getty Images)

onto a Zeke through a climbing turn. He fired, saw smoke, and lost sight of the Mitsubishi as it seemed to fall into the clouds.

Next Lindsay jumped the tail of another Zeke, fired from directly astern, and got immediate strikes. His final burst set the enemy plane alight.

Lieutenant (jg) George M. Williams tried following an agile Zeke through a turn, stalled in the attempt, and spun out. He shoved the stick forward, countered the spin with rudder, and providentially recovered behind another Japanese aircraft. Williams pursued through a wide turn, firing steadily with convincing results. The Zeke gushed smoke and flames, spiraling toward the ground.

Regaining precious altitude, Williams latched onto another opponent, matching the enemy pilot's evasive maneuvers. Williams' gunfire drew flames from the target, followed by an explosion.

Flying number four in the division was Lieutenant (jg) Elwood K. MacDonald. With the sun behind it, a Zeke began an overhead run but MacDonald defeated the pass by an aggressive turn, maneuvering onto the enemy's tail just above the cloud deck. After absorbing about six bursts, the Japanese dived into the undercast, his plane trailing smoke and shedding parts.

Another Zeke lost its six o'clock low advantage by overshooting the Hellcats and pulling up ahead of them. MacDonald accepted the gift, hammering the Mitsubishi with four bursts. Streaming smoke, it rolled on one side as MacDonald put in two more volleys, watching his victim drop into a flaming spin.

With his head on a swivel, MacDonald glimpsed a third assailant diving in from three o'clock high. He turned starboard to face it, forcing the Zeke to cross his nose. Applying ample deflection, MacDonald triggered a lethal burst that skewered the airframe from prop to rudder, recalling, "The Jap plane seemed to fly apart as he fell toward the clouds." But MacDonald wanted to ensure a kill and fired again, exploding the Mitsubishi.

The few remaining Japanese poked their noses down, disappearing into the undercast. The brief combat netted "Fighting 49" seven confirmed and two probable victories without loss. That figure doubled the unit's total, as there had been little opportunity to engage airborne Japanese since May.[22]

Seafires and Avengers

The lone British carrier, HMS *Indefatigable*, was "on loan" to McCain while her Royal Navy team mates withdrew, preparing for later operations. At dawn on August 15, "*Indefat*" launched against Kisarazu Airfield 30 miles south of the capital where, unknown to the Allies, Japan was testing its nascent jet program. Six Avengers, escorted by eight Seafires, were unable to find the field beneath a cloud layer so they diverted to the alternate target, a chemical plant.

Crossing Odaki Bay, the escorts sighted two Zeros below the formation. Suspecting that the vulnerable Japanese were bait, the Seafire pilots swiveled their heads to sight perhaps a dozen other Zeros approaching from above and behind. Most of the British pilots had enough time to jettison their heavy drop tanks, shove up the power, and turn to engage.

An exception was 22-year-old Sub-Lieutenant Freddie Hockley, whose plane took repeated hits on the enemy's first pass. He reached up, pulled the ball to release the canopy, and went over the side.

Hockley's wingman, Sub-Lieutenant R.A. Gorvin, was doubly damned. His belly tank refused to drop and one of his two 20mm cannon jammed. He escaped with damage to his Seafire, heading for the safety of the sea.

From there the combat degenerated into a series of small dogfights. Belle of the brawl was Sub-Lieutenant Victor Lowden, who had repeated opportunities and registered hits on five opponents. The young Scot closed from 800 down to 450 yards to destroy his first Zero, despite one of his cannon jamming. Then he dropped a second and shared a third with Sub-Lieutenant W.J. Williams, who had destroyed a Zero moments before.

Maneuvering against three Mitsubishis, Lowden's airspeed degraded and the agile Japanese began gaining a favorable angle on him. He left the fight in a 70-degree dive, pushing 420 miles per hour.

Sub-Lieutenant G.J. Murphy dueled with two Japanese and outfought them despite the Zero's fabled maneuverability. Conserving his ammunition, he hit them with deflection shots in the turns, claiming both shot down.

Section leader, Sub-Lieutenant R.C. Kay, flying close escort to the bombers, cut off a Zero threatening the Avengers and hit it hard, igniting a fire in the wing root. Next Kay accepted a 60-degree deflection shot, applied proper lead – and blew its tail off. Then he hit another Zero but ran out of cannon shells before he could complete the kill. He was the only Seafire pilot to expend all his 20mm ammunition, and out-climbed two remaining Zeros to achieve an altitude haven.

Kay's wingman, Sub-Lieutenant D.N. Duncan, fought a textbook battle – literally. Recalling the Seafire's tactical notes, he retained his drop tank despite the 360-pound penalty and kept his airspeed above 250mph. He shot at three enemies, destroying one despite yet another jammed 20mm.

The Seafires had claimed eight against one loss in their last combat against four Axis powers: Germany, Italy, Vichy France, and Japan.

Meanwhile, the Avengers fought their own battle. The initial Japanese attack pressed through the escort to engage the second bomber flight. Lieutenant L. Baldwin's turret gunner, Petty Officer A.A. Simpson, scored .50-caliber hits on one assailant – likely Kay's first victim. But the Avenger's sturdy airframe coped with loss of the starboard horizontal stabilizer, with the starboard wing punctured by cannon shells. All six bombers continued to the secondary target, bombed successfully, and turned for home.

Nearing the task force, Baldwin's Avenger expired. A fire had erupted, forcing him to ditch alongside an American destroyer. The bomber crew gratefully accepted Yank hospitality.

Nor was that all. Because of continuing Japanese probes, the Americans were wary of any inbound aircraft. Victor Lowden was threatened by Corsairs making menacing gestures, so he lowered wheels and flaps, banking steeply to show his Seafire's distinctive elliptical wing with blue and white markings.[23]

The Final Bomb, August 15, 1945

At 6:14 a.m. – 45 minutes after Strike One had launched – Halsey was having breakfast aboard the *Missouri*. From the operations plan he knew that Two Able was within five minutes of its target time when Commander Doug Moulton burst in, waving a message form. "Admiral, here she is!"

It was a top-secret message from Nimitz, highest priority. "Air attack will be suspended X Acknowledge." It also contained the transcript of President Truman's announcement.*

The fleet commander was struck by the symmetry. Horace Douglass Moulton, Annapolis class of 1931, had spent most of the war with Halsey, receiving repeated medals for his staff work. On the morning of December 7, 1941 then-Lieutenant Moulton had interrupted Vice Admiral Halsey's breakfast aboard the USS *Enterprise* (CV-6), when the aircraft carrier had been approaching Pearl Harbor.

Now, Halsey wrote that his first thought was, "Victory!" His second was, "'God be thanked, I'll never have to order another man out to die.' And my next was, 'I am grateful for the honor of being in command of the Third Fleet on this day.'"[24]

Over Japan, the world-shaping news came too late for many; men continued to die. *Ticonderoga* (CV-14) pilots in all likelihood dropped the last bombs of World War II. Twelve Hellcats led by Lieutenant Commander Charles W. Gunnels were unable to find their primary objective due to cloud cover so they diverted westward. Gunnels assigned each of his four-plane divisions to separate targets – an airfield, a gunnery school, and an industrial plant. About 6:30 Gunnels was just recovering from his 60-degree dive when he heard an astonishing call from the task force: "All Strike Able planes return to base immediately. Do not attack target. The war is over!"

Nonetheless, the Hellcats were already committed, and a premature pullout could have exposed them to medium-altitude flak. The aviators pressed home their runs on each target. Lieutenant (jg) John McNabb, a 23-year-old Pennsylvanian, was the last pilot in line, and his 500-pound bomb almost certainly was the last one dropped over Japan.

---

* Truman's announcement of Japan's surrender acceptance was broadcast on national radio at 7:00 p.m. Eastern Daylight Savings Time on the 14th (see Chapter 4, p. 161).

TASK FORCE 38'S LAST ENCOUNTERS

Yorktown and Intrepid

At 49, Rear Admiral Arthur W. Radford already had a stellar career, and he was bound for greater things as an eventual commander of the Pacific Fleet and the second Chairman of the Joint Chiefs of Staff. But this Wednesday his Task Group 38.4 was the greatest ever assembled, both in terms of size and success rate, with six U.S. fast carriers.

Early that morning *Shangri-La* had launched 12 Corsairs to strike airfields in the Kasumigaura area, some 30 miles northeast of Tokyo. However, due to weather they were only able to attack Kashima on the coast. The VBF-85 pilots descended through holes in the undercast, bombing, rocketing, and strafing. They claimed five grounded planes destroyed and "hangar area covered with bombs."

Lieutenant (jg) John C. Dunn had earned a Navy Cross the month before, bombing a Japanese battleship in Kure Harbor. But his plane took hits to his engine and, losing oil pressure, he lacked altitude to glide to the coast. Following ditching procedure, he cinched up his shoulder harness, locked his canopy back, lowered his flaps, and made a water landing in Kasumigaura Lake. Dunn escaped from his sinking Corsair and deployed his life raft as his friends departed.

Later a "dumbo" rescue plane with a *Yorktown* (CV-10) escort searched the area. The VBF-88 pilots noted an oil slick where Dunn had ditched, and concluded that he had been captured.

Yorktown's fighter-bombers fashioned themselves as "The Gringos," with a mustachioed desperado brandishing a poker hand and a six-shooter displayed on their aircraft. In only three aerial encounters, the squadron logged five victories over the Japanese Home Islands during the last three weeks of hostilities. Sweeping the area for targets of opportunity in the morning hours of the 15th, three "Gringos" were outbound over Hokoda Airfield when Lieutenant (jg) George B. Lewis spotted two planes taking off. They were immediately recognizable: Nakajima Myrt reconnaissance aircraft distinctive by their long, lean profile. The

Japanese pilots could not have been caught at a worse moment. Lewis rolled in on the nearest bandit from about 1,100 feet, firing at full deflection from starboard. He recovered behind the Myrt, fired again, and saw it blow up just before crashing.

The flight leader, Lieutenant Raymond C. McGrath, gained extra altitude and dived onto the second Myrt's tail, firing one lethal burst from about 500 feet. The victim exploded in McGrath's face, forcing him to honk back on the stick to avoid most of the fireball. Meanwhile, Lieutenant (jg) Robert J. Wohlers dispatched a third Myrt in two passes. McGrath regrouped his flight and returned to escort the rescue aircraft clear of the coast.[25]

Unknown at the time, Dunn had been captured to join two shipmates, one who had been downed in early June and another downed more recently when strafing an airfield on August 13.

Before the strike could return to base, Task Force 38 announced that the Japanese had agreed to surrender.

Whether from ignorance or anger, numerous other Japanese airmen continued resisting the intruders. Hardest hit was *Yorktown*'s Fighting Squadron 88, flying a joint mission with 24 Corsairs off *Shangri-La* and *Wasp*. Lieutenant Howard M. Harrison's dozen Hellcats became dispersed in worsening weather, leaving six intact upon penetrating a cloud front.

"Howdy" Harrison was enormously popular with his shipmates. They considered him, "The friendliest, straightest guy you could ever meet."[26]

Overflying Tokurozama Airfield northwest of Tokyo when the ceasefire message was broadcast, Harrison was about to reverse course when the roof fell in. An estimated 17 enemy aircraft – reportedly a mixed bag of Imperial Army and Navy types – dropped onto the Grummans from above and behind. It was a near perfect "six o'clock" attack.

Japanese records are incomplete or contradictory, but the attackers were most likely from the 302nd Air Group at Atsugi, inland from Yokohama. The 302nd had scrambled eight Zekes under Lieutenant Yutaka Morioka, a former dive bomber pilot with four victories to his name. Also, he may have led four

Kawanishi Georges – big, rugged fighters with four 20mm cannon.

Morioka set up the bounce well, hitting the Americans at 8,000 feet. Spotting the threat, Harrison knew there was no choice but to fight. His pilots shoved throttles to the stops, countered the threat, and opened fire. In that first frantic pass, the Yorktowners thought they had dropped four bandits. Then the formations were shredded in the head-on charge.

Lieutenant (jg) Theodore W. Hansen, wingman to Lieutenant (jg) Maurice Proctor, exploded a fighter head-on, then claimed a second. Proctor himself shot the wing off another assailant.

Flying the U.S. Navy's patented Thach Weave, the two Hellcats afforded mutual support despite the odds.* Banking hard right, Proctor and Hansen glimpsed a bandit shooting at Lieutenant (jg) Joseph Sahloff. Proctor fired from longish range – about 700 feet – and the assailant exploded. Then he radioed Sahloff to head his smoking plane toward the safety of the coast.

"Fighting 88" was a tight-knit outfit. The week previously, Maury Proctor and Joe Sahloff had volunteered to cover "Howdy" Harrison down off Miho, only about 50 miles northeast of Tokyo. They had led the rescue amphibian to Harrison's tiny life raft, knowing that otherwise it was unlikely he would be found. Their devotion to their friend paid off, and he had rejoined the squadron.

Now, as Proctor assumed a protective position on Sahloff's damaged Grumman, tracers streaked past Proctor's wings. He turned hard to starboard and Hansen shot the Japanese off his tail. Maury Proctor and Ted Hansen rejoined above Sahloff, observing two more Japanese afire but could not identify the victors. Abruptly Proctor was boxed in: six bandits ahead and one astern. Unaccountably, the attackers on his nose pulled up, allowing him to engage the stalker behind him. He scored decisive hits, sending the enemy down burning.

---

* This maneuver could be used if one pair of aircraft were threatened from behind; they would turn into the other pair, giving the second duo a shot at the attackers.

By the time the previous sextet returned, Proctor had enough of a start to dive toward some protective clouds. The Japanese hit his plane but he evaded through the weather, reaching the coast. There Proctor saw Joe Sahloff's crippled Hellcat spin out of control and dive into the sea. But Proctor knew nothing of the others. He radioed his shipmates for a rendezvous, though only Hansen replied.

Hansen returned to *Yorktown* alone, sick at heart, believing he was the lone survivor. His spirits lifted slightly when Proctor snagged an arresting wire a few minutes later. In the debrief of the hard-fought combat they claimed three and two kills, respectively. Subsequently, the intelligence officer awarded one each to New Yorker Sahloff, Howard Harrison from Columbus, Ohio, and Ensigns Wright "Hybrid" Hobbs of Kokomo, Indiana, and Eugene Mandeberg of Detroit. It was Hobbs' 23rd birthday.[27]

Another debriefing was held by the 302nd Air Group in Atsugi. The Japanese lost Zero pilot Lieutenant Mitsuo Taguchi plus two Georges. The only confirmed success went to Morioka, giving him ace status on the last day of combat.[28]

All Allied offensive operations were then canceled at 7:00 a.m. but fleet defenses remained on full alert.

Incredibly, some men missed the news. Aboard the carrier *Intrepid* at Eniwetok, recently repaired from her April kamikaze damage, some tired Corsair pilots were sleeping in. Recalled Lieutenant (jg) Roy Erickson:

One of my buddies, Ensign "Boots" Liles, had just learned of the Japanese reconciliation and the war had ended. Armed with this magnificent news, he went charging up to "Boys' Town" to find them in their favorite pastime, making ZZZs. With tumultuous zeal and at the top of his lungs he announced the most important, momentous event in human history. "Hey! Wake up! The Japs have surrendered! The war is over! The war is over!"

Almost in unison he was rebuffed with, "Shut up Liles, get the hell out of here and let us get some sleep." Amused, Liles left the room not really surprised at the light-hearted response to the conclusion of a chapter in history in which they had played such an active and dangerous role. To his amazement, no one believed him and they all told him to go soak his head in the toilet, as they rolled over and went back to sleep. I guess Boots had cried wolf once too often.[29]

Cavalla Delays Celebration

Far to the west an impromptu celebration erupted in Task Force 38.

Nobody agreed on the general reaction; it was too varied, too personal. At sea, men either shouted and pounded the backs of shipmates or stood frozen in place, trying to absorb the message. Reported *Hancock*, "Ships steaming in orderly columns broke out in disorderly blasts on powerful steam whistles and men on their bridges took turns, in child-like anticipation, each giving vent to his emotion with the sounding of three short and a long – the symbol of Victory."[30]

Beethoven's Fifth Symphony intro – *dit dit dit dah* in Morse Code – never was more heartfelt.

In some airborne squadrons, discipline unraveled. Pilots jettisoned ordnance, broke formation, and indulged in joyful aerobatics at the sheer thrill of being alive. To fighter pilot Lieutenant (jg) Richard L. Newhafer – a future novelist and screen writer – the message brought "all the hope and unreasoning happiness that salvation can bring."[31]

Meanwhile, the submarine USS *Cavalla* (SS-244), 11 days out of Freemantle, Australia, on its sixth war patrol, circled outside Tokyo Bay. The skipper was Commander Herman J. Kossler, a popular 33-year-old Virginian from the Annapolis class of 1934. Exceptionally experienced, he had made nine previous patrols in *Guardfish* (SS-217) and *Cavalla*, receiving a Navy Cross and three Silver Stars. More than that, he was a survivor: 31 of his classmates died in the war, seven in submarines and three at Midway, while Commander Richard H. O'Kane – America's leading submarine skipper – became a prisoner when *Tang* was sunk in October 1944.

By 1945, *Cavalla* already had a distinguished record: 14 months previously Kossler had sunk the Japanese carrier *Shokaku*, one of the six that had launched against Pearl Harbor.

That morning offshore Kossler's log entry noted, "1115: received 'cease firing' order from ComSubPac [Commander,

Submarine Force, U.S. Pacific Fleet]. All hands highly elated that this damn war is finally over, but unfortunately 25 miles off the coast of Japan is a hell of a place to celebrate it."

Since the patrol station's fighter escort had departed, the submariners logically thought that a celebration was in order. Around noon, running surfaced, the skipper approved distribution of beer when radar noted a single aircraft straight ahead at six miles, closing to four. Kossler reported:

> It went into a dive just after we sighted it, and at about 1,500 feet altitude it dropped a 50- to 100-pound bomb. Increased to full speed and cleared the bridge. The bomb missed our starboard quarter about 100 yards. I was so busy watching the bomb that I didn't see the [Japanese] markings on the plane. Everything happened too fast for all of us. The plane did not strafe, but when about a mile astern commenced turning to come back on us. I lost interest in everything but deep submergence.

Cavalla "pulled the plug," remaining under for almost two hours, and Kossler decided that his crew would defer celebration until the surrender was signed. He was prescient: *Cavalla* was one of 12 fleet boats in Tokyo Bay when the war officially ended two weeks later.[32]

The Last Kamikaze

At noon – airborne nearly four hours and slated for relief – *Shangri-La*'s Lieutenant Bayard Webster and Ensign Falvey M. Sandige received a 300-degree vector, 15 miles from their controlling destroyer. They made the tally-ho at 12,000 feet, a Yokosuka Judy dive bomber leading a fighter about 1,000 feet behind.

Sandige was closest to the Judy, attacking from 4 to 5 o'clock, scoring hits on the cockpit and engine. The bomber went into slow rolls "burning vigorously with pieces coming off." Sandige disengaged at 4,000 feet.

Webster closed on the fighter for several good bursts into the left wing from the 6:30 position. Smoking heavily from the wing root, the escort dropped into cloud, credited as damaged.

The action report variously called the fighter a navy Mitsubishi Jack or an army Nakajima Frank – the latter seeming extremely unlikely to accompany a lone naval bomber.[33]

The penultimate victims splashed early that afternoon when *Wasp*'s four-plane division of VF-86 skipper Cleo Dobson, the Pearl Harbor survivor, received a radar vector over the task group. The "Watchdog" controller sent Dobson and his wingman to 25,000 feet while the second section descended to 12,000.

The section lead, Lieutenant (jg) Ora E. Myers, glimpsed a bogey breaking out of clouds about ten miles on the nose at 14,000. Myers and Lieutenant (jg) C.W. Baker shoved up the power, closing on the hostile, now clearly a Zeke. Myers executed a high firing run from 500 feet astern, scoring hits on the engine and fuselage. With the Zeke visibly burning, Myers pulled up and reversed for another pass. He hit the engine again, increasing the flames. Baker joined in, scoring hits with a short burst. Then Myers closed on the Mitsubishi's tail, pursuing down to 4,000 feet, and watched his victim dive into the sea.

Meanwhile, from 25,000 feet, Dobson and Lieutenant (jg) Mahlon J. Morrison orbited for half an hour. Then they received a steer from the controller and sighted a lone bogey 8,000 feet directly below. Dobson could not spot it so he ceded lead to the youngster. As the two Grummans descended, Dobson got a look at the dark-green intruder, a single-engine bomber. He recalled:

Morrison made a firing run on it and I saw some of his incendiary bullets hitting him. A bit of smoke came out of him. The Jap pushed over and headed for the water and I closed on his tail and really let him have it. His left wingroot blazed and he went into a spin. After falling about 1,000 feet his left wing came off and more flames came from his plane. We followed him down and saw him splash in the drink. Boy, he really made a splash. That was my first shot at a Jap in the air and I'll tell you it really was a thrill.

As the day wore on Dobson speculated, "Maybe they are going to keep us in danger for a while. Well, we got lots of pilots who want to shoot hell out of them, and I am one of them."[34]

Dobson's intelligence officer reported, "This plane was the last enemy aircraft of the war to be shot down." But Air Group 86 did not know about a subsequent event in Task Group 38.1.

Half an hour after Dobson and Morrison's kill, a *Belleau Wood* pilot won the race to the last kamikaze. At 2:00 p.m. three VF-31 divisions were flying CAP when a radar vector put the dozen Hellcats onto a single hostile 20 miles out. From 7,000 feet the Judy dive bomber saw its peril, jettisoned its bomb, and reversed into a steep wingover. With an altitude advantage the *Belleau Wood* fighters quickly overhauled their prey, catching it at 4,000 feet. The Hellcat leader was drawing a bead when the Japanese pilot abruptly throttled back, forcing the American to overshoot. It was a clever move but only bought a few seconds' reprieve.

The second section leader, Ensign Clarence A. Moore, dived to attack and hauled into range. He fired two bursts into the wing root, torching the Judy. It was Moore's first kill and the 34th credited U.S. aerial victory of the day.

Engine Shut-Down
While the second wave of carrier-based attackers was recalled, the third shut down engines on their carriers' flight decks. Among the inbound strikers was *Essex*'s air group. Ensign Donald McPherson, a Nebraska ace, said:

> We VF-83 pilots were part of a large attack force that was approaching the Tokyo Bay area when we were informed by radio of the "cease fire." We were to proceed back over the ocean and to jettison our bombs and rockets. After following those orders we broke formation and "celebrated" by doing all kinds of aerobatics! What a great feeling to have ended the conflict victoriously![35]

Farther off Tokyo, *Shangri-La* pilot Lieutenant Richard DeMott, owner of a Navy Cross from the Kure strikes, led a low-level search for downed squadron mates. "On our way to the target area, word was passed of the official announcement from Pearl and CinCPac of the end of the war. What a time to hear it – en route to Tokyo!"

Upon return to the "Shang," DeMott was summoned to the flag bridge to give the task force commander a personal update. The aviator noted that McCain was "slightly burned up at the Japs for continuing to send their planes out after us. He's a funny little guy. Everyone is all smiles and happy aboard, although it's almost too hard to believe the news."

Later, with time to gather his thoughts, DeMott journaled, "Brother, I am thankful that I am alive this day and got to see the end of the war from the front seat. I hope to spend the rest of my life enjoying everything and being at peace with the world. Kick me if I don't."

Dick DeMott kept his pledge, dying in Pennsylvania 61 years later.[36]

✳   ✳   ✳

Earlier in the day, the airborne strikes had returned by 10:20; therefore, Third Fleet ordered the carriers to stow bombers on hangar decks and maintain fighters ready to launch if needed to reinforce CAPs. As Halsey noted, "My trust in the Japs was still less than whole-hearted, and I was taking no chance that a kamikaze would seize a last-minute opportunity to win honor for his ancestors. In fact, I had our fighter directors call our CAP pilots and instruct them, 'Investigate and shoot down all snoopers – not vindictively but in a friendly sort of way.'"

Just before 11:00, Third Fleet received the notice to all Pacific Ocean commands, validating Halsey's order. Barely 30 minutes later Nimitz's command clarified the situation. Whereas the previous information was to suspend operations, now "Offensive operations against Japanese forces will cease at once X Continue searches and patrols X Maintain defensive and internal security measures at highest level and beware of treachery."[37]

Throughout Third Fleet in the pre-noon hour, sailors hoisted oversize battle colors while *Missouri*'s signalmen broke out the admiral's four-star flag. On the bridge, Captain Stuart S. Murray ordered the whistle and siren to sound for 60 glorious seconds, and the rest of the fleet emulated "Mighty Mo" in celebration. Soon thereafter the fleet commander ordered the "Well done" signal run up *Missouri*'s halyard.

And then the killing continued.

Final Splashes
Like every other ship present, aboard the destroyer *Stembel* (DD-644) the crew listened to ComThirdFleet's announcement:

At 1300 Admiral Halsey addressed the fleet personally over voice radio. His speech, not long, and direct, was a simple statement of his thanks and congratulations to all the men under him who helped bring the war to its end. His final words were: 'Again and again I say, God bless you, and well done.' During the address four Jap planes were splashed near the task force.[38]

Monitoring the fighter director net, Halsey and his staff heard repeated calls. As Halsey himself recorded:

1125: The high CAP called in, "Tallyho! One bandit diving!" But almost immediately afterwards the same voice reported, "Splash one Judy." [Actually a Kate]
    Even as I was speaking a battle royal raged overhead:
    1303: CAP splashed one Zeke and one Judy [actually 1300]
    1316: CAP splashed one Judy [probably 1331]
    1325: One Judy splashed by picket destroyer's gunfire.
    Before the day was done our CAP and AA had shot down eight planes trying to bomb us or dive into us. I was certain at the time that those Japs were irreconcilables, fighting a private war; but when I went ashore and saw the utter ruin of Japan's communications system, I became convinced that they simply never received the word.[39]

Japanese aircraft had become rare sights over Third Fleet; in the last six weeks of hostilities, shipboard gunners only claimed 11 shootdowns. The final encounter came early that afternoon when four picket destroyers were attacked by a lone Judy dive bomber 100 miles offshore (Halsey's 13:25 call).

Radar tracked the intruder until it broke out of the clouds at 8,500 feet, range eight miles, nosing into a 20-degree glide. The destroyers accelerated to 25 knots.

The *Heermann* (DD-532) was a blooded veteran with nine battle stars dating from 1943. She had earned lasting fame in the October 1944 battle off Samar, defending the escort carriers of "Taffy Three" in Leyte Gulf. Despite heavy damage, she had survived a gun and torpedo duel with Japanese cruisers and battleships.

Heermann was fast on the draw, opening fire at a slant range of 8,000 yards. A five-inch proximity-fused round knocked off part of the wing or tail, flipping the Judy into a slow spin. *Black* (DD-666) and *Bullard* (DD-660) also claimed hits. The target swerved to the right and splashed about 200 yards from *Bullard*.

The commanding officer of *Heermann*, commenting on the action, reported: "In accordance with verbal instructions from Commander Third Fleet, the Judy was splashed 'in a friendly manner.'"[40]

The fleet commander further reflected, "I hope that history will remember that when hostilities ended, the capital of the Japanese Empire had just been bombed, strafed and rocketed by planes of the Third Fleet, and was about to be bombed, strafed, and rocketed again. Last, I hope it will remember that seven of the men on strike Able One did not return."[*, 41]

"*Hanna*'s" war diary summarized:

In all TF 38 planes tangled with approximately 45 Jap aircraft over the Tokyo area before their recall, shooting down 26 of them. Returning strike planes overtook and shot down three bomb-carrying Japs

---

[*] Halsey's figure may have been premature. There were four missing *Yorktown* pilots and one from the *Independence*, status uncertain, but the other aircraft losses did not involve aircrew casualties so possibly other pilots were in fact saved.

heading for the fleet. CAP shot down five more, including our Kate, and AA from a Tomcat destroyer got another. Of these planes, one was our Kate splashed 1123 at 353 deg, 32 miles.

Task Force 38's known losses were 13 planes and *Yorktown*'s four pilots.

DENIAL, ACCEPTANCE, AND ATROCITY

On the morning of the 15th, at Omura naval air station on Kyushu, Captain Minoru Genda's elite fighter unit learned of an upcoming imperial announcement. Genda, who had overseen much of the training for the Pearl Harbor attack, was among the most-respected leaders in naval aviation. He had built his 343rd Air Group into a potent force flying the rugged, powerful Kawanishi *Shiden-Kai*, called "George" by the Americans. But the "squadron of aces" had taken severe losses recently, including nine pilots and ten planes fighting P-47 Thunderbolts on the 8th.

Before noon on the 15th about 100 personnel assembled to hear the broadcast. They heard the voice of popular Japanese Broadcasting Corporation (NHK) announcer Shinken Wada, partly known for broadcasting sumo wrestling matches. But this day he intoned, "This will be a broadcast of the gravest importance. All listeners please rise. His Majesty the emperor will now read the imperial rescript to the people of Japan. We respectfully transmit his voice."[42]

After the national anthem, *Kimagayo*, the audience heard Hirohito's spoken words for the first time. But the marginal quality of the recording coupled with the scratchy loudspeaker prevented many listeners from following closely. The situation was compounded by Hirohito's archaic language.

He began, "To Our Good and loyal subjects: after pondering deeply the general trends of the world and the actual conditions obtaining in Our Empire today, We have decided to effect a settlement of the present situation by resorting to an extraordinary measure."

Then, in less than five minutes, Hirohito indulged in some of the most disingenuous statements uttered in the 20th century. "We declared war on America and Britain out of Our sincere desire to secure Japan's self-preservation and the stabilization of East Asia, it being far from Our thought either to infringe upon the sovereignty of other nations or to embark upon territorial aggrandizement." Which of course was exactly what Japan had done in China from 1937 and across the Pacific from 1941, especially infringing upon the sovereignty of the Philippines and the oil-rich Dutch East Indies.

Continuing with a colossal understatement, the emperor conceded that "the war situation has developed not necessarily to Japan's advantage."

The rescript concluded that Tokyo "accepts the provisions of the joint declaration" issued by the U.S., Britain, China, and the Soviet Union.[43]

Hirohito's lawyerly obfuscation left millions of Japanese uncertain of what the emperor actually meant. Because he had not specifically alluded to surrender, many military men and civilians wondered what lay ahead.

At Omura, proud but tired fighter pilots fumed. Genda himself said, "It was my thought we would continue the war on the soil of Japan, for as long as the Japanese nation existed, even if it took ten, twenty, fifty or one hundred years!"

Warrant Officer Yoshio Nakamura, wounded in the Solomons in 1943 after nine victories, spoke for many: "I could not understand the meaning of the broadcast. Though we heard from the command that Japan was defeated, I did not think that the war would end." However, Warrant Officer Masao Sasakibara reflected that most pilots showed "an expression of relief on their faces."[44]

Genda wanted to confirm that hostilities had in fact ended. Therefore, he led a four-plane flight to Oita Base, headquarters of the Fifth Air Fleet, 100 miles east. It is unlikely that Genda met the commanding vice admiral, as Matome Ugaki had already reached an irrevocable decision.

Rather than endure the grief of surrender, Ugaki chose death. Previously he had written, "We can make the enemy finally give up the war after making it taste the bitterness of a prolonged conflict." Aged 55, Ugaki – who had survived being shot down on a 1943 mission with Admiral Isoroku Yamamoto – removed his rank insignia, indicating his intent. Late that afternoon Ugaki made a final entry in his diary, noting that because he had not received a ceasefire order, he would lead a final kamikaze mission in partial atonement for the deaths of so many aircrew. He shared sake with his staff, including his naval academy classmate and friend of three decades, Rear Admiral Takaji Joshima, who tried to dissuade him:

> I know that, as commanding officer, you accept full responsibility for the Fifth Air Fleet. But, in addition to what is past, you must consider the future. There, too, you have duties and responsibilities. I have been told of your present intention and am in complete sympathy with your feelings. Nevertheless, for the good of everyone concerned, I urge you to call off this sortie.[45]

Undeterred, Ugaki climbed into a Judy dive bomber piloted by Lieutenant Commander Tatsuo Nakatsuru. Wearing a dark-green uniform and carrying a short sword from Yamamoto, the admiral crowded into the rear seat with the radioman, Warrant Officer Akiyoshi Endo. Nakatsuru's bomber was one of ten on the mission but three returned with faltering engines. The others flew southward toward Okinawa. Around 7:25 p.m. Endo sent a message reporting that the crew was diving on an American naval vessel. Nothing more was heard from any of the aircraft, although a U.S. seaplane tender may have sustained minor damage in the attack.

The next morning American sailors from the landing ship tank *LST-926* examined a wreck on an islet off Okinawa. Oddly, the two-seat bomber contained three bodies. The third occupant, whose skull was crushed and whose right arm was missing, wore a dark-green uniform with a short sword beside him.

The unidentified bodies were buried in the sand.[46]

Surrender was also too much for some other imperial warriors. In an act of atonement, the kamikaze master, Vice Admiral

Takajiro Onishi, committed *hara-kiri* on the floor of his residence the night of the 15th. He botched the job, lingering in agony until about 6:00 the next morning.

About three hours after the emperor's broadcast, in a dingy prison near Fukuoka between Hiroshima and Nagasaki, 17 B-29 crewmen were dragged from their cells and murdered in an exhibition of outrage at Hirohito's capitulation. Fukuoka became notorious for casual killings: as many as 16 POWs had been hacked to death in two separate episodes on June 20 and August 10. That afternoon the Americans were slain in three locations, most apparently bearing a sense of resignation. It is possible that they did not know of Hirohito's broadcast.

Eight killers were subsequently tried and three sentenced to death but seven escaped execution, partly owing to Douglas MacArthur's postwar "big picture" philosophy that pardoned some atrocities. The most senior officer, Lieutenant General Isamu Yokoyama, died in hospital.[47]

Nor was that all. Freddie Hockley, the British pilot who had bailed out of his stricken fighter over Odaki Bay on August 15, was a terribly lonely stranger in an alien land. He was a world away from his home in Littleport, Cambridgeshire. Intelligence briefings to aircrew stressed that civilians would kill Allied fliers on sight – far better to surrender to the military. However, Hockley's first opportunity was a civil defense organization, a quasi-military unit, but presumably preferable to a mob.

The civilians delivered the flier to an army regimental headquarters after Hirohito's radio address. Seeking clarification, Colonel Tamura Te'chi phoned division for information on how to proceed. Major Hirano Nobou, the 147th Division's intelligence officer, ordered Colonel Te'chi – a superior – to dispose of the Englishman that night. Consequently, Captain Fijino Masazo led a detachment into the hills where the soldiers dug a grave. That night, nine hours after the surrender announcement, the Japanese murdered Hockley by pistol and sword.

Subsequently, fearing prosecution, Te'chi ordered Hockley's body cremated. Nonetheless, the truth eventually emerged, and in 1947 the three most senior Japanese were tried as war criminals in Hong Kong. Te'chi and Nobou were hanged, and Captain Masazo was sentenced to 15 years.

The British prosecutor, Major Murray Ormsby, was so taken with Hockley's case that he determined the pilot should not be forgotten. "I thought it was such a tragic case that it should be brought to people's attention." Forty years later he began paying for a memorial notice in the *Daily Telegraph* each August 15th until his own death in 2012.[48]

That same afternoon as Hockley was being murdered, Shigeko Araki, the pregnant widow of a kamikaze pilot, walked alongside an open field. Like many Japanese workers, she spent her days off wandering the countryside seeking food. She noticed an older couple digging in the dirt, retrieving containers that probably held valuables. Upon addressing them, she was tersely answered with, "The war is over. The Emperor announced it on the radio."

Araki, whose husband had reputedly ended his life against an American destroyer off Okinawa three months before, seized on a sliver of hope. "You mean we've won?"[49]

MACARTHUR AND TOKYO

In Manila on the morning of August 15, General of the Army Douglas MacArthur received word that he would become Supreme Commander of the Allied Powers. His headquarters attempted to communicate with Tokyo using War Department signal facilities, but when he received no reply, he turned to the Army Airways Communications System (AACS). The AACS Manila station tapped out MacArthur's instructions to the Japanese on a frequency normally used to transmit uncoded weather information.

From Supreme Commander for the Allied Powers to the Japanese Emperor, the Japanese Imperial Government, the Japanese Imperial General Headquarters Message Number Z-500. I have been designated as the Supreme Commander for the Allied Powers (the United States, the Republic of China, the United Kingdom and the Union of Soviet Socialist Republics) and empowered to arrange directly with the Japanese authorities for the cessation of hostilities at the earliest practicable date.

It is desired that a radio station in the Tokyo area be officially designated for continuous use in handling radio communications between this headquarters and your headquarters. Your reply to this message should give the call signs, frequencies and station designation.

It is desired that the radio communication with my headquarters in Manila be handled in English text. Pending designation by you of a station in the Tokyo area for use as above indicated, station JUM on frequency 13705 kilocycles will be used for this purpose and Manila will reply on 15965 kilocycles. Upon receipt of this message, acknowledge. Signed, MacArthur.

Tokyo replied in less than two hours, the first direct communication between the Allies and Japan.[50]

Amid the worry and uncertainty, Tokyo continued to play musical chairs. On the 17th, Prime Minister Suzuki's four-month tenure ended with replacement by Prince Naruhiko Higashikuni, twice uncle by marriage to Hirohito. A four-star general, he had led a checkered career, accused of authorizing the use of poison gas in China yet opposing war with the West.

Higashikuni would ultimately occupy the office for only 54 days but lasted beyond the crucial early September period. His cabinet's dual priorities were ensuring the military's compliance with demobilization and assuring the nation that "the imperial institution" would endure.[51]

PHILIPPINE END GAME, AUGUST 8–17

By August the American public largely assumed that MacArthur's forces had nailed down Japanese resistance in the Philippines. He had announced full liberation on July 5 but in fact two Army divisions remained in combat, conducting "mop-up" operations on the large southern island of Mindanao.

The 24th "Victory" and 31st "Dixie" Infantry Divisions originally went ashore in late April, conducting an arduous four-month campaign against the geography and weather at least as much as the Japanese. Only six degrees above the Equator, Mindanao was rainy, hot, and humid, crossed with a hatchwork of jungle ravines affording excellent defensive terrain. The road network was minimal to primitive in many places, and soldiers who ventured very far afield sometimes slogged through knee-deep mud.

Little known was that Japanese civilians accompanied the Imperial Army in the islands. That fact was grimly evident to Lieutenant Colonel Thomas Hoke Compere, a prewar Chicago attorney, among the 24th Division officers who met in August to form the postwar division association. He wrote to his wife Elsie:

> My dear sweetheart... News correspondents will go anywhere when there is lots of action but when the drudgery of mopping up in distant mountains, gorges, jungle and impassable trails begins they depart. The plight of the Jap here is most pathetic. They have ceased to fire and merely exist – both the soldiers and civilians, men, women and children. The Japanese civilians retreated from Davao with the army... We find bodies of men, women and children who died along the trails from starvation or disease. It's tragic but that's the way they have chosen to conduct themselves and we have a most difficult time trying to convince them that life is much easier in an internment camp.[52]

The finale on the island of Mindanao was witnessed by Master Sergeant Aubrey Paul Tillery of the 124th Infantry in the 31st Division, an old soldier by that summer. Drafted in early 1941, he had made his sixth stripe in the fall of 1943 and observed the final operations with the weary eye of a 26-year-old veteran:

> The 31st Division commanding general [Clarence A. Martin] accepted from the Japanese general surrender of all troops

on Mindanao. The word went out by various means to the Japanese soldiers in the remote sections of the mountains that the war was over. Through experience we had learned to be very cautious and leery of this enemy; therefore caution was taken to be sure that there were no surprises. The first large group was ordered to come down from the mountains and stack their arms in a designated area on the other side of a river. I was there on our side of the river with a truck convoy to take them to a compound. I noticed that we had plenty of American troops there on our side of the river – just in case.

Our Army Engineers hooked up a barge on some cables stretched across the river. By tilting the barge sideways the river current would force the barge back and fro across the river. This means was used to bring the Japanese soldiers across to our side. The operation went along without any hitches and they loaded on our trucks where we took them to a compound. There they awaited transportation back to Japan.[53]

Five days earlier, an unlikely airborne drama had played out. American-born Second Lieutenant Minoru Wada of the 100th Division staff had been captured earlier in the war. Reputedly a graduate of both the University of Tokyo and Kyushu Military Academy, despite the origins of his birth, in fact he only spoke limited English. However, as a prisoner of war he reluctantly considered an offer to guide U.S. Marine Corps bombers to his division headquarters of Lieutenant General Jiro Harada. Finally, speaking through a bilingual Marine gunnery sergeant, Wada concluded that any Japanese losses would be offset by an early end to the fighting, saving lives on both sides.

As such, on August 10 at Moret Field on Zamboanga, Wada had boarded a North American PBJ bomber, the naval variant of the Army's fabled B-25 Mitchell. Flying in the lead PBJ, augmented by Corsair fighter-bombers, he provided detailed navigation to well-concealed headquarters locations. The flying leathernecks bombed accurately, effectively decapitating the division's command structure. Major Mortimer Jordan stated, "The Japanese officer put us zero on target and we did the rest, though maybe we overdid it."

The Marines expended bombs, napalm, rockets, and machine gun ammunition on each portion of the headquarters.

Survivors became a disparate group of stragglers who five days later accepted the general surrender announcement.

After the war, Wada received a false identity to protect him from Japanese retaliation should his complicity become known.[54] His story is one of the very few incidents of Japanese collaboration with the Allies on the road to the final victory.

PACIFIC CELEBRATIONS

Iwo Jima's black sand had absorbed the blood of nearly 7,000 dead Marines in the process of conquering the sulfurous eight square miles, and some 19,000 Japanese defenders. Since securing Iwo Jima in March, the Americans had expanded or built three airfields crammed with a variety of Army, Navy, and Marine Corps planes. Regardless of their uniforms, the young men shared a common attitude based upon a single question – when would the war end?

When the word finally came down, perhaps Iwo's most relieved personnel were radio operators who had monitored the on-again-off-again reports for about 24 hours. On or off duty, they had been pestered, badgered, and harassed by men earnestly pleading for more "inside dope" than the radiomen had been able to provide. At length the vigil was over.

Contrary to joyous outbursts back home, Iwo's residents – like most of those elsewhere in the Pacific – generally slumped in grateful respite from the numbing fatigue. Many – perhaps most – took off and hit the sack.

An Army correspondent observed that sudden peace "was essentially an indwelling experience... They had bitched and bitched, a bitching that was just short of neurotic in a war that thrived on bitching. They hoped more desperately for the end of the war than men on other islands where life was somewhat easier."[55]

However, some newcomers had not yet succumbed to the "rock happy" attitude of other veterans. The Thunderbolt pilots of the 437th Fighter Squadron, only ashore five weeks, generously contributed 65 quarts of whiskey to the enlisted men's club, with predictable results. Many soldiers and airmen who had previously been denied anything approaching such largess reacted in gratitude:

> There are few incidents the enlisted men can recall after uncorking the first bottle.
>
> [A sergeant] tried walking down the club steps using his beard instead of his feet. His beard is curly now.
>
> A private thought he could walk through a shower wall that proved he couldn't.
>
> Thursday 16 August came much too soon for us all. With splitting headaches and aching bones, we went back to work at noon.[56]

Flying continued, both as a precaution and for proficiency. But groundcrew noted that many pilots changed their previous pattern, keeping closer to shore. Nobody wanted to risk a bailout or ditching with peace imminent, but the upshot was greater peril. With more planes crowding the beaches, Iwo airspace became more congested and therefore more dangerous.

In the Marianas, the B-29 command stood down and Colonel Paul Tibbets' crews shelved plans for delivering a third atom bomb. Around 10:00 p.m. came confirmation that the war had finally reached its end. Typically working late, LeMay and his staff had just finished dinner, sitting on the screened porch of his quarters, when the glorious news was broadcast by loudspeaker.

There followed some shouting, running, and irresponsible behavior as two or three sentries shot into the air. But in a matter of minutes the lights flicked off, and an eerie quiet descended upon the base. LeMay understood why: during the last two months his aircrews had logged about 30 flight hours a week and the ground crews had worked around the clock to keep the Superforts airworthy. Most men were simply too tired to celebrate.[57]

However, LeMay had the energy to take himself to a card table. As he explained to his wife Helen:

We celebrated VJ Day last night with a little poker game at General Spaatz's that is pretty fast company for me, but I managed to come out about $250 ahead. Don't spend your share right away as I may not keep it long. I still haven't caught up on my sleep and I would much rather have gone to bed.

I received a nice wire from General Arnold today…

The part you played in developing and commanding the 21st Bomber Command represents one of the outstanding personal achievements of this war. You and the men under your command has (sic) indeed made clear to the world the full meaning of strategic bombardment. Your imagination, resourcefulness and initiative have reflected credit on the entire Army Air Forces. We are intensely proud of what you have done.

LeMay added in his next letter, "Things were very quiet here although there were six men killed and 60 wounded in Okinawa when they heard about the surrender offer. Everyone shot off the AA guns and everything else, I guess."[58]

At the 348th Fighter Group on Ie Shima, 22-year-old First Lieutenant Robert Stevens realized that he had never fired his .45 automatic. Like many fighter pilots, he had swaggered around with the hefty Colt in a shoulder holster, vowing, "The Japs will never take me alive." So on VJ night he unlimbered the pistol, chambered the first round, pointed skyward, and pressed the trigger.

Click.

He repeated the process until the magazine was empty.

The next day Stevens went to the armory and learned that he had been issued a sidearm with a broken firing pin. He later commented, "The Japs would've got me after all!"[59]

On nearby Okinawa, 21-year-old Private First Class Eugene Sledge and his fellow Marines recorded their relief at not having to attempt an invasion of the Japanese Home Islands: "We viewed the invasion with complete resignation that we would be killed – either on the beach or inland."

Army Lieutenant Paul Fussell, also 21, was a previously wounded platoon leader in Europe. Anticipating deployment to the Pacific, he wrote, "We would not be obliged to run up the beaches near Tokyo, assault-firing while being mortared and shelled... we cried with relief and joy. We were going to live. We were going to grow up to adulthood after all."[60]

In the Philippines, First Lieutenant Sally Hitchcock Pullman wrote to her parents, describing the response in her Army field hospital:

> For the past few days I've been dying to write you – THAT IT'S ALL OVER, that this terrible war has ended and what it was like over here when word first came over the radio. My wards were bedlam. What a time! I wouldn't have missed it for anything... that first night when the news of the surrender came over.
>
> My four wards went wild. I have never been hugged or kissed or spun around so many times in my whole life. Even had a dance with a cute young guy who had been over here 28 months and says that this was his first dance in all that time! How wonderful it was to see such pure, unadulterated joy and bedlam, and real smiles and laughter!!
>
> Above all was the relief we would not have to invade Japan. We all knew there would have been terrible casualties if we had to invade. And so it's over. Now the talk is how and when we will get home.[61]

Though Manila has been partly destroyed in fighting, residents still belted out "God Bless America."

Australia proclaimed "Victory in Pacific Day" (VP Day), marking the end of the Pacific War. VE Day barely four months previously had been subdued, with so many Australians still fighting in the Pacific. On VP Day pubs were closed, as per VE Day, but Aussies were dedicated celebrants and usually found a way. As one summary noted, "joy still managed to break out. Crowds gathered in the streets and strangers danced together."

Melbourne's Asian community observed "VC Day" for victory in China to the tune of numerous fireworks. Spotting a traditional Chinese parade with dragon floats, Australian sailors cheerfully joined the throng.[62]

Near Melbourne Miss Lois Anne Martin donned the red, white, and blue VP vest she had knitted for the occasion – and never wore again. She emphasized the effect by printing VP on her forehead in lipstick.[63]

New Zealanders learned of Japan's capitulation at 11:00 a.m. on the 15th. National and local celebrations sprouted with two days of sirens sounding, parades, music, and heartfelt prayers of thanksgiving.

And more.

In Auckland, "the city went out to enjoy itself the moment the factory whistle sounded. At first it was simply people drinking, dancing and scattering confetti. Then some rowdy people began throwing bottles. Windows were smashed and people were hurt. By evening, fifty-one people had been taken to hospital and fifteen tons of glass lay in the roads."[64]

Peace or no peace, the war still exacted a toll as the ordinary cost of doing business. The AAF lost six aircraft in overseas accidents, including two P-47s at Ie Shima. Others were written off in China, Burma, India, and Germany.

Attrition was even worse at home. The Army lost 28 planes in the continental U.S. on the 14th.[65]

Chinese people jubilantly touched off firecrackers in Chungking, the provisional capital since 1937, while celebrants "almost buried Americans in gratitude."[66]

For many men the reality did not sink in until sunset. That evening Task Force 38 ships steamed with lights ablaze, no longer zig-zagging to avoid enemy submarines. All over the Pacific, carriers and air groups stood down to begin savoring – to begin believing – in the hard-won peace. And not only off Japan, but at Okinawa, Manus, Guam, Adak, and Pearl. Big new ships like *Boxer* (CV-21) and *Antietam* (CV-36) en route to the Western Pacific had only just missed the air war over Japan, and many aviators privately regretted losing the chance to put their long training to use.

But to most, it was enough to be young and alive and to have a future on the day the shooting stopped.

✳   ✳   ✳

Yet in reality the shooting was not quite over. On the night of the 14th, an Ie Shima-based P-61 Black Widow named *Lady in the Dark* took off to patrol for last-minute attackers. The Northrop was huge for a fighter – a twin-engine nocturnal predator as big as a B-25 medium bomber, possessing both radar and potent armament. The crew of Lieutenants Robert Clyde and Bruce LeFord intercepted a single-engine Japanese Army fighter north of Okinawa but never fired a round, chasing the Nakajima into the water. The victory went uncredited for reasons still unknown.

Late the following night, the 15th, Captain Solie Solomon* and First Lieutenant John Scheerer, flying *Lady in the Dark*, closed to visual distance on a lone bogey, following it through several evasive maneuvers. Although the Japanese – probably in a Nakajima Tojo – released batches of metallic foil to jam U.S. radar, the Widow hung on. Scheerer lost contact for ten minutes in ground clutter until the ground controller regained the bogey. Solomon pushed his throttles forward, exceeding 300mph, to close the range. The persistent Scheerer regained and lost air-to-air contact four times, finally with no further radar image. Subsequently a nearby radar station confirmed a crash.

Thus, the same Black Widow scored the Army Air Forces' last two aerial victories – the latter in a war already concluded – without expending one round of 20mm ammunition.[67]

In the Third Fleet one long-serving officer spoke for all. In *Essex's* final wartime newspaper, senior chaplain Victor H. Bowman wrote:

The long days at sea are ended. Only in restless dreams we will hear "Set Condition One in the Gunnery Department" or "Pilots, man your planes." We are on the way back.

---

* Solomon later changed his name to Lee Kendall.

As the years lead us forward memory will, with increased fondness, recall the shipmates who proved their worth at Rabaul, Truk, the length and breadth of the Philippines, at Tarawa, Iwo Jima, Okinawa and on to the heart of the Empire. Those who flew in planes and fought them, those who kept them flying, those who fought the ships, those who performed their countless duties that enabled the ship to make a mighty record, all these have made the *Essex* glorious. All of us shareholders in the fame of the Mighty E.[68]

4

Around the World

August 1945

The word flashed across the North American continent on Tuesday, August 14: apparently the war was ending. After Station KGEI in San Francisco had monitored Domei's message around midnight on the Monday, events had accelerated. President Truman was due to make a radio address Tuesday evening, evidently confirming the joyous news.

Jubilant, and sometimes violent, celebrations broke out worldwide among the planet's 2.3 billion people. In London a multinational conga line of Allied soldiers and British civilians danced down Regent Street. Americans and French citizens clogged the Champs-Elysées in Paris, singing "Don't Fence Me In." But perhaps the most heartfelt sentiment was among GIs in Germany, suddenly freed of the specter of deployment to Japan.

However, the response in Moscow was remarkably subdued, as the Soviet invasion of Manchuria continued steamrolling its way over the Japanese defenders.

Near Seattle "a rootin' tootin'" festival erupted with sailors and workers spilling out from Bremerton Navy Yard. Servicemen rioted from Massachusetts to California, clashing with police for as much as three days.

Meanwhile, in New York City the greatest crowd ever was assembling in Times Square. Nearby, Austrian-born dental assistant Greta Zimmer worked in Dr. J.L. Berke's office near 33rd Street and Lexington Avenue. During her lunch break she went outside, wearing her white dress, hose, and shoes, leaving her cap behind. She wanted to see the *Times* news "zipper" with moving type providing continuous updates. There it was: apparently Japan was about to surrender.

Among the throng, Navy Petty Officer First Class George Mendonsa had orders to rejoin his destroyer *The Sullivans* (DD-537), named for the five Iowa brothers who had died on the light cruiser *Juneau* (CL-52) off Guadalcanal in 1942. He was due to depart for San Francisco that evening and intended to enjoy the balance of his leave to the fullest. Wearing custom-tailored blues, he took his girlfriend Rita Petry to Radio City Music Hall, viewing Henry King's *A Bell for Adano*, based on John Hersey's Pulitzer Prize novel. But the screening was interrupted when an usher broke in: the war was ending!

The lid was off. The theater emptied, spilling joyous, elated patrons into the crowded street. Drawn to Times Square, Mendonsa and Petry ducked into a restaurant where the bartender poured whatever was available for whomever could stand up.

Repeated slugs of booze – whatever they were in whatever quantity – seized hold of the sailor. Minutes before he had faced an uncertain destiny in the Western Pacific. Now he had a happy future – and better than that – a certain present. He took off down the street at a high rate of knots uncertain of his destination, Rita vainly trying to match his long strides.

Lost in the crowd was one of several *Life* photographers, 51-year-old Alfred Eisenstaedt. A German veteran of World War I, he had come to America in 1935 and spent the last four years covering the home front. Eventually he shot 90 *Life* covers and now held a prime assignment: show readers what the end of World War II looked like, and felt like. He found it at Broadway and Seventh Avenue, leading to Times Square.

The photographer glimpsed what he instantly knew was "The Shot": a fast-walking sailor approaching a young woman in white.

Greta Zimmer had not planned on meeting anyone. She was merely seeking confirmation that the rumor was true – Japan had surrendered. Then Petty Officer Mendonsa entered her life.

Mendonsa was a tall, well-built 21-year-old son of Portuguese immigrants. He grasped the pretty brunette – also 21 – who he assumed was a nurse, holding her close while she leaned back, her left arm dangling. She realized that resistance was futile and went with the moment. It came and passed in seconds, but Eisenstaedt's shutter clicked in time. Taken with the scene, he quickly snapped three more shots, including the iconic image published in the August 27 issue.[1]

In 2005 Greta Zimmer Friedman told an interviewer:

> I was grabbed by a sailor and it wasn't much of a kiss, it was more of a jubilant act that he didn't have to go back, I found out later, he was so happy that he did not have to go back to the Pacific where they already had been through the war. And the reason he grabbed someone dressed like a nurse was that he just felt very grateful to nurses who took care of the wounded.

She added, "I felt he was very strong, he was just holding me tight, and I'm not sure I – about the kiss because, you know, it was just somebody really celebrating. But it wasn't a romantic event. It was just an event of thank God the war is over kind of thing."[2]

The rejoicing continued for hours, leading to days. Then at 7:00 p.m. Eastern Daylight Savings Time on the 14th, President Truman went on national radio to announce Japan's surrender acceptance. His entire statement took one minute and seven seconds, beginning, "I have received this afternoon a message from the Japanese government in reply to the message forwarded to that government by the secretary of state on August 11. I deem that reply a full acceptance of the Potsdam Declaration."

Truman added that General Douglas MacArthur would become the Supreme Allied Commander to receive the formal surrender. "The proclamation of VJ Day must await upon the formal signing of the surrender terms by Japan."

The United newsreel announced that 2 million New Yorkers jammed Times Square. "It's all over, total victory. All night long the rejoicing continues. Never before in history has there been greater reason to be thankful for peace."[3]

There were "peace riots" across the nation, from coast to coast. In Boston, *Yank*, the Army weekly, reported, "A million people crammed narrow, twisting downtown streets and the famous Common in the wildest riot of noise in the city's long history." Residents compared the occasion to 50 New Year's Eves in one.

"The most general impulse seemed to be to shout, sing and hug passers-by. For men in uniform the celebration seemed to be more of a kissing fest than anything else. They were seized by girls and women of all ages…"

Amid the joy, nearly 200 people required medical treatment though few appeared serious. Meanwhile, more sedate Bostonians crowded hundreds of churches, however briefly, to reflect and give heartfelt thanks.[4]

Probably the worst "peace riots" erupted in San Francisco. A local account summarized, "A huge mob mostly composed of drunken sailors on a three-night binge degenerated into an orgy of vandalism and violence. When it was over 13 people were dead, more than 1,000 were injured, at least six women had been raped – the true total was no doubt far higher – and Market Street was in shambles."

Belatedly Mayor Roger Lapham took note. On the 17th the *Chronicle* reported, "San Francisco officials, flanked by high-ranking Army and Navy authorities, spent most of yesterday locking a badly battered barn door and indulging in recriminations."

Apparently no charges were filed in the wake of the deaths or rapes, and many incidents went uninvestigated.[5]

PRISONERS REPRIEVED

VJ Day also was Survival Day to large numbers of prisoners of war and internees in Japanese hands. In August approximately 150,000 Allied personnel were thought held captive in some 130 camps throughout Asia. However, a complete accounting revealed 775 facilities in the Japanese Empire; 185 in Japan itself.

The prisoners represented not only the U.S. but Britain, Australia, New Zealand, Canada, the Netherlands, and India. Approximately 36,000 soldiers and sailors were sent to Japan itself with most of the balance in the Philippines, China, Korea, Burma, Malaya, Java, and various Pacific islands. Japan also held large numbers of civilian prisoners and internees, as many as 125,000, mainly in the Dutch East Indies and Philippines, with more than 10 percent in China and Hong Kong. That figure excluded Nationalist Chinese personnel. Frequently the Imperial Army killed Chinese prisoners as a matter of policy.[6]

One quarter to one third of Anglo-American prisoners held by Japan had died in captivity, with about 12 percent dying in the Home Islands. In contrast, about 3 percent of Western POWs perished in German *Stalags.* War crimes investigators later determined that 27 percent of Allied POWs in the Pacific died in captivity – officially seven times the rate of Western POWs in German camps.[7]

Bushido, the philosophical "way of the warrior," had evolved from antiquity, emphasizing the samurai virtues of fealty, sacrifice, and skill at arms. The concept was institutionalized in school texts early in the 20th century, but after the death of Emperor Meiji, Hirohito's grandfather, in 1912, the feudal service concept lost much of its grip in Japan's rush to industrialize. However, during the 1930s ultra-conservative factions reinvented *Bushido* for their own purposes, notably in the Army.

A pillar of *Bushido* was no surrender, to win at all cost or to die with honor. Therefore, the notion of elite warriors committed to victory or death cast enemy prisoners as the lowest of the low – disgraced soldiers who had lacked the courage to kill themselves. Their only purpose was to serve the empire, and thousands endured years of slave labor amid appalling conditions. They included those exploited by Japanese corporations that paid the government for their services.[8]

Allied POWs existed in a hellish world of perennial malnutrition during Japan's food shortage amid disease and routine brutality. Postwar investigators often referred to ritual or informal executions but the killings were largely extrajudicial or, to put it bluntly – murder.[9]

Though Tokyo had signed the Second Geneva Convention in 1929, the government had never ratified the agreement regarding treatment of prisoners of war. After a qualified pledge to abide by the convention in early 1942, Japan quickly reverted.

Prisoners endured horrific conditions in captivity, eventually subsisting on 600 calories per day. What few Red Cross parcels arrived often were confiscated by the captors. The situation could hardly have been improved in the final months of the war, however, because in mid-1945 virtually all Japanese civilians were also malnourished.

Allied planning for repatriating military prisoners and civilian internees began well before Tokyo's capitulation. But wherever they were held, POWs slept the sleep of the saved: a year previously, Tokyo had laid plans for wholesale killing of Allied prisoners. In August 1944 the Vice Minister of War, Lieutenant General Kyoji Tominaga, authorized prison camp commanders in occupied territories and Home Islands to execute POWs.

Postwar investigators concluded that the kill orders probably were in response to queries from POW administrators on Formosa. A camp commander asked clarification as to circumstances under which he should act on his own, anticipating an American invasion and a breakdown of communications with Tokyo. Tominaga authorized camp commanders to kill all POWs if "an uprising of large numbers cannot be suppressed without the use of firearms" or "when escapees from the camp may turn into a hostile fighting force" and "not to allow the escape of a single one, to annihilate them all, and not to leave any traces."[10]

Given the depleted condition of the POWs, no such resistance was possible. More likely the order was intended to prevent survivors testifying against their captors for deaths and brutal treatment.

A copy of the murder order was found in the files of the Japanese Governor-General of Formosa, Richiki Ando, who subsequently was sentenced to a term in prison.[11]

Some POWs had withstood horrific conditions for more than three years. In the murderous Bataan Death March of April 1942, the Japanese prodded thousands of U.S. and Filipino soldiers nearly 70 miles, on foot. Accounts vary but conservatively 600 Americans and at least 5,000 Filipinos perished from malnutrition, dehydration, and casual brutality.

Those who survived did so in part by setting small, achievable goals for themselves. Then-Private Zoeth Skinner, a survivor of the Death March, was asked who survived. "The kids and the lifers," he said. "Kids are dumb and resilient, they can stand almost anything. The lifers were old timers who know that you can't do everything, you have to pace yourself."[12]

A long-term prisoner was Sergeant Lester Tenney, survivor of a tank battalion captured in the Philippines also that April. Subsequently shipped to Japan, he worked as a slave laborer in a coal mine at Omuta alongside other Allied personnel, usually 12 hours a day. He recalled:

Getting out of work in the coal mine was a real challenge. Not only did a man have to break a bone, get caught in a mine cave-in, or develop ulcers on his legs, but he wanted to be sure that, whatever happened, it happened in the mine. That way, if he stayed in camp on sick call, he would still get full rations. If he had an accident while in camp that prevented him from working in the mine, he would only get half rations. And if he got sick, he only got two meals a day.[13]

Among the northern Honshu POW camps was Ohashi on the coast, holding nearly 400 prisoners who endured forced labor in a nearby mine. About half were Canadians captured in Hong Kong, including 23-year-old George MacDonell from Alberta. He recorded the news of August 15 with a mixture of joy and concern due to uncertainty over how the Japanese would react.

We knew that the camp commander – First Lieutenant Yoshida Zenkichi – had written orders to kill his prisoners "by any means at his disposal" if their rescue seemed imminent.

Lieutenant Zenkichi seemed angry and felt humiliated by the surrender. But he appeared willing to negotiate our status. And after some stressful hours, we reached an agreement: the Japanese guards would be dismissed from the camp, while a detachment of *Kempeitai* (the much feared military police) would provide security for Zenkichi, who would confine himself to his office.[14]

Although local farmers agreed to barter food for some "luxury" items the POWs had looted from the camp's supplies, it was not nearly enough to sustain 400 men. However, some innovative prisoners had built a radio that monitored channels likely to broadcast information on U.S. operations to recover POWs. Morale surged further when the POWs learned that American planes were flying grid searches for camps, and the men followed instructions to place large "P.O.W." signs on a rooftop.

Two days later, with food expended, the prisoners heard an engine from the east. A single-engine carrier plane – a Hellcat, it turned out – overflew the compound at about 3,000 feet. MacDonell prayed, "Please God, let him see our camp."

And he did. The VF-6 pilot reversed course and flew down the valley, descending nearly to treetop level. "We all went wild. Our prayers had been answered."

The naval aviator dropped a container with a streamer inside the compound. The men found strips of colored cloth with instructions for what each represented: medicine, food, or general support. The note was signed, "Lieutenant (junior grade) Claude Newton, USS Hancock. Reported location."

Newton was good to his word. Several hours later some two dozen Avenger torpedo planes each made two parachute drops, providing a ton or more of food and medicine. Among the largess was something none of the POWs knew about – something called penicillin.

Further aid came the next day in the form of B-29s delivering 60-gallon drums of food, clothes, shoes, and other supplies. Some barrels snapped their lanyards and crashed through roofs of camp buildings but no fatalities resulted.

Before leaving Ohashi, MacDonell and his fellow survivors, including British and Dutch, paid their last respects to comrades buried in the camp cemetery.[15]

Simultaneously, prisoners and internees rejoiced well beyond Japan. Internees at Weihsien in Shandong Province, just inland from the Yellow Sea, in mainland China, had led an erratic existence amid routine privation. The 1,400 Americans, Australians, Canadians, Belgians, Dutch, and even Italians, officially were civilian internees rather than POWs. They included Arthur Hummel, Jr., a future U.S. ambassador to China; Mary and Arthur Wright, Yale professors; and had also included Eric Liddell, Scottish Olympic medalist who had died in February 1945.

Based in a large prewar missionary compound, the internees were perennially short of food, medicine, and clothing, living in often squalid conditions amid filth and flies. The internees had 23 toilets – some frequently inoperable – with little running water. In retrospect an American prisoner, then 12-year-old Mary Previte, described the medical situation as "serious," as the Japanese provided no treatment, leaving the few civilian doctors and nurses to improvise as possible.

Toward the end, Allied intelligence and internee letters through the Red Cross brought some relief. Swiss delegates finally were allowed to deliver some drugs with cereal and tinned milk.[16]

The prisoners became masters of improvisation. They scrounged books for a library, organized club activities, and even formed a Salvation Army band.

On the 17th the detainees heard a multi-engine aircraft approaching; many rushed into the compound for a better look. The distinctive four-engine, twin-tailed shape of a B-24 Liberator rumbled into view at about 400 feet, and seven parachutes began blossoming beneath it.

Thus arrived the Office of Strategic Services' "Duck Mission." The 14th Air Force bomber delivered a joint Army-Navy-Chinese team under Major Stanley Staiger, including linguists Sergeant Tad Nagaki of Nebraska, and Chinese volunteer Wang

Chenghan, called "Eddie." They alighted in a nearby cemetery to a joyous reception.

On the 60th anniversary of liberation in 2005, Mary Previte, now a New Jersey assemblywoman who had been held as a child with her brothers and sister, recalled, "Weihsien went mad. Oh, glorious cure for my diarrhea! I raced for the entry gates and was swept off my feet by the pandemonium. Prisoners ran in circles and pounded the sky with their fists. They cursed, wept, hugged, danced. They cheered themselves hoarse."

She added, "Wave after wave of prisoners swept past the guards into the fields beyond the camp. A mile away we found them – six Americans and a Chinese interpreter standing with their weapons ready. Advancing toward them came a tidal wave of prisoners intoxicated with joy – free in the open fields."

Those men with sufficient strength seized Major Staiger and hoisted him shoulder high, carrying him to the gate. The camp's band even turned out to play appropriate national anthems.[17]

The prisoners – especially children like Previte – could not get enough of the liberators, asking for buttons and patches. One woman waylaid Tad Nagaki long enough to clip his hair as a souvenir.

With additional support it took two months to transfer all internees, but Mary Previte and her siblings finally were reunited with their parents, whom they had not seen since 1939.

Almost lost amid war's end was the residue of its origin: Japan's conquest of the Dutch East Indies' petro-wealth. In 1940 Tokyo had requested half of the Dutch oil exports, but officials in the capital Batavia replied that existing commitments permitted little increase for Japan. That response set the Pacific afire. With only two years' oil reserves on hand, and denied imports from the U.S. and Java, Tokyo's warlords launched themselves on an irrevocable course.

The Japanese had to sort out a large, diverse population of some 70.5 million. Upwards of 250,000 were Dutch, mostly *blijers*, Dutch citizens born in the East Indies. Around 1.3 million Chinese had enjoyed preferred relations with the Netherlands' hierarchy, but there was also a small Japanese population.

Conquest of the archipelago only took 90 days, ending in March 1942. Japan pledged Indonesian independence in 1943 but never honored it. And despite the Asia for Asians theme of the Greater East Asia Co-Prosperity Sphere, Indonesians suffered terribly under Japanese rule. The new rulers interned all Dutch military personnel and 170,000 civilians. Conditions were appalling: approximately 25,000 died in captivity. Estimates range between 2.5 and 4 million total deaths, more than half of whom perished during the Java famine of 1944–45.[18]

Additionally, millions of Javanese were pressed into servitude elsewhere, notably on the Burmese railroad.[19]

Elizabeth Van Kampen, the 19-year-old daughter of a Dutch plantation manager, recalled the end of internment:

Something strange was going on. We received a little more food than usual, and maybe it was just a tiny bit better in quality as well. It was very silent in the Japanese corner. We could see them moving, but for several days they didn't come anywhere near us.

At last we were told that the war was over. Japan had surrendered to the Allies on the 15th of August, nine days earlier. Nine long days the Japanese had kept this wonderful news to themselves. They knew that they had lost the war and that they should have given their Dutch prisoners their freedom, but they didn't.

Not long after, we were ordered to stay inside the prison because groups of *pemuda*, or youth defending the newly proclaimed Indonesian Republic, were trying to kill Dutch prisoners, or so we were told. With Sukarno now the proclaimed President of the Republic, his supporters among the *pemuda* and others refused to accept Dutch rule. Again the gate of our prison was closed. We now had Japanese soldiers protecting us against angry young nationalists. The lovely Javanese lady who had been so kind towards my mother, sisters and me was no longer allowed to enter our prison; we missed her.

Japanese guards remained for about two weeks until Gurkhas in the British Army took over. Red Cross supplies began arriving, and at year's end Western internees were finally released on the condition they left Indonesia.[20]

The most notorious venue of Japanese POW treatment remains the infamous "Bridge on the River Kwai," the subject of an extremely successful 1957 movie. Located on the rail line from Bangkok to the Burma border, the bridge was constructed mainly by Commonwealth personnel in 1942–43. Precise numbers of deaths appear unknown, but 1,379 names are carried on the memorial at the Chonk-Kai War Cemetery on the site of a railway POW camp.[21]

Allied prisoners in Thailand (then Siam) were slated for death on August 21. Survivors related that they had dug mass graves in preparation for execution of the order.

Few of the internees realized the source of their salvation. Elizabeth Van Kampen recalled:

One morning Henny and I saw one of the Japanese soldiers who was protecting us... crying his heart out. Someone asked the Japanese why he was crying. They told us that a terrible bomb had killed his whole family. We felt very sorry for him, but we didn't know anything about the big bomb they were talking about. Only much later did we learn about the atom bombs dropped on Hiroshima and Nagasaki.

OPERATION *BLACKLIST*

Besides freeing imprisoned Allied military personnel and civilians, plans were laid for supplying POW camps before they were liberated. Detailed work on Operation *Blacklist* dated from August 10, promulgated by U.S. Army Forces, Pacific. Though Navy planes made supply drops (as noted previously), the carrier aircraft lacked the Army bombers' huge payload. The *Blacklist* notice stated in part:

> Upon unconditional surrender or collapse of the Japanese Government and High Command, emergency supplies will be air-dropped to prisoners of war and internees of United Nations held in known Japanese camps. Emergency supplies will be flown from bases in the Philippines, Okinawa, and the Marianas. By arrangement with the Commanding General, China Theater, emergency supplies will be flown from Philippine bases for dropping to camps located on the China coast...

The number and location of Japan's POW camps was uncertain for much of the operation. An early August list showed 60 known in Japan plus 38 in China and Formosa, excluding Korea. Fifty-one were suspected or unconfirmed in Japan.[22]

The humanitarian operation eventually involved nearly 1,000 B-29s which began dropping food and medical supplies to an estimated 63,500 prisoners in 154 far-flung prison camps in Japan, China, and Korea. In less than a month the Superforts delivered nearly 4,500 tons of supplies to starving, elated POWs and internees.

But even humanitarian missions in the final days of war and the first days of peace involved risk. The 497th Bomb Group reported a 44 percent rate of failure: 203 of 458 parachutes malfunctioned, failing to open or only partly arresting their package's descent. In perhaps the war's ultimate irony, eight bombers crashed with nearly 80 fatalities, and some prisoners were killed by falling bales owing to a shortage of cargo parachutes.

On August 29, First Lieutenant Joseph W. Queen, flying *Hog Wild* of the 500th Bomb Group, was delivering supplies to a POW camp in Korea. The compound held about 350 prisoners – mostly British and Australian – needing assistance. But apparently the controlling Soviets received no warning of the American mission. Over the coast, four Russian fighters intercepted and signaled the B-29 to land. Queen later said, "Our guns were loaded and ready to talk but I told the crew to hold their fire. Then the Yaks made a pass and hit the number one engine."

Six of the crew safely parachuted into the water while seven others "rode her down" to a forced landing at Hamhung. Upon examination, the three-month-old *Hog Wild* required a new engine and propeller.

After regrouping the crew next day, Queen was received by a Russian lieutenant general who apologized and provided the Americans with vodka. *Hog Wild*'s fliers returned to Saipan on September 16.

General Douglas MacArthur sent an angry message to the Soviet command:

> On August 28 (sic) at Kanko, Korea, a United States Army B-29 while engaged in dropping supplies to prisoner of war camps at Hosen was shot down by Russian fighters. The American plane was plainly marked and its mission could not fail to have been identified as purely benevolent. The circumstances of the case cause me the gravest anxiety and I request that immediate and decisive steps be taken to prevent any recurrences of so deplorable an incident. A prompt reply is requested pending which the much-needed dropping of supplies to prisoners of war in this area has been stopped.

Eventually the U.S. military mission in Moscow forwarded a response from Russia's directorate of Allied relations. An appended American report said, "the attack occurred before the Japanese had ceased resistance and suggested as justification for the attack that Japanese might have been flying a B-29 that landed in Japan."

Moscow granted permission for an American transport aircraft to land with mechanics and replacement parts, but *Hog Wild* was stripped and left to the Russians, who already had interned other B-29s.[23]

However, the wider POW supply operation was a major success, providing survivors with more than enough materiel to last until relief columns arrived.

OCCUPIERS, THE OCCUPIED, AND ATOMIC DOUBTS

As the first occupation forces spread out across Kyushu and Honshu, cooperation by Japanese authorities was almost universal. American soldiers were carefully briefed on civilian relations, emphasizing that GIs should regard themselves as much liberators as victors. The situation in Japan contrasted with the postwar environment in Germany, where residual resistance units committed isolated acts against Allied forces for months.

Relatively few Japanese troops surrendered during hostilities – perhaps 50,000 were captured by the Allies among more than 8 million who served, with 2 million dead. Most Japanese POWs were held in Australia, New Zealand, and India, with some in the U.S.

In America, Prisoner Number One reflected on his nearly four-year journey. Ensign Kazuo Sakamaki, aged 26 by August 1945, had piloted his midget two-man submarine into Pearl Harbor on December 7, 1941, but became stranded on an Oahu beach. The crew abandoned ship in high waves and one drowned before Sakamaki was captured. Sakamaki had spent the war in prison camps in four states, passing from morose at being captured to acceptance and finally easing other POWs' tendencies for suicide. He was released in 1946.

But there were other prisoners, however defined. In the U.S. more than 100,000 American citizens of Japanese ancestry were unconstitutionally sent to detention camps after the Roosevelt Administration's panicked order of February 1942. Eventually some 20,000 served in the U.S. Army, including the highly decorated 442nd Infantry Regiment in Europe. The Supreme Court declared the removals illegal in December 1944, although the War Relocation Authority had already arrived at that decision. However, the order was not publicly rescinded until after the November election, when Roosevelt was returned to office.

Over 20,000 Canadians of Japanese heritage also were detained, and many were forcibly returned to Japan.

*　　*　　*

During the war the Bishop of Chichester had worried that Britain might "lose the moral high ground" by bombing German cities – the sources of Nazi production. There were some similar attitudes in the U.S., although it was widely understood that an invasion of Japan would result in enormous casualties.

While welcoming the peace, some American religious leaders questioned the use of atomic bombs. In August 1945 the U.S. Council of Churches wired Truman with similar sentiments. Samuel McCrea Cavert, the council's secretary, said, "Many Christians deeply disturbed over use of atomic bombs against Japanese cities because of their necessarily indiscriminate destructive efforts and because their use sets extremely dangerous precedent for future of mankind... Respectfully urge that ample opportunity be given Japan to reconsider ultimatum before any further devastation by atomic bomb is visited upon her people."[24]

The president, a self-described "lightfoot Baptist," replied with typical bluntness:

> Nobody is more disturbed over the use of Atomic bombs than I am but I was greatly disturbed over the unwarranted attack by the Japanese on Pearl Harbor and their murder of our prisoners of war. The only language they seem to understand is the one we have been using to bombard them.
>
> When you have to deal with a beast you have to treat him as a beast. It is most regrettable but nevertheless true.[25]

At the time, 69 percent of Americans believed "it was a good thing that the atomic bomb was developed." Seventeen percent were opposed while 14 percent had no opinion. In mid-September George Gallup summarized, "Even though such bombs with their destructive power contain a threat to the security of mankind, in the public's mind the atomic bomb hastened the end of the war and pointed the way to useful development of atomic energy in the future."[26]

The controversy persists more than seven decades later.

❋   ❋   ❋

At Los Alamos a fever pitch spiked in the high New Mexico desert when the news of peace broke out. When word arrived, the scientists, engineers, carpenters, plumbers, and families spilled into the streets as work screeched to a halt. The Tech Area's siren blared, accompanied by automobile horns and happy-tearful exchanges. People shook hands, hugged, cried, and exchanged hearty back slaps. Neighbors eagerly knocked on doors, ensuring that everyone knew the joyous news.

An impromptu party arose at the home of Robert Bacher, head of the physics division – later dubbed "The Gadget Division" – where 11 teams had developed various aspects of the bomb. One of Bacher's crew, 44-year-old Russian émigré George Kistiakowsky, had earned his chemistry doctorate in Germany in the 1920s, then emigrated to America and became a citizen in 1933. He knew everything worth knowing about explosives and headed the team that developed explosive lenses for the plutonium-fueled implosion bomb that destroyed Nagasaki. After an appropriate time imbibing at the Bacher residence, he and some "well lubricated" colleagues adjourned to a nearby field to detonate more than 1,000 pounds of TNT.

The celebration continued through the dinner hour. "The hill" was remote from normal facilities so alcohol was a treasured commodity, stashed in pantries and secret drawers for suitable occasions. And if ever an occasion was suitable, this was it. A few favored couples went all out, producing hoarded bottles of prewar champagne.

Enjoying the festivities perhaps more than most was 25-year-old Robert Krohn, a physicist from the University of Wisconsin. He had arrived in 1943, living with the Manhattan Project for two frantic years. Krohn's superior was Kenneth Bainbridge, a PhD from Princeton, who had assigned the youthful Krohn to design and construct a filter to collect airborne samples of radioactive materials following Hiroshima and Nagasaki. Since the third bomb was expected in a matter of days, Krohn had no time to waste, as he recalled:

I had one week to get the filter built and then I would take it to Tinian on a military plane and install it on a B-29... I could put a hole in the side of the plane if necessary... I got the shop started the next day, then got a call from Bainbridge that... it appeared that Japan was ready to surrender.[27]

Los Alamos residents reacted with a mixture of relief and sorrow, delight and profound distress. Their emotions were in such a tumultuous state that it was hard to know how to feel or act. Only the GIs seemed to celebrate with total abandon, piling en masse onto Army trucks and jeeps and riding around cheering wildly.

Other celebrations followed, but they were more subdued. There was something unseemly, almost "ghoulish" as physicist Otto Frisch put it, "about celebrating the sudden death of so many people, even if they were 'enemies.'"

Frisch continued, "Few of us could see any moral reason for dropping the second bomb. Most of us thought the Japanese would have surrendered in a few days, anyhow."[28]

Many, perhaps most, approved of Hiroshima but, unaware of intelligence reports that would be concealed for a quarter century and which ultimately drove the decision, they felt that bombing Nagasaki was an unnecessary step too far.

5

Uneasy Peace

August 16–31

Tokyo had accepted surrender. But a twilight zone of not-quite-peace ensued, stretching into the next two weeks. During that period, plans great and small were under way.

Admiral Sir Bruce Fraser, commander of the British Pacific Fleet, came aboard USS *Missouri* on August 16 to present Halsey with the Knight Commander of the Order of the British Empire. It was an ornate decoration held by no more than 300 recipients at a time. Knights received the red and gold sash or mantle with a blue and gold cross at the throat and an eight-pointed silver star pinned on the left breast.

Of greater importance, "Mighty Mo" contributed a 200-man landing party to her sister *Iowa* for the first occupation troop landings at Tokyo slated for the 21st. Third Fleet's landing force comprised a regular Marine regiment plus three battalions of Marines and sailors from Task Force 38 and one from the British Task Force 37. Additionally, a reserve of five battalions was formed in event of Japanese resistance.

As Halsey noted, "We had assembled groups of specialists and artificers to operate captured Jap facilities and equipment, and to establish temporary shore facilities of our own. We were prepared even to occupy and develop the naval base and air station at Yokosuka, to demilitarize enemy installations, to drop supplies at POW camps, and to rescue and evacuate prisoners."[1]

While contingency plans went ahead, flight operations over Japan continued.

HOSTILE SKIES

The Dominators' End Runs
An often-neglected player in World War II aviation was Consolidated's B-32 Dominator. Intended as an alternative if the B-29 failed or was delayed, the four-engine Dominator arrived late, logging a handful of missions that overlapped VJ Day.

First flown in September 1942 – almost the same day as the prototype B-29 – the Consolidated used the same Pratt & Whitney R3350s as the Superfortress. Thus, the Dominator suffered development problems that kept it out of combat until May 1945, when it began operating in the Philippines.

The only Dominator combat unit was the 386th Bomb Squadron, attached to the 312th Bomb Group. On August 13 the unit moved from the Philippines to Kadena Airfield, Okinawa.

One of the requirements for enforcing the surrender terms was monitoring Japanese disarmament before the Allied occupation. Therefore, U.S. reconnaissance flights covered many military facilities in metropolitan Japan, frequently photographing bases to gauge compliance with the surrender terms.

B-32 photo missions began on August 16 with two Dominators assigned to scout airfields in the Tokyo area. One plane aborted with mechanical trouble but Japanese radar pinged the other, dubbed *Hobo Queen II*, which completed the assignment without interference.

Four more sorties were scheduled the next day, led by 25-year-old Lieutenant Colonel Selmon Wells, commander of the 312th Bomb Group. Despite his youth, Wells possessed two years' experience, having flown some 150 missions with the group. As he later told historian Stephen Harding, "I knew the Japanese were tenacious fighters who had no problem pulling dirty tricks on their enemies." He suspected that something untoward still might happen.[2]

He was right. Some Japanese commanders and pilots believed that no U.S. overflights would occur until the formal surrender was signed.

Wells's Dominators departed Kadena early on the 17th, briefed to photograph the area northeast of Tokyo. His formation arrived over the southern portion of Tokyo Bay at 10:15, four and a half hours after takeoff. Then each Dominator turned for its designated area.

The intrusion into homeland airspace drew an immediate response from Imperial Navy pilots at Atsugi and Yokosuka. At Yokosuka one-eyed Ensign Saburo Sakai was a veteran of eight years of Darwinian combat and wartime flying. He recalled:

Our commander told us that the war was over and that we were not to go looking for trouble. But he also added that should the Americans dare fly over us and we wanted to get them, he wouldn't stop us. Then around noon, we received word that some American bombers were flying over Tokyo. That really provoked us and we said, 'Let's go get them!' and piled into our planes.

Sakai and his friend, Warrant Officer Sadamu Komachi, both multiple aces, led the scramble.[3]

Wells's plane attracted a lone fighter – probably one of Sakai's Kawanishi Georges misidentified as an army Nakajima Tojo – that slow-rolled beside the bomber. Then the Japanese pulled downward into a split-ess and returned for a gunnery run from the right front. Wells's nose gunner returned fire and the interceptor broke off.

Subsequently Wells's and other B-32s drew flak, with his plane taking fragments in a wing and engine nacelle near Kisarazu Airdrome. Approaching Yokosuka, flak thickened and attracted more fighters.

Two other Dominators were intercepted in the Yokosuka area, where they were prevented from photographing facilities by an undercast. One bomber counted as many as ten interceptors "rat racing" south of the base; then the Japanese began a series of single-plane attacks, mostly from 12 o'clock at 20,000 feet. The combat continued, with the gunners claiming a probable kill and a damaged, receiving 20mm cannon and machine gun rounds in the right wing. Descending under power, the B-32 evaded further attack heading for the coast.

The third Dominator also received unwanted attention near Yokosuka. Five or six fighters ran in from astern, one exposing itself to the rear upper turret. The gunner was on target, seeing tracers impact before the assailant nosed over trailing smoke into the cloud deck.

However, the tail turret had malfunctioned and, lacking return fire, other Japanese attacked from six o'clock. The shootout continued for about 15 minutes before the fighters disengaged, leaving the Americans to claim two probably destroyed and at least one damaged by 4,000 rounds of machine gun ammunition.

The B-32s regrouped and turned for Okinawa at 12:15, after an eventful two hours over Japan.

At Kadena the mission report was received with deep concern. American officers wondered if the interceptions were part of Tokyo's policy or the result of confusion or command failure. The only way to know was to repeat the process, hoping to photograph the previous objectives.

The next day, the 18th, two unescorted B-32s were led by First Lieutenant James Klein in *Hobo Queen II* and First Lieutenant John R. Anderson in an unnamed Dominator. To maximize the opportunity, extra observers and photo specialists augmented both crews. Flying with Anderson were Second Lieutenant Kurt Rupke, Sergeant Joseph Lacharite, and 19-year-old Staff Sergeant Anthony J. Marchione. It was the first mission in a B-32 for each of them.[4]

The Dominators droned through the atmosphere near Tokyo, completing their assigned routes without interference. But the contrails of the two American planes enraged Komachi and other Atsugi pilots. As many as 14 fighters responded.

With an unobstructed view, one of Klein's gunners reported that Japanese planes were taking off from Yokosuka. At 20,000 feet Klein felt safe for the moment, but he expressed concern for Anderson, "a good 10,000 feet below us."

Sergeant John Huston, Anderson's tail gunner, spotted the interceptors as they reached his altitude. Attacking from astern, three or four Japanese bored in, so Huston placed his sight reticle on the nearest. "One fighter came so close I couldn't miss. I gave him about fifty rounds and saw hits on the wings and fuselage. He kept coming until he was within about 100 feet, and then he just blew up."[5]

Sergeant Benjamin Clayworth, in the top forward turret, engaged a fighter attacking from high and right. As it absorbed a stream of .50-caliber rounds, Clayworth saw it tumble beneath the bomber; he shouted a victory yell that it exploded.

Anderson's nose gunner also traded fire with enemy pilots, who kept coming. One was 25-year-old Sadamu Komachi, who thoroughly knew his trade. He had flown with the Pearl Harbor task force, fought in three 1942 carrier battles, and survived the massacres at Truk Atoll in February 1944 and the Marianas that June.

Rolling inverted, Komachi pulled into a frontal overhead pass and held his fire until well in range. Stephen Harding subsequently reckoned that Komachi's 20mm cannon knocked out the left inboard engine and blew the plexiglass off the upper rear turret, wounding the gunner.

Down in the fuselage, looking to the right, Sergeant Lacharite saw the assailant that had shot him. Machine gun rounds had struck both his legs, knocking him to the catwalk. Despite the shock and pain, he was clear-headed enough to improvise tourniquets from a baggage cord and an interphone line. Tony Marchione hefted his friend, laying him on a cot.

Moments later another fighter scored heavily. A cannon shell penetrated the Dominator's thin aluminum skin and struck Marchione, tumbling him against the far side of the fuselage. He slid to the floor, immobile.

Lieutenant Rupke was the first to arrive, appalled at the gaping hole in Marchione's chest. Rupke thought Marchione muttered, "Stay with me," and reassured him. Four other crewmen joined Rupke, applying pressure to the wound, providing blood plasma, and strapping on an oxygen mask.

Both bombers put their noses down, accelerating for the sanctuary of the sea, outpacing their tormentors.

Half an hour later, cradled in Kurt Rupke's arms, Tony Marchione died a long, long way from his hometown of Pottstown, Pennsylvania.[6]

The B-32s limped into Kadena that evening, Anderson's on three engines with about 30 holes in the airframe. The wounded were cared for and Marchione's body was buried, eventually repatriated to Pottstown in 1949.

Years later Sakai reputedly described his reason for the attacks:

It may appear that we committed an illegal act… While Japan did agree to the surrender, we were still a sovereign nation, and every nation has the right to protect itself. When the Americans sent over their B-32s, we did not know of their intentions… by invading our airspace they were committing a provocative and aggressive act… It was most unwise for the Americans to send over their bombers only a few days after the surrender announcement! They should have waited and let things cool down.[7]

Assuming that Sakai's statement was accurate, the facts were lacking. Japan had agreed to "unconditional" surrender, while the emperor, who had both approved the war and the peace, remained on the throne, and Tokyo had agreed to Allied occupation. Any notion of "self-defense" clearly was invalid.

Consequently, Allied officers required the propellers to be removed from all Japanese aircraft.

On the 28th the B-32 continued its descending career spiral. Although only 118 were produced, the Convair bomber still contributed to the final act of World War II. Before dawn the Okinawa-based 386th Bomb Squadron prepared to launch a two-plane flight to the Tokyo area. Twenty-nine-year-old First Lieutenant Leonard Sill of Wisconsin began his takeoff from Yontan, heavy with extra fuel for the long flight. Before reaching flying speed the right inboard engine failed, prompting Sill and copilot, 25-year-old Glenn Bowie of Kansas, to abort the run, doubtless concerned about the extra gasoline. With throttles cut to idle and the brakes locked, Sill and Bowie experienced stomach-churning horror as Number 544 raced toward the end of the runway.

Speed barely abated, the Dominator skidded off the runway, plunging 80 feet into a gravel pit. The bomber exploded on impact, killing the entire nine-man crew and the two intelligence officers who were passengers.[8]

Close behind was the veteran *Hobo Queen II*, running up its engines before taking the runway. Just then the control tower flashed a red light, indicating an abort. Colonel Frank Cook, with at least six Dominator missions behind him, squealed to a halt in his jeep, waving the "cut engines" signal to Lieutenant Joe E. Elliott.

Number 544's fatal crash forced a delay in the flight schedule, but later *Hobo Queen* scouted Atsugi for proof that propellers had been removed from all Japanese aircraft. Low clouds prevented a positive assessment, but the crew noted for the first time the extensive camouflage measures, with entire painted streets and buildings. Meanwhile, the airspace over Tokyo Bay drew considerable interest with Army Air Force transports and Navy carrier planes.

On the return leg the Dominator developed electrical problems that caused a fire in the bomb bay, spewing smoke into the fuselage. Elliott and his copilot feathered one engine and continued their landing approach, with another engine trailing smoke.

That day First Lieutenant Collins Orton's plane, Number 528, and another Dominator dubbed *The Lady is Fresh*, patrolled the Tokyo area, only taking about 40 photographs due to an undercast below 3,000 feet. After turning for Okinawa, Orton's crew began transferring fuel from the ferry tank to the wing tanks when the left inboard engine lost power. About four hours later the right outboard also began failing. The crew started considering its options.

Despite jettisoning extra weight, it appeared that 528 was not likely to reach base. Shortly thereafter the fliers spotted a glorious sight – two U.S. Navy destroyers east of Amami O Shima, north of Okinawa. Orton's crew began an organized bailout, all jumping clear of the bomber. However, Staff Sergeant George Murphy sustained fatal injuries and Sergeant Morris Morgan's parachute apparently failed. Murphy was buried at sea by USS *Aulick* (DD-569).

Nor was that all. Twelve days later, on September 9, the troubled *Hobo Queen* was undergoing maintenance when a ground crewman accidentally flicked the switch to retract the nose wheel. The bomber sustained significant damage, requiring a crane to hoist the fuselage enough for extension of the wheel. Two days thereafter, a crane crew dropped the *Queen* twice, compounding the damage. With the war over, there was no point repairing the abused bomber, which was scrapped.[9]

August 19

Four days after Hirohito's broadcast, one of the most obscure places on Planet Earth became the focus of one of the most significant events. Tiny Ie Shima off Okinawa's west coast amounts to barely nine square miles, with only three runways long enough for bombers. But radio communications between Tokyo and the Allied Command thrashed out details for a meeting. Two Japanese aircraft bearing 16 military and civilian representatives would land on Ie Shima on the 19th; then the delegates would be flown to MacArthur's headquarters in Manila.

The Japanese had trouble filling out the 16-strong surrender delegation. Said historian William Manchester, "Every time sixteen officers and officials assembled, one of them would run away." But finally the roster was complete, and flight arrangements were made. American aircraft would meet the two Mitsubishi Betty bombers south of Kyushu and lead them to Ie Shima.[10]

The escorts were B-25s from the 345th Bomb Group, a long-serving unit of the Fifth Air Force dating from mid-1943. Known as the Air Apaches, the group flew and fought its way from New Guinea to the Philippines to Okinawa, establishing a reputation for competent aggressiveness. Colonel Glenn A. Doolittle (no relation to the Eighth Air Force commander) was new in the job, having only assumed command at the end of June. He brought with him a strong reputation from his bombing missions in the far-off Aleutians in 1942. "Cyclone" Davis's 8th Fighter Group also escorted the Japanese delegation to Ie Shima, alongside the Air Apaches.

To avoid any confusion, the Allied Command directed that the Japanese planes be painted white overall with green crosses.* They left Kisarazu Airfield near Tokyo with the required paint already wearing thin – some of the original rising suns peeked through the layers.[11]

The Bettys from the Yokosuka Air Group were led by Lieutenant Den Sudo, an experienced bomber pilot. The Americans required the white-painted planes to bear radio call signs "Bataan One" and "Bataan Two," a not-so-subtle dig from MacArthur dating from the 1942 battle.

The Air Apaches sent three two-plane teams to meet the inbound Japanese, each Mitchell bomber with a full ammunition loadout. The team led by Major J.C. "Jack" McClure spotted the distinctive Mitsubishis and established garbled communication on the designated frequency. He replied, "We are Bataan One's watchdog. Follow us." McClure recalled:

At one time they went off course, so when they couldn't understand the corrections I gave them, I took over the lead and had them fly formation with me.

Before the flight we had been told that a pilot would be court-martialed if he came within a thousand feet of their planes, so I kept my distance. Once in the lead, however, I glanced back and there was the number one Jap plane tucked in close with his wing less than twenty feet from mine. Major Decker joined us, and we came in over the field. I gave the Jap plane landing instructions and prepared to land myself. The Jap still kept on my wing – I couldn't shake him – and, as we went around in the

---

* This color scheme was largely limited to the peace delegations as propellers had been removed from Japanese planes not authorized to fly.

traffic pattern, a P-38 cut in. The Jap called that he saw a P-38, so I told him to land after the Lightning, which he did. It was a big thrill to be in on the final show.[12]

During his landing approach, Lieutenant Sudo in Bataan One found that his flaps refused to lower. With a greater-than-normal landing speed, Sudo successfully wheeled his Betty onto the runway without harm.

Thousands of American servicemen crowded both sides of the landing strip, watching the historic moment. Military police could barely restrain them from swarming the two planes, seeking a closer look or perhaps souvenirs.

With minimal fanfare the Japanese disembarked from the two bombers and approached MacArthur's personal transport, the gleaming aluminum C-54 dubbed *Bataan* in memory of his Philippine service. Leading the delegation was Lieutenant General Torashiro Kawabe, sporting a long sword and spurs. Besides Kawabe and a major general were six other army officers including two interpreters, a rear admiral with four other navy men, and three civilians. The senior diplomat present, Katzuo Okazaki, had been a runner in the 1924 Paris Olympics.

The Douglas Skymaster loaded its human cargo and headed 920 miles south.

In Manila, skirting angry Filipino crowds, the entourage motored to an apartment building that, unlike City Hall, had survived the liberation relatively intact. The Japanese received a pointed message from the conqueror: they were not present to negotiate. Their purpose was simply to learn the specifics as to the terms of surrender and protocol of the impending ceremony. Keeping himself remote from the discussion as befitted a budding emperor, MacArthur allowed his intelligence chief, Major General Charles Willoughby, to conduct much of the meeting. Willoughby asked Lieutenant General Kawabe, vice chief of the Imperial Army, what language they should speak, to which the multi-lingual general replied, "German." That suited Willoughby – he had emigrated from Germany as a child in 1910.

The details were thrashed out with minimal problems. MacArthur's staff intended to land at Atsugi in four days, to which the Japanese objected for practical reasons. It was a kamikaze base and "a hotbed of revolt against the cease-fire." Lieutenant General Richard K. Sutherland, MacArthur's perennially abrasive chief of staff, refused to shift venues but allowed five days instead.[13]

During an interval between numerous meetings, while looking at downtown Manila, a Michigan GI of Japanese descent, Technician Fourth Grade Raymond Katayama, struck up a conversation with the delegation secretary, Shuichi Mizota. "These ruins aren't so bad as Tokyo," the diplomat observed. Katayama asked in Japanese if it was true that the atom bomb had destroyed Hiroshima.

Mizota replied, "Hiroshima has not been destroyed. It has vanished from the face of the earth."[14]

Upon completion of the meetings, with details for the official surrender on September 2, the Japanese remained in Manila overnight. The next day the delegates reboarded *Bataan* for the five-hour return to Ie Shima.

However, while taxiing for takeoff, one of the Bettys ran off the runway, damaging the landing gear. Therefore, the Japanese delegation divided, with five junior members remaining on the island until repairs were completed in a day or so.

The Air Apaches were assigned to escort the other Betty partway back to Kyushu, and both sides indulged in some comradely airmanship. One of the Americans was Sergeant George Givens, who recalled:

After we were airborne for awhile, one of the Japanese planes started easing toward us on the left side. I was on that side at the waist gun position. As he got closer the Japanese pilot [more likely copilot] met my eyes and he smiled at me. I patted my .50 caliber and smiled back. He got so close to us that his wing was tucked in a few feet under ours. I called my pilot on the interphone and asked if he knew what was going on. He said that he saw everything and seemed unconcerned. After a while the Japanese pilot eased away. Not long after that, we turned back to Ie Shima.[15]

However, the senior delegates fetched up short of their destination. The remaining Betty coughed into silence with fuel exhaustion 130 miles short of Tokyo. Apparently the American flight line crew was confused about liters and gallons, and had shortchanged the Betty, although presumably the crew also neglected the takeoff check list. The pilots managed a safe ditching in shallow water off Honshu. Aided by fishermen, the officials splashed ashore for delivery to the capital by rail the following day.[16]

August 21
Meanwhile at sea, probably the last naval engagement of the war was fought off the China coast. On the morning of August 21 two sailing junks with American-Chinese crews were en route from Haimen to Shanghai. They were attached to the clandestine Sino-American Cooperative Organization, supporting guerrilla operations in Asia.

Lookouts sighted a large junk ahead; then the stranger came about, unmasking its armament, and opened fire.

Unknown to the two U.S. skippers – Navy Lieutenant Livingston Swentzel, Jr. and Marine First Lieutenant Stuart L. Pittman – their black-painted rival was a potent adversary. It carried a 75mm-pack howitzer, six machine guns, and more than 100 rifles for the 83 Japanese soldiers on board. Swentzel was a 35-year-old New Yorker with a degree from William and Mary whose excellent academic education ill prepared him for the situation.

The enemy's first round was eerily accurate, severing Swentzel's foremast to the consternation of most of his crew. Four Chinese were killed or wounded and the rudder damaged. However, Swentzel radioed Pittman, who coordinated the response. And in a brief moment of recalled glory from the age of sail, Swentzel hoisted the Stars and Stripes before returning fire.

Closing to 100 yards, the Yanks opened up with their heavy weapons – two bazookas intended for antitank action rather than naval warfare. One of Pittman's sailors took two rounds to get the range, then knocked out the Japanese cannon, but both sides retained automatic weapons. After holing the enemy vessel,

Swentzel directed Pittman alongside the Japanese and gave an order that John Paul Jones would have approved 170 years before: "Prepare to board!"

Hull to hull, Pittman's half of the seven Americans and 20 Chinese led their attack with a hail of hand grenades to kill or disperse the superior Japanese numbers. With the Marine in the lead, a brief, violent skirmish subdued most of the remaining enemy, driving others below decks. More grenades followed down the hatches, forcing the survivors to surrender.

After 45 minutes the issue was settled, climaxing when the opposing skippers clashed hand to hand, with Pittman victorious. Before he expired, the Japanese officer told the Chinese that he had thought the junks were pirates.

Americans and Chinese sorted the Japanese casualties, reckoned at 44 dead and 35 wounded. The Allies lost four dead and six injured.

Swentzel and Pittman reversed helm for Haimen, and delivered their prize and prisoners to the Chinese before proceeding to Shanghai. Both skippers received Navy Crosses for their utterly unique action.[17]

August 24

Anchored in Buckner Bay, Okinawa, were hundreds of vessels of all types, awaiting events. On August 24, five battleships and other combatants left for Tokyo Bay, allowing ample time for the 950-mile voyage.

Aboard the light cruiser *Montpelier* (CL-57), Seaman First Class James J. Fahey was one of 1,255 officers and men who had lived in a sweltering world of hunger, sleep deprivation, violence, homesickness – and friendship. "Mighty Monty" was a veteran with 13 battle stars dating from January 1943: she had shelled Japanese-held islands on 53 occasions, supporting 26 amphibious landings.

Fahey also was a veteran: he had enlisted in October 1942, and six weeks later, fresh out of recruit training, he was assigned to the brand-new, 12,000-ton warship on an antiaircraft crew. Since then he had kept a surreptitious diary in violation of security regulations. On August 24, the 23-year-old New Yorker noted,

"All the crew talk about now is when we will go home. The *Montpelier* has fired over 100,000 rounds of five- and six-inch shells. By the time we reach the States, we will have traveled almost 200,000 miles. Of that total approximately 95 percent was spent in enemy-infested waters."

The crew – like servicemen everywhere – hung on every news report, including the progress of the Japanese peace delegation from Ie Shima to Manila. But the impending end of hostilities did not end the peril. Fahey wrote, "The fellows returned from recreation at 5:30 p.m. They said that one sailor was killed and another had his arm blown off when they came across some Jap booby traps."

With the official end of a long war imminent, many ships and units took farewell photographs. At Buckner Bay some skippers polled their crews as to what to wear. One was *Montpelier*'s Captain William Gorry. A handful advocated dress blues as befitting the occasion but as Seaman Fahey noted, "It's too warm to wear any clothes at all. This morning at 7 a.m. the temperature was 107 degrees. The bulkheads were so hot that I could not lean against them. This is the hottest time of the year and it seldom rains. The sun beats down all day."[18]

August 25

Third Fleet's original plan had been to enter Sagami Wan on the 25th, but an approaching typhoon forced a two-day delay. The Western Pacific was a weather factory, sometimes blowing 13 typhoons and as many tropical storms in the long season from April to early December. Task groups were free to maneuver as required to avoid the worst of the storm: 38.1 and 38.4 north and east of Tokyo; 38.3 south and west.

Ninety-five miles off Shikoku, Captain Wendell Switzer's aircraft carrier USS *Wasp* bucked 80-knot winds that could whip signal flags to tatters while taut halyards moaned a harmonic wail. Wind-driven mountainous waves buckled steel and splintered Douglas fir over the forward 35 feet of the flight deck.

The next day the task force dodged a second storm riding in the low-pressure trough of the first. Radar operators tracked its passage, a miss by 40 miles as it "recurved" from northeast to northwest.

Despite the foreshortened flight deck, on the 27th "Windy" Switzer's aviators launched on photo missions over Nagoya on Honshu followed by relief flights dropping supplies to POW camps from the 28th to the 30th. It was her final act of the war.

On the 31st, as *Wasp* left for repairs, *Indefatigable* signaled, "Good luck. It has been a pleasure to see you work. Presume you are going to have your face lifted."[19] This was a humorous reference to the repairs necessary to fix *Wasp*'s highly visible damage.

Bragging Points: Landing in Japan

In the heady days following Tokyo's announcement, a few American aviators landed in Japan without official approval. On August 25 two P-38 Lightnings from Okinawa alighted at Nittagahara Airfield on Kyushu when the wingman's plane started siphoning fuel. The 49th Fighter Group leader, Colonel Clay Tice, exercised some initiative and radioed for a bomber to land and transfer gasoline. The Japanese responded cooperatively, the local mayor dashing to the scene on his bicycle, wearing top hat and frock coat. The Americans took off and returned to Okinawa.

According to Halsey, two days later a brash *Yorktown* pilot landed at Atsugi and provided the Japanese a banner to be erected for the benefit of the first GIs ashore: "Welcome to the U.S. Army. From the Third Fleet." Halsey wrote that shortly thereafter American airborne troops apparently saw the greeting but there is no record of a Japanese reaction.[20]

Neither *Yorktown*'s air group commander nor the fighter squadron commander heard of the incident. Retired Captain Seth Searcy wrote, "It makes a good story but I rather doubt that it actually happened."[21]

Another hardy soul grasped a rare opportunity – Lieutenant Commander Walter Michaels, the 29-year-old skipper of a Navy privateer squadron on Iwo Jima, who had been in command since mid-July. VPB-116 had been flying 1,200-mile patrols from Tinian, generally uneventful outings, before moving to Iwo in April. When the Navy fliers learned of General MacArthur's plan to land at Atsugi on August 30, they saw an opportunity. And they seized it.

Michaels cajoled the island's supply officer to donate 1,000 pounds of rations, ostensibly for delivery to POWs in Japan. The Army officer agreed – if he could go along. Done deal. Without the burden of official approval, Michaels' crew plus one lifted off Iwo and set course north – destination Atsugi.

The mission was not just an impetuous lark. Michaels had scanned reconnaissance photos and memorized Atsugi's runway layout. His information included the location of bomb craters that might interfere with a landing.

Navigation was fairly simple, as Atsugi lay just inland from Yokohama. Arriving overhead his destination, Michaels had his radioman call Iwo pleading an "oil leak." With that cover story established, the four-engine Privateer descended onto Japanese soil, probably the first U.S. Navy aircraft to do so. It was aptly named *Peace Feeler* with a near life-size pinup girl wearing half a sarong. The Navy pilots had upstaged the Army by four days.

While some aircrew removed a cowling in a pantomime of engine repair, others kept watch. Soon they noticed two reception committees: some civilian vehicles and a line of military trucks headed for an upwind position on the runway. That settled it. Michaels said, "Let's go while we still can." The sailors and their Army guest buttoned up the cowling, scrambled aboard, and started engines. Contrary to their cover story, all four Pratt & Whitneys fired up. The Liberator undoubtedly left some querulous Japanese in its slipstream.[22]

After the one-upmanship was over, Task Force 38 squadrons turned their attention from defensive patrols to seeking new "targets" inland. Recalled then-Ensign Don McPherson aboard *Essex*:

The fleet retired to the replenishment area to await further orders. On August 25th our task group 38.3 returned to the Japanese coastal waters and we fighter pilots were assigned duty through the 28th to fly low-level searches over some of the Japanese cities to chart POW camps and to drop small parachute packets containing food, cigarettes, etc. for the prisoners plus leaflets to inform the POWs that the war was over![23]

SWEEPING THE BAY

August 27
For three quarters of a century, Pacific Fleet sailors have argued over whose ship first entered Tokyo Bay. The subject was confusing because dozens of vessels arrived in Sagami Wan, the outer bay, before others penetrated Tokyo Bay proper. To those unfamiliar with the area, navigating into Sagami Wan could be mistaken for entering Tokyo Bay.

Halsey certainly knew the difference but wanted to make an early impression. As historian Samuel Eliot Morison noted, he ordered major units of Third Fleet into Sagami Wan, "under the shadow of Mount Fuji."[24] There representatives and harbor pilots from the Japanese Navy in destroyer *Hatsuzakura* ("Early Blooming Cherry") rendezvoused with *Missouri* at the entrance on the 27th. *Hatsuzakura* was brand new, only commissioned in May. She made a study in contrast with her 1,300 tons alongside "Mighty Mo's" 48,000.

Halsey's staff provided detailed directions to prepare for occupation of Yokosuka in exchange for hydrographic information and a chart of the bay's minefields. *Missouri* and Admiral Fraser's flagship *Duke of York* steamed into Sagami Wan, anchoring at assigned berths.

Doctrinally, the Imperial Navy regarded mines mainly as defensive weapons, although offensive types could be delivered by submarines and aircraft. But with Japan's waning fortunes, defensive mines had begun development in late 1944.[25]

Naval mines came in different flavors, activated by impact with a ship's hull, a vessel's magnetic field, the sound of an engine and propeller, or the pressure of displaced water by a passing ship. However, even with German data apparently the Imperial Navy did not develop magnetic mines, and postwar investigation found that acoustic mines were only deployed in limited areas.

By far the most common Japanese mine was the "Hertz horn" variety with contact detonators. If a ship broke one of the horns, acid was released that activated a battery for detonation. Many were large and potent, weighing 1,500 to 2,000 pounds with 200 to 400 pounds of explosive.[26]

Minesweeping could be nerve-wracking work with ever-present tension driven by the prospect of running into one of the vessel's prey. Throughout the war, the U.S. Navy lost nearly 50 minesweepers to all causes, including at least 22 by enemy mines.

Both Sagami and Tokyo Bay had to be swept so that safe lanes were available to the large numbers of Allied ships inbound, both for passage and for anchorage. That crucial mission seldom received much publicity, prompting Lieutenant Commander James L. Jackson to comment, "Minesweeping was considered about the most unglamorous job you could have. But we didn't feel that way… Not one of those cruiser or destroyer officers wanted to be aboard with us!"

Leading the sweeping parade was the two-year-old, 900-ton minesweeper *Revenge* (AM-110). Lieutenant Commander Jackson's 100-man crew had seen action in the Philippines and Okinawa, learning to appreciate their skipper. Hailing from Georgia Tech, the personable, drawling Jackson had initially chosen Navy Reserve Officers Training Corps (ROTC) while a student "because they furnished uniforms." He had served in the Atlantic and Caribbean before assuming command of *Revenge* in Hawaii. Then, between Guadalcanal and Pearl Harbor, he had played Christmas carols on his accordion.[27]

Tokyo Bay was fairly shallow, averaging about 40 feet deep, though some U.S. minesweepers operated sweeps to 60 feet. Often two minesweepers towed a submerged wire between them, on a line weighted forward and aft beneath a buoy showing the sweep's position. When the sweep encountered a moored mine, it cut the chain or cable, allowing the weapon to surface where it could be destroyed.

Typical armament of a U.S. minesweeper was a .50-caliber machine gun plus two each 20mm and 40mm cannon. All were fully capable of destroying a floating mine, but the latter pair were more suited to air defense. However, the dispersion of automatic weapons fire could bracket a mine without destroying it, requiring more ammunition expenditure. Therefore, precision rifle fire sometimes was employed with home-grown marksmen perhaps from Montana or Kentucky to hit a horn with .30-caliber rounds.

Jackson's Unit 24 had lost two sweepers just before the operation, detached with engine problems. But they were replaced by three more, and the nine vessels entered Sagami Wan the afternoon of the 27th. They remained underway through the night despite an alteration to the operations order.

For the foray into Sagami Wan and Tokyo Bay, Jackson had a Japanese Navy lieutenant aboard who spoke perfect English. Small wonder – he had attended Yale. He brought charts of the 20-mile approach leading to Tokyo Bay including an unmined channel for passage of Japanese vessels. The sweepers confirmed that no mines were sown in that area.

At first light on the 28th the sweepers proceeded to Tokyo Bay itself. Jackson said, "The most exciting thing I saw first was a sign hanging on a warehouse building and it said, 'Welcome U.S. Navy. Come and get us. Prisoners.'"

Immediately thereafter Jackson's vessels proceeded to their assigned areas. Typical was Task Unit 23, which swept anchorage "Easy" for moored mines to a depth of 60 feet with negative results.

However, two of Unit 24's small YMS vessels (a Yard-class minesweeper) fouled their trailing gear, forcing them out of action. *YMS-467* snagged three mines and had no choice but to cut the wire. Of the three mines, one was exploded by rifle fire, another by 20mm cannon, and the third drifted toward the beach.

Meanwhile, *YMS-426* fouled a buoy while fighting a strong current and had to leave formation. The other sweepers completed their task, clearing 85 percent of their assigned area. The units continued sweeping Areas Baker and Charlie over the next two days.[28]

August 28

Before the supreme commander could take over, he required an essential element: communications.

Planning focused on a small communications unit that exerted importance far beyond its size. On the 28th Colonel Gordon A. Blake's detachment arrived at Naval Air Base Atsugi, about 20 miles southwest of Tokyo, just inland from Sagami Wan. Blake's mission was to provide radio contact with Okinawa plus navigation and weather information in addition to local air traffic control.

Blake, a 35-year-old Iowan, hailed from the West Point class of 1931. Initially assigned to fighters, he had been in communications since 1934. Serving in Hawaii from 1939, he had survived Pearl Harbor and had risen quickly, becoming a full colonel in November 1942. He seemed to be everywhere, serving in the Central Pacific, Alaska, New Guinea, the Solomons, and Philippines.

Blake selected five men from the 68th Army Airways Communications System Group to establish his Atsugi facility. They arrived with about 150 others in the advance party crammed into two dozen C-47s so heavily laden that the Skytrains only carried enough fuel to reach Japan, where presumably more gasoline was available.

The "Gooney Birds" landed at the bombed-out base with rubble strewn either side of the active runway.

Taxiing off the ramp, the Americans saw what appeared to be hundreds of Japanese sailors lining the parking area. Some of the Yanks fingered their carbines and pistols, wondering what to expect. But upon deplaning, Blake and his colleagues were greeted by courteous, English-speaking officers who explained that the ranks of sailors were a welcoming honor guard.

Blake and company immediately set to work erecting a control tower, as the Japanese had merely used a platform atop the operations building. Literally overnight his crew, supporting personnel, and Japanese laborers finished a tower, complete with radio antennas and wind sock, operational the next day.[29]

Within a few hours, the first C-54 Skymaster of the official occupation forces landed. The Honshu atmosphere continued thrumming with the constant drone of radial engines as U.S. aircraft arrived and departed, often at two-minute intervals. Before noon on the 29th Blake's controllers had directed nearly 350 takeoffs and landings, and by the next day Atsugi probably was the busiest airport on Earth.[30]

The first arrivals on the 30th were five more C-47s carrying components for the first airborne radio station in Air Force history.

Weather prevented the original schedule for arrival of MacArthur's staff in Japan. After two days of waiting, on the 28th a fresh breeze blew in, to the relief of the Japanese. Two lieutenant generals, a navy captain, and a diplomat headed the welcoming committee while a hand-picked detachment of naval security troops stood guard, armed with truncheons.

Most of the Far East Air Forces' transport planes were committed to lifting the 11th Airborne and 27th Infantry Divisions from Okinawa, so the first Americans to arrive used whatever was available. At 8:30 a.m. – half an hour ahead of schedule – the lead Curtiss Commando touched down, followed by 15 more twin-engine transports. They carried paratroopers, a communications crew, and a small hospital unit.

First off the lead plane was MacArthur's assistant chief of staff, Colonel Charles T. Tench (ninth among 299 in the West Point class of 1929), sporting a .45 pistol in a shoulder holster. His aides – six Army officers including a translator and a Navy captain – also wore casual khakis with sidearms or carbines.

Lieutenant General Seizo Arisue, chief of imperial general headquarters intelligence and a former attaché to Rome, conducted Tench and company to a reception area, offering food and drink. Tench declined with thanks, as his entourage had brought rations with them. Meanwhile, the first Okinawa airlift continued landing until about 150 Americans were assembled, beginning the process of reconnaissance and examination of Atsugi as the base for further operations.

Beneath a blue blanket of Navy fighters, two more lifts totaling 30 AAF transports landed before noon. The last C-46s and C-47s delivered fuel, oil, and maintenance gear to support the increasing traffic. Americans observed that the Japanese were especially impressed when Hellcats folded their wings while taxiing to a parking area, ready for contingencies.[31]

The need for a prompt U.S. presence on the ground drove Third Fleet to form Task Force 31. A regiment of the 6th Marine Division – the original 4th Regiment had been lost in the Philippines – augmented by members of shipboard Marine and British detachments, totaled some 5,400 men under Brigadier General William T. Clement, a Virginia Military Institute (VMI) product with postgraduate education as a bush fighter in Haiti and an old China hand. The Royal Navy provided a battalion of sailors and a battalion of Royal Marine Commandos.

The task force entered Tokyo Bay with Rear Admiral Oscar Badger aboard the antiaircraft cruiser *San Diego* (CL-53) leading an armada of minesweepers and support craft.

San Diego too was a blooded veteran. Commissioned in January 1942, her 18 battle stars – second only to the carrier *Enterprise's* 20 – included Guadalcanal, the Solomons, the Gilberts and Marshalls, the Marianas, the Philippines, and Okinawa. Her skipper, William E.A. Mullen, had been with her since July 1944.

Before the Americans arrived, the Japanese at Yokosuka were informed that any resistance "would be severely dealt with." None ensued.[32]

Badger's advance force anchored off Yokosuka on the 28th, hosting Vice Admiral Michitaro Tozuka, a 35-year veteran and former torpedo specialist. Though not a flier, he held several aviation commands including part of the Pearl Harbor task force. As commander of the Yokosuka Naval District he formally surrendered the facility to Badger and Rear Admiral Robert Carney, Halsey's chief of staff.

In charge of the Third Fleet Naval Landing Force, Commander L.T. Malone issued a memorandum that stated in part, "We are operating in fast company – men of two nations that are seasoned in combat and inspired by many memorable and historical campaigns... The foe has capitulated. We have tested him and we now go into his inner sanctum sanctorum to raise the American Flag and occupy his territory. Our responsibilities are great and our obligations tremendous."[33]

Admiral Tozuka and his subordinates kept their word, as the Marines found the forts guarding the bay entrance had been neutralized as per instructions.

Another turnover was even more significant historically. A 98-man nucleus crew boarded *Nagato*, the last Japanese battleship still afloat. The 16-inch main batteries had been disarmed while the secondary and antiaircraft batteries were removed. The Japanese skeleton crew cooperated fully with the Americans.

Captain Thomas J. Flynn, *Iowa*'s executive officer, reported, "At no time was any antagonism, resentment, arrogance or passive resistance encountered; both officers (including the captain) and men displaying a very meek and subservient attitude. It seemed almost incredible that these bowing, scraping, and scared men were the same brutal, sadistic enemies who had tortured our prisoners, reports of whose plight were being received the same day."[34]

Even in the period of prospective peace, bizarre incidents claimed lives. On the 28th a New Zealand flying boat alighted at Rekata Bay in the Solomons for a relaxing picnic while inspecting the formerly enemy-occupied area. But Leading Aircraftsman Leslie Angus Ellen disappeared while swimming, probably victim of a saltwater crocodile. Ellen's squadron sent Catalinas back to the area for days thereafter, dropping depth charges in vain hope of dislodging his body. The 21-year-old flier was never found.[35]

August 29

Fleet Admiral Chester Nimitz favored the huge Consolidated PB2Y Coronado. Frequently he toured the Pacific Theater in the U.S. Navy's standard four-engine flying boat of the war. On August 29 he and part of his staff set down in Tokyo Bay, transferring to the battleship *South Dakota* (BB-57).

That same day LeMay wrote his wife Helen that he had just landed after a 50-mile flight over Japanese-occupied Rota. "Didn't see any Japs. But needed to keep flying hours up for flight pay." In those days, flight pay was not automatic for generals as it is today. Nor was it an insignificant increase. In 1945 two-star officers (major generals and rear admirals) with more than 15 years of service received $666.67 per month. Flight pay was 50 percent more.[36] And while certainly the monthly bonus was welcome, a better explanation was that Curtis LeMay simply liked to fly.[37]

In the run-up to the formal surrender, the Americans needed to decide where the ceremony would be held. General of the Armies George C. Marshall and Fleet Admiral William E. Leahy asked the commander-in-chief for his opinion.

As Truman recalled in his memoir:

> I suggested, without hesitation, that the official act of surrender should take place in Tokyo Bay, aboard a naval vessel, and that ship to be the USS *Missouri*. I thought it wise to hold the ceremony within view of the Japanese capital in order to impress the fact of defeat on the Japanese people, but it also seemed desirable to remain offshore until we could be assured that there would be no last-minute outbursts of fanaticism.

Not only was "Mighty Mo" named for Truman's home state but his daughter Margaret had christened the huge warship in January 1944, and the then-senator had spoken on the occasion.[38]

Among *Missouri*'s crew was Seaman John C. Truman, the president's nephew. Days after Uncle Harry assumed the office the sailor candidly wrote, "I still find it difficult to realize you are the President."[39]

Earlier, on August 19, Truman had drafted a statement marking a national day of prayer to recognize what was about to become official, saying in part:

> Our global victory has come from the courage and stamina and spirit of free men and women united in determination to fight.
>
> It has come from the massive strength of arms and materials created by peace-loving peoples who knew that unless they won, decency in the world would end.
>
> It has come from millions of peaceful citizens all over the world – turned soldiers almost overnight – who showed a ruthless enemy that they were not afraid to fight and to die, and that they knew how to win.

It has come with the help of God, Who was with us in the early days of adversity and disaster, and Who has now brought us to this glorious day of triumph.

Let us give thanks to Him, and remember that we have now dedicated ourselves to follow in His ways to a lasting and just peace and to a better world.[40]

August 30
At 6:00 a.m. on the 30th a flock of C-54s descended on Atsugi Airfield, bringing the advance element of the 11th Airborne Division.

In February 1943 then-Brigadier General Joseph M. Swing stood up the division, leading it through highly successful maneuvers, then left to observe airborne operations in the Mediterranean. Upon return his advocacy and reasoning were credited in some quarters with preserving U.S. airborne forces as employed during World War II. Perhaps it was a small surprise – he had graduated from West Point in 1915, "The class the stars fell on." Standing 38th of 164 graduates, he ranked with a record 59 generals including Dwight Eisenhower and Omar Bradley.

The troopers had fought in the Philippines from November, including a January jump on tiny Corregidor at the entrance to Manila Bay, seizing the small island though outnumbered. It was among the most impressive airborne performances of the Pacific Theater.

Subsequently Swing's staff had four days' notice for deployment to Japan. The planners worked a minor miracle involving 600 aircraft to lift 11,100 men and 120 vehicles to complete the operation.

Once on the ground, regimental headquarters were established, with the troopers poised to establish a perimeter extending toward the urban area. Japanese military and civilians were evacuated within a three-mile radius toward Yokohama, a huge city with nearly 1 million residents. Nearly a week of shuttle flights brought the rest of the division to Japan, with reinforcements from the 27th Infantry Division.

Meanwhile, one of MacArthur's favorites, the First Cavalry Division (the Cav, also known as the First Team), had served in the Pacific a full two years, with initial action in the Admiralty Islands in February 1944. Under Major General William C. Chase, the First Team saw its final combat in the Philippines in early July, sustaining a total 4,000 combat casualties during its campaigns.

A former Rhode Island National Guard cavalryman, Chase had pursued Mexican bandit *jefe* (boss) Pancho Villa in 1916 as had Charles Swing, his airborne counterpart. Then, Chase survived the meat grinder of the Great War's Western Front. In the Pacific since July 1943, the division also was blooded in the Admiralties alongside the 11th Airborne.

The former horsemen embarked from the Philippines on August 25 and arrived at Yokohama by sea on September 2. Some cavalrymen believed they were first into Japan, a notion that remained part of the division's lore for decades. The 11th Airborne history records that the division band greeted the Cav unloading dockside with a rendition of "The Old Gray Mare Ain't What She Used to Be." However, the cavalry was in fact first into Tokyo, with General Chase first across the demarcation line.[41]

MACARTHUR DESCENDS

That day, General of the Army Douglas MacArthur also alighted upon Nippon's soil. With the supreme confidence that characterized his life and career, the supreme commander decided on a grandiose gesture. He flew into Atsugi with perhaps 1,000 Americans in the area amid tens of thousands of Japanese troops. When he descended the stairs of his C-54 Skymaster transport, named *Bataan* in honor of his 1941–42 Philippines service, he exuded a calmness not universally shared among his staff. However much he knew of mutinous sentiments among Japanese units in the previous weeks, he believed that Hirohito's edict would be obeyed. And he was proven right.[42]

MacArthur explained his reasoning based on long experience in Asia. "Years of overseas duty had schooled me well in the ways of the Orient."

No less an authority than Winston Churchill – who knew about personal courage – observed, "Of all the amazing deeds of bravery during the war, I regard MacArthur's personal landing at Atsugi as the greatest of the lot."[43]

The new supremo was chauffeured to Yokohama's New Grand Hotel for three days, preparing for the official surrender ceremony on September 2. The hotel, built after the devastating earthquake of 1923, somehow had survived Curtis LeMay's searing B-29 attacks.

While Tokyo accepted the Allies' requirements for peace, the war continued. The Third Fleet maintained a watchful waiting in Japanese waters, but massive violence continued on the Asian mainland. Soviet tanks, infantry, artillery, aircraft – and especially a huge logistics train – continued steamrolling as before.

RECLAIMING AN EMPIRE

The far-flung interests of Britain and Japan remained intertwined even after the formal surrender. Admiral Louis Mountbatten, Supreme Allied Commander in Southeast Asia since August 1943, oversaw the process.

Mountbatten represented a world in transition from the colonial to the post-colonial era. Born in 1900 – the year before his great-grandmother Queen Victoria died – he was christened Louis Francis Albert Victor Nicholas Battenberg. He was the son of German nobility, Prince Louis of Battenberg and Princess Victoria of Hesse. His godparents were Queen Victoria and Czar Nicholas of Russia.

Like many of his relatives, "Dickie" entered the Royal Navy at a tender age. He saw combat against the Kaiser's fleet, prompting the family to drop the Battenberg surname in favor of the Anglophonic Mountbatten. An early talent, he finished the war as the 18-year-old executive officer of a 600-ton sloop.

Between the wars Mountbatten attended Cambridge, studied electronics, and specialized in communications, mostly serving aboard battleships, and assumed command of a destroyer in 1934. Subsequently he was naval aide to King Edward VIII before returning to sea in his defining command, the destroyer HMS *Kelly* in June 1939. Three months later he was again at war with Germany.

Leading a destroyer flotilla, Mountbatten was forced off *Kelly* due to torpedo damage near Norway in May 1940 and shifted his flag to HMS *Javelin*, torpedoed in the English Channel that November. Mountbatten returned to *Kelly*, which was sunk by the Luftwaffe off Crete in May 1941.

Thereafter, although not an aviator, Mountbatten commanded the aircraft carrier HMS *Illustrious* undergoing repair in Norfolk, Virginia. That September he grasped the chance to visit Pearl Harbor and made the 4,900-mile trek. He was astonished at finding a poor state of readiness, which he reported to Washington. As a reader of history, he knew that Japan had begun wars by surprise attack and predicted the events of December 7.[44]

Soon thereafter Mountbatten began nearly two years of planning Allied combined operations, including the highly successful St. Nazaire raid and the disastrous Dieppe landing of 1942. His value was evident in appointment to a position on the Chiefs of Staff Committee with preliminaries for the Normandy invasion of 1944.

In August 1943 Mountbatten was named to lead South East Asia Command (SEAC) as a full admiral. Thus, he spent the last two years of the war directing Allied operations in the region, most notably Burma.

Mountbatten's wartime experience led to a lifelong aversion to Japan, excepting a brief meeting during Hirohito's U.K. visit in 1971, at Queen Elizabeth's urging.

The Japanese had seized much of Burma, a British colony, in a short campaign during 1942, leading to a prolonged Allied effort to regain former possessions. Mountbatten's field commander, Lieutenant General Sir William Slim, faced a complex strategic and operational challenge involving Indian and Chinese allies as well as Thai forces backing Japan. A series of battles ensued in the region's jungle wetness where soldiers saw their weapons rust and their uniforms mold almost overnight.

Mountbatten's deputy was the acerbic General Joseph Stilwell, the senior U.S. officer in Asia, who had done much to bolster the Chinese Army. But his relationship floundered with Chiang Kai-shek, whom he described as "the peanut." Stilwell was recalled to Washington in late 1944 and subsequently given command of the Tenth Army on Okinawa. He was replaced in Asia by Lieutenant General Albert C. Wedemeyer, who three years prior had been a lieutenant colonel. Wedemeyer had a rapport with Mountbatten, having been a planning officer for Normandy, and remained in Asia for the duration of the war.

Mountbatten, the European commando exponent, was receptive to bold innovation, including airborne insertion of troops far behind enemy lines, and supplied by air. Both British and American units such as the Chindits and Merrill's Marauders proved effective, although the Japanese rebounded in the spring of 1944 with a briefly successful incursion into eastern India.

Slim and his American counterparts completed the reconquest of Burma with an airborne and amphibious landing at Rangoon in May 1945.

That August a succession of British amphibious operations with esoteric names like *Tiderace*, *Jurist*, and *Mailfist* were planned to reclaim territory lost in the early days of the Pacific War. They were aimed at Singapore, Malaya, and Penang. In Operation *Jurist*, Japan's Penang garrison in northwestern Malaya surrendered on September 2 with Royal Marines occupying Penang Island the next day.

But much of the reclamation of British interests occurred after the Tokyo Bay ceremony. In *Tiderace* an Allied fleet arrived at Singapore on the 4th and accepted the Japanese forces' capitulation, formalized in the city on the 12th. In that event Mountbatten, resplendent in dress whites, personally accepted the surrender of General Seishiro Itagaki. Subsequently Itagaki was indicted for war crimes, convicted on eight counts for atrocities in Manchuria and Southeast Asia, and hanged in 1948. More immediately, the British brought food and medicine to thousands of former POWs.

Mailfist never came about; it was a contingency plan to liberate Singapore before a Japanese surrender.

However, Indian Army troops – among the most capable available to Britain – occupied the coastal areas of Malaysia between September 9 and 12.

Some 2,500,000 Indians served in the British Indian Army and the Royal Indian Navy. Without that huge contribution many Allied victories on the ground throughout Asia would not have been possible. But ground combat largely ended by January 1945 when the first Allied supply convoy drove the Ledo Road from India to Kunming, China. Otherwise, relatively small operations included an unopposed airborne-amphibious assault that seized Rangoon, Burma, in early May, just ahead of the seasonal monsoon.

INDIA EMERGENT

Despite the vast majority of Indians deciding to support their old colonial master, undoubtedly with an eye toward a future democratic India, a far smaller minority had sided with the Japanese. The effort manifested itself in the Indian National Army (INA) formally allied with the Axis powers. With some 40,000 men and women, the INA operated alongside the Japanese in Burma and India from 1943 onward, led by the anti-colonial organizer Subhas Chandra Bose. Bearing a multi-faceted political philosophy, Bose had consorted with Nazi Germany and the Soviet Union while seeking support for his organization. His more conventional older brother, Sarat Chandra Bose, became postwar leader of the majority Indian National Congress.

With collapse of the INA in August, Subhas Bose sought refuge where he could. He boarded a Japanese aircraft on Formosa but died from injuries received in a takeoff crash on August 18.

That same month the subcontinent was wracked with controversy over plans for postwar organization and realignment. The Indian National Congress's spiritual and political leader

Mahatma Gandhi, aged 75, advocated an integrated Hindu-Muslim India, but separatist elements exemplified by Muslim leader Muhammad Ali Jinnah insisted in separating Pakistan. Fractious policy disputes led to a general election in December and postwar partition of a separate Muslim Pakistani nation. Subsequently India and Pakistan fought two wars.

Gandhi's separatist movement probably could only have succeeded against postwar Britain. Certainly his pacifist approach would have found little success against the French, let alone the Japanese. Yet he achieved enormous moral authority based on decades of experience and activism.

With a law degree from University College London, from 1893 Gandhi began representing Indian residents in South Africa. Repeatedly arrested, the social and political discrimination he endured only sharpened his resolve. In order to demonstrate Hindus' capabilities alongside Muslims, he formed a 1,000-strong ambulance service supporting British troops during the Boer War, and was decorated for his efforts. Yet his trademark pacifism germinated in South Africa. Throughout the years of World War I he waged a series of nonviolent protests. He had already established his ideology in his 1909 treatise, noting that Britain had gained control of India with the compliance of the population, and the arrangement would endure only as long as the 240 million subjects obeyed the crown. His message was clear: that situation, harking back to the 17th century, was ending.

Upon return to India in 1915, Gandhi began organizing rural and urban factions protesting property taxes and outright discrimination. After rising to leadership of the Indian National Congress in 1921, he broadened his efforts in seeking eventual independence from colonial rule.

Gandhi's public image was deceptive. With his almost emaciated stooped posture, gap-toothed smile and traditional garb – broadcloth knotted about the waist and legs, often bare above the waist – he appeared more a peasant than a revolutionary. But in 1945 he sat on the edge of eternity for the entire subcontinent.

Conflict in China

No less fractious was the situation in China. President Franklin Roosevelt had endured an often-tense relationship with Chiang Kai-shek, the Chinese Nationalist ruler.

At 57, Chiang presided over the Republic of China (ROC), formed in 1912 after deposing the last imperial dynasty. Chiang was a well-tutored politician, having studied in Japan and Russia, and he wielded both political and military power. Following a succession of leadership disputes, he emerged on top to establish his capital in Nanking in 1928. He was Director General of the Kuomintang Nationalist Party from 1937 until his death 38 years later.

For a brief period in the 1920s Chiang's Kuomintang faction was supported by the Chinese Communists and the Soviet Union. However, he soon turned away from those sometime allies, expelling Russian advisors and killing Chinese opponents in large numbers, perhaps hundreds of thousands. Thus, the Kuomintang became a single-party dictatorship whose effectiveness was limited by perennial feuding with the Communists, warlords, and Japan.[45] Full-scale civil war broke out between Nationalist and Communist forces in 1927. The bitter civil war would continue despite the Japanese invasion of Manchuria in 1937 and throughout the entirety of World War II.

Chiang recognized opportunities. While enthusiastically slaying Communists, he confiscated property of capitalists and largely prevented them from gaining influence within his party and parliament, while moving toward government control of industry. Philosophically agile, he appeared equally wary of Russia, Germany, Britain, and America.

However, facing full-scale war with Japan, from 1937 onward Chiang proved a rare mixture of spiritualist and hard-eyed realist. Having converted to Christianity in 1930 to please his wife's powerful family, he read the Bible daily, yet decided to breach the Yellow River dikes in 1938, flooding a vast area to impede the Japanese advance on Wuhan. In addition to Japanese losses, the disaster claimed perhaps half a million Chinese lives and displaced as many others.

Chiang moved toward better relations with Washington. That year he contracted with a former U.S. Army captain, Claire Lee

Chennault, to build a more competent ROC air arm. The result was the American Volunteer Group (AVG), a mercenary fighter wing composed of furloughed U.S. military pilots and maintenance men equipped with American-built aircraft. Famed as the Flying Tigers, the AVG arrived in 1941 and entered combat soon after Pearl Harbor. It was disbanded in July 1942 when sufficient U.S. Army units arrived in the China-Burma-India Theater.

Chiang was ably aided by his wife, Soong Mei-ling, sister-in-law of Sun Yat-sen, founder of the Kuomintang party and first premier of the Republic of China. A 1917 Wellesley graduate in English literature and philosophy, she was popular in America where she smoothly combined Chinese subtlety with southern charm.

Chiang Kai-shek's occasional ally and bitterest enemy was Mao Tse-tung, head of the Chinese Communist Party. Born to an upper-class peasant family, Mao briefly served as a teenage soldier before Sun Yat-sen's Chinese Republic was established in 1912. Mao completed his education and moved into politics, evolving from republicanism to Marxism. In 1921 he participated in the foundation of the Chinese Communist Party, while recognizing the desirability of cooperating with the Nationalists. However, Chiang's brutal suppression of workers and peasants in 1926 forced a change in Mao's priorities. Nationalist forces executed the second of Mao's four wives in 1930, and he lost three brothers to Nationalists and warlords between 1929 and 1943.

Mao's "wilderness period" lasted 22 years, beginning with a three-year building phase developing guerrilla tactics with army commander Zhu De. In 1930 the Communist Central Committee ordered expansion from the countryside into urban centers, but Mao saw the results were counter-productive and withdrew. Although scoring some successes against the Nationalists, in 1934 Mao and Zhu De took between 70,000 and 85,000 people on the 12-month "Long March" to northwest China. Perhaps 8,000 survived the arduous trek to Shaanxi Province in the fall of 1935.

The following spring the Communists formally allied themselves with the Nationalists against the Japanese, but Mao's forces largely operated independently.

Over the next four years Mao's literary production increased, a combination of personal-professional reflection and an account of the campaign against Japan. His philosophy sharpened into the "Sinification" of Marxism, focusing on Chinese applications while rejecting many Soviet aspects as "foreign dogmatism."[46]

Amid the long Japanese war, in 1943 Mao rose to Chairman of the Politburo, a position he held until his death in 1976.

Until the final defeat of Japan in August 1945, China remained a country divided three ways: Chiang's Nationalists controlled the southwest, Mao's Communists controlled the northwest, and Japan held Manchuria and much of the coastline.

Under whatever regimes, China suffered appalling losses. Although the precise numbers remain unknown, the civilian deaths are reliably estimated at 12 million between 1937 and 1945. In those eight years (3,000 days) the average mortality was 4,000 per day – the equivalent of more than an infantry regiment.[47]

During August the warring factions engaged in nearly nonstop combat during half a dozen campaigns and at least five independent battles in seven provinces, notably Jiangsu and Shandong on the coast. Several of the clashes overlapped.

From August into September the Nationalists fared poorly. Numbers vary, of course, but Chiang's forces likely lost from 17,000 to 20,000 men, the large majority captured. Some of them became cannon fodder for use against the Americans in the subsequent Korean War. The Chinese used whole captured and side-switching ex-Nationalist divisions and corps ("armies") in Korea, especially to lead head-on assaults. However, two thirds of repatriated Chinese POWs went to Taiwan.

Numbers vary with sources, but in 1945 the Communists probably drew upon some 3 million men, heavily militia units. The Reds controlled about a quarter of China's land area with one third of the people. The Red Army's role in defeating Japan certainly was less than Chiang's Nationalists, but Mao's forces also made contributions. No less a Cold War warrior than General Curtis LeMay expressed gratitude to Mao for succoring downed American fliers in northern China.

Even before Tokyo's capitulation, Chiang proposed meeting with Mao to discuss postwar arrangements and essential reconstruction. Near month's end Mao and veteran U.S. diplomat Patrick Hurley arrived in Chungking, where several weeks of negotiations produced "an agreement in principle" for reuniting China. However, a combination of sensitive military and political subjects were still being drafted when full-scale combat broke out.

Lacking manpower to enforce his will throughout so large an area as Henan Province in the east, Chiang formed an alliance of convenience by directing the remaining Japanese forces and their puppet regime's allies to oppose the Reds until he delivered reinforcements. Because many of the Chinese units owed allegiance to regional warlords, command and control proved nearly impossible.

Computing the odds, Chiang seemed to recognize that he might have things his way regardless of the outcome. If he absorbed nominally Nationalist warlords and those formerly allied with Japan, he stood to reduce the long-term problem of warlords throughout China. Conversely, if the Communists defeated the warlords, the Nationalists also gained an advantage.

Whether Chiang realized the downside of a victory, he had to cope with years of local resentment for abandoning large areas to Japanese brutality and warlord opportunism. Thus, he was caught in a dilemma that had been years in the making, considering that his withdrawals had been militarily justified.

In any case, the Nationalists suffered one defeat after another. In a two-day battle at Yin Village (Yinji) on August 26 and 27, the Communist 5th Division launched a double envelopment from east and west. Deploying methodically in darkness, the Reds decimated the outermost Nationalist regiment and, having pierced the perimeter, defeated the second regiment at an outlying village.

With little option, many survivors escaped in daylight, although about 800 were captured with substantial heavy weapons.

The Huaiyin-Huai'an campaign of August and September cost Chiang valuable ground despite outnumbering the Reds approximately 14,000 to 11,000. The location was worth the effort: central Jiangsu Province where the Yangtze meets the East China Sea.

Shandong on the Yellow Sea had been scoured during the Japanese occupation, suffering under the "Three Alls" policy from 1941: kill all, burn all, loot all. Other provinces were doubly damned, as the Nationalists adopted a scorched earth policy to deny support to the Japanese, including poisoning wells.[48]

Recognizing the importance of Huaiyin as a city and river port, the Communists besieged the defenders between August 26 and September 7. Following that success, the New Fourth Army set its sights on Huai'an beginning on September 13. After defeating a Nationalist attempt to break out, the Communists sent massive forces against the city with artillery support, breaking through the defenses in about two hours. The bitter, hard-fought mop-up operation occupied several more hours before General Huang Kecheng's red banner was raised throughout the city.

Chiang's major garrisons sustained disastrous losses including well over 12,000 Nationalist troops captured against a Communist claim of merely 200 casualties. Among perhaps 1,000 Nationalist dead were the generals commanding each garrison – testament to the tenacity of the often-disparaged Nationalist forces.

From August 21 to 23, amid the accelerated internecine feuding in China, the first major Japanese surrender ceremony in the country was held at Zhijiang Airport in Hunan Province. A major transport hub with the Allies' second-largest airport in the Far East, Zhijiang also was a major base of the U.S. Fourteenth Air Force, though the original commander, Claire Chennault, had been replaced.

In surrendering to the Kuomintang, the Japanese delegation was led by 61-year-old General Yosuji Okamura who had spent most of his 41-year career on the Asian mainland and had commanded the China Expeditionary Army since November. But Zhijiang was only a first step. In Nanking on September 9, Okamura's signature assured the surrender of Tokyo's forces in China, Formosa, and northern Indochina, but not Manchuria. Simultaneously Japan's surrender in Korea was formalized, effective south of the 38th Parallel.

Tokyo's capitulation throughout Asia involved a huge task of disarmament and repatriation. There were 1.6 million Japanese military in China among a total 3.5 million outside the Home Islands. Another 2.9 million civilians were numbered in those areas, some attached to army or navy organizations.[49]

These numbers give some inkling of the irrevocable effects of Japan's Manchurian invasion and continued occupation during the war. It had caused untold hardship and depravation while changing the nation's political landscape.

August 1945 did not herald peace for the people of China. The end of World War II in China and the defeat of the Japanese only meant the beginning of full-blown civil war.

6

Tokyo Bay

August 31–September 2

Preparation for Japan's surrender and occupation proceeded apace as Allied warships entered Sagami Wan, Tokyo's outer bay, on August 27. During the night, *Bon Homme Richard*'s (CVN-31) air group logged the last combat air patrols. The next evening, with increased confidence, Third Fleet ran illuminated.

On the 28th two of Vice Admiral John H. Towers' Task Force 38 staff rode a *Shangri-La* Avenger to Atsugi to initiate discussions with Japanese authorities. Towers had relieved John S. McCain a few days prior.

On the 31st U.S. Marines landed at Tateyama Naval Base to scout the landing area ahead of Army troops. The base commander assured Marine Brigadier General William Clement that "all hot heads and others considered unable to abide by the Emperor's decree had been removed." Meanwhile, British Royal Marines secured other facilities in the channel.[1]

The next day two civilian internment camps were found in Tokyo. Survivors were quickly evacuated to a hospital ship.

Although *Missouri* got the ink, *South Dakota* did much of the work. "SoDak" had been commissioned in March 1942, barely 90 days after Pearl Harbor, and saw wide service in the Atlantic and Pacific with combat from Guadalcanal to Okinawa. As lead ship of her class with three sisters, *South Dakota* had two five-inch gun turrets removed to provide more staff space. Therefore, a parade of senior admirals strode her deck in Tokyo Bay. Strangely, both battlewagons were commanded by former submariners.

A native Texan, Stuart S. Murray graduated from the Naval Academy in 1919 and began World War II with a submarine division in the Philippines. Subsequently he served on SubPac staff in Australia before returning to Annapolis as commandant of midshipmen. Captain "Sunshine" Murray became "Mighty Mo's" second skipper in May 1945.

Hailing from Minnesota, "Swede" Momsen was one of the most accomplished naval officers of his generation. Graduating near the top of his Annapolis class in 1920, he was popular with contemporaries, as noted in the yearbook: "Meet The Swede and you'll like him; make a liberty with him and you'll swear by him for he's always the same likable gentleman from St. Paul."[2]

Momsen qualified in submarines in 1922 and devoted years to devising methods of escape and rescue of crews from sunken subs. He was best known for the individual rebreather that bore his name, although he collaborated with a chief petty officer and a civilian. He was decorated for testing the Momsen Lung from as deep as 200 feet, and subsequently he worked on a successful diving bell capable of bringing eight men to the surface at a time.

In 1939 Momsen gained public acclaim for his role in the recovery of sailors from the sunken submarine *Squalus* in 240 feet off the New Hampshire coast. All 33 men who survived the sinking were rescued.

During the war Momsen had commanded two submarine squadrons, developing wolf pack tactics against Japanese convoys. He assumed command of *South Dakota* in December 1944, remaining through August 1945.

In preparation for the surrender ceremony, Sunshine Murray's sailors broke out holystone bristles, paint remover, and polish. "Mighty Mo's" warpaint gave way to scraping gray from the teak decks and fittings while brass work was rubbed to peacetime glory.

ABOARD "MIGHTY MO"

The formal surrender came two weeks after the emperor's announcement. On September 2 *Missouri* was one of more than 260 Allied warships anchored in Tokyo Bay. They included 15 British, ten Australian, and one New Zealand vessel. In a show of Allied unity, when *Missouri* had entered Sagami Wan she was closely attended by HMS *Duke of York*, Admiral Fraser's flagship in Task Force 37.

Halsey allowed just one U.S. fast carrier in Tokyo Bay, the light carrier *Cowpens* (CVL-25) which his daughter Margaret had christened in 1943.

Preparations for the surrender were detailed with a tightly drawn timeline in *Missouri*'s plan of the day. The site was the "veranda deck" on the starboard side just aft of the huge number two turret. The location allowed access via the captain's in-port cabin, an advantage given the large number of dignitaries.

Contrary to legend, "Mighty Mo" did not hoist the American flag that had flown over the White House (or the Capitol building) on December 7, 1941. In a 1974 interview retired Admiral Murray discounted reports that *Missouri* flew the colors that had wafted the Sunday breeze nearly four years before. He bluntly stated, "They were hard up for baloney, because it was nothing like that. It was just a plain, ordinary GI-issue flag and a Union Jack (at the bow). We turned them into the Naval Academy Museum when we got back to the East Coast in October."[3] But one noteworthy flag was the 31-star banner that Commodore Matthew Perry had flown during the opening of Japan to more Western powers in 1853–54. The historic flag, in a glass case, was flown for delivery to *Missouri* with an officer courier from the Naval Academy.

General MacArthur and Admiral Nimitz arrived with their staffs at 8:00 a.m., proceeding to Halsey's spacious cabin. There the principals got their first look at the surrender documents, carried by an Army colonel from Washington, D.C.

Meanwhile, reporters and photographers arrived literally by the boatload, in total two destroyers' worth. Murray, being realistic about the journalism profession, assigned "escorts" to keep the newsmen in their designated spaces, lest they interrupt the ceremony. Apparently only one got out of hand – a Russian correspondent who broke ranks to climb the rungs of the number two turret for a better view. He was seized by two Marines with Colt pistols on their hips who fetched him down by the legs and thereafter kept close attendance. A Soviet general, witnessing the antics, exercised his limited English, exclaiming to Nimitz, "Wonderful, wonderful!"[4]

A Royal Navy contribution to the event came courtesy of Admiral Sir Bruce Fraser who delivered "a beautiful mahogany table and its two nice chairs." But reality intervened. The U.S. signatories immediately recognized that the ornate table was too small for the 40- by 20-inch documents, forcing a quick change of plans. Murray said, "I called the four nearest sailors and we headed for the wardroom, which was the deck below my cabin." But the wardroom table was bolted to the deck so the search party descended to the next level where mess cooks were still cleaning after breakfast. Despite the seniority of the visitor, some dedicated sailors objected. "They didn't want their table taken away from them. They didn't know what it was all about, but they did know that was their mess table and they were supposed to clean up and take care of it. We waved them down and said, 'You'll get it,' and took it on up."

Headed topside, Murray scooped up a coffee-stained green cover off a wardroom table and finished the arrangement moments before the designated time.[5]

Shortly after 9:00 a.m. Douglas MacArthur as Supreme Allied Commander began the brief ceremony with 11 representatives from Japan and nine Allied nations. The American forces were represented by 35 Army generals, 28 admirals and seven commodores, plus three Marine Corps generals. Crowding available deck space were 44 flag officers from Britain, Australia, New Zealand, Canada, China, the Soviet Union, the Netherlands, and France.

Chief among the American delegation was Chester Nimitz, representing the United States. Among others was Lieutenant General James H. Doolittle, who had moved the headquarters of his fabled Eighth Air Force from Britain to Okinawa. It was his second trip to Tokyo, the first being three and a half years earlier during his famous carrier-launched mission in B-25s. He reflected, "It was hard to believe that the long months of killing and dying were over." Standing nearby, representing a bombing bookends arrangement, was Major General Curtis LeMay, whose command had ended the air campaign against Japan.[6]

The Signatories

Japan's representatives were delivered to *Missouri* by a destroyer. Reaching the top of the accommodation ladder, they noted the dozen "sideboys" lined up, six each left and right, requiring visitors to pass between the obviously healthy young Americans, reportedly all six feet tall or more.

Once on deck, the Japanese delegation was directed to stand in a group facing the draped table where Douglas MacArthur waited in starched khaki elegance. The battleship's two forward turrets were trained 20 degrees to starboard, ostensibly to permit more deck space, although some observers noted that the six huge barrels – with muzzles 16 inches in diameter – literally placed the arrivals "under the gun."

As if that weren't enough, other symbolism was apparent. The Japanese could not have missed the battlewagon's scoreboard with 11 rising-sun flags signifying enemy aircraft shot down. Less obvious emblems showed four shore bombardments.

Tokyo's delegation was led by 58-year-old Foreign Minister Mamoru Shigemitsu, signing on behalf of the emperor. A former consul to Seattle and ambassador to Moscow, he moved slowly, having lost a leg in a 1932 assassination attempt.

MacArthur tactfully "invited" the Japanese to sign the surrender document "at the places indicated." Shigemitsu was first, on behalf of the emperor and the government, followed by General Yoshijiro Umezu, Army Chief of Staff representing the military.

Though Shigemitsu had incurred Imperial Army resentment for initially opposing war with America, he seemed determined to prolong the inevitable. He removed his top hat and gloves, fumbled with his cane, and appeared to search for a pen. Finally, an aide produced one while Admiral "Bull" Halsey silently fumed in the khaki ranks. Afterward he admitted to MacArthur, "I wanted to slap him and tell him, 'Sign damn you, sign!'"[7]

Umezu was a 42-year veteran of the Imperial Army, of long service in China and a general for 15 years. He became chief of staff in July 1944, a hardliner opposing surrender by the supreme war council. However, he could not ignore Hirohito's order to sign the surrender document. Later found guilty on five counts for war crimes, he died in prison in 1948.

Many of the signatories were veterans of World War I, excepting France, the Netherlands, China, and Russia. Fleet Admiral Nimitz, signing for the United States, had no combat experience, but General of the Army MacArthur was highly decorated for his World War I service in France.

The Allied signatories inked their signatures in order after the United States:

China

General Xu Yong Chang represented the Republic of China, certainly holding the record among signatories for war with Japan. Graduating from the Beijing Military Institute in 1909, during the long war he held two army commands, reporting to former warlords in each case, and subsequently was raised to a province chairman. Later he became president of his alma mater and Chiang Kai-shek's minister of defense. At 59 he could anticipate a postwar career, but he might not have expected the Communist victory in four years' time.

Great Britain

At 57 Sir Bruce Fraser was a full admiral commanding the British Pacific Fleet from Sydney. As previously noted, in that capacity he oversaw Task Force 37 or 57, depending upon whether it was subordinate to the U.S. Third Fleet or Fifth Fleet. A veteran of World War I, he had been captured by Bolshevik forces while a volunteer British representative with the White Russian Caspian Flotilla in 1920. However, clearly not one to bear a grudge, he became noted for his effectiveness at working with his allies, be they Soviet or American. As commander of the Home Fleet he had sunk the famous German battleship *Scharnhorst*, having turned down the position of First Sea Lord for the opportunity to do so.

Soviet Union

Lieutenant General Kuzma Derevyanko, a 51-year-old Ukrainian, was chief of staff of the 35th Army on the First Far East Front. His escort was a 19-year-old Nebraska sailor, Seaman Robert McGranaghan, who had dropped out of high school to join the Navy. He drew the VJ assignment when the Russian boarded the destroyer *Nicholas* (DD-449) for delivery to *Missouri*. McGranaghan later mused at his selection, "I didn't speak Russian and he apparently didn't speak English." The youngster stepped aside when other Russians met the general, but retained his rare perspective to a world-changing event, standing 40 feet from General of the Armies Douglas MacArthur.[8]

Australia

Australia's General Thomas A. Blamey was a lifelong soldier. He enlisted as a "ranker" in 1906, almost immediately was commissioned, became a noted marksman, and was decorated for heroism at Gallipoli and on the Western Front. He advanced quickly in wartime, finishing as a brigadier in 1918.

Between the wars Blamey helped establish the Royal Australian Air Force, left in the 1920s for police work, and led the militia-staffed Third Division. He resigned from the Victoria police under accusations of wrongdoing but later earned admiration for his work on the manpower committee that doubled the militia ranks.

Blamey's World War II service included Greece and the Middle East before assuming command of Allied ground forces in the Southwest Pacific Theater. His relationship with the supreme commander sometimes was contentious, as were his relationships with subordinates, especially in the New Guinea and Solomons campaigns. At 61 he was older than all the Allied signatories except MacArthur.

Canada

Canada's representative was by far the most junior – the only signatory not a flag officer – but arguably the most combat experienced. Colonel Lawrence Moore Cosgrave had just turned 55, owning a stellar record as a World War I artilleryman. He had lost the use of one eye, but with two Distinguished Service Orders (second only to the Victoria Cross) he was among fewer than 800 "DSO and Bar" heroes from nearly 10,000 recipients of the DSO during World War I.

Between the wars Cosgrave was trade commissioner in Britain and Australia, returning to uniform as Canadian military attaché to Canberra.

According to Cosgrave's grandson, he and Shigemitsu tacitly acknowledged one another during the signing, as they were previously acquainted from their diplomatic posts at Shanghai in the 1930s.

Perhaps owing to his poor vision, or because of a momentary distraction, Cosgrave signed the Japanese copy of the surrender document on the line designated for France. The error was corrected by MacArthur's chief of staff, Lieutenant General Richard Sutherland, who manually amended the lines, adding one for New Zealand at the bottom.[9]

France

At 42, General Philippe LeClerc was the youngest signatory of the document ending World War II. To give his full name, Philippe François Marie Leclerc de Haueclocque was perhaps France's most successful field commander of the war. Scion of an aristocratic family, he was commissioned out of Saint-Cyr Military Academy in 1924, serving on occupation duty in Germany and then in Morocco.

Following France's surrender in 1940, Leclerc removed himself to Britain, joining Charles DeGaulle's Free French movement. He commanded troops in Africa, most notably Libya, then returned to France leading the 2nd Armored Division in the joyous liberation of Paris in August 1944. Twelve months later he was in Tokyo Bay. Immediately after VE Day he was given command of the Far East Expeditionary Corps based in Indochina.

The Netherlands
Lieutenant Admiral Conrad E.L. Helfrich signed for the Netherlands. Rising to four-star rank, he had missed action in World War I due to Holland's neutrality but saw extensive service in the Pacific. As overall commander in the Netherlands East Indies from 1939, he had imbued his small force with an aggressive spirit, and by contemporary reckoning, in the early phase of the war his submarines sank more Japanese ships than both the U.S. and Royal Navies.

Helfrich was given command of the American-British-Dutch-Australian (ABDA) navies in the region, and his scratch-built ABDA force suffered heavy losses in the February 1942 battle of the Java Sea. The command was disestablished shortly thereafter and Helfrich moved to Ceylon, planning postwar administration of the East Indies. His selection to sign the surrender aboard *Missouri* capped his 38 years of service at age 58.

New Zealand
New Zealand's Air Vice Marshal Leonard M. Isitt, aged 54, had an impressively varied World War I record. Son of a minister, Isitt suffered a head wound in 1916, the year his brother was killed in action. He was discharged from the New Zealand Army and joined the Royal Flying Corps, serving two tours in France through 1918 with the new Royal Air Force.

Upon return home in 1919, Captain Isitt found a deplorable situation with only four military aircraft in-country. When the expanded air arm was eventually separated from the army in 1937, he became a wing commander responsible for personnel.

Through most of World War II Isitt served in senior staff positions including a seat on the Empire Air Training Scheme, and attended Allied conferences in Washington, London, and Ottawa.

"These Proceedings Are Closed"
MacArthur led the Allied signatories, using six pens. He gave two of them to long-term senior POWs: his Philippines successor

Lieutenant General Jonathan Wainwright, and British Lieutenant General Arthur Percival, commander at Singapore. Both appeared incongruously thin, almost emaciated, in fresh new uniforms. Nimitz signed on behalf of the U.S., followed by representatives of China, Britain, the Soviet Union, Australia, Canada, France, and the Netherlands.

The final signature, by New Zealand's Air Vice Marshal Leonard Isitt, was inked at 9:22. Thus ended nearly four years' expenditure of blood and treasure in barely 20 minutes.

While the last signatories were inking their names, MacArthur whispered to Halsey, "Start them now!" Third Fleet radioed the word to aircraft formations orbiting nearby, beginning a huge flyover with some 460 B-29s and 350 carrier planes – an aerial parade of nearly 2,200 powerful engines thrumming the atmosphere over Tokyo Bay.

MacArthur solemnly concluded, "These proceedings are closed." Then "Operation Airshow" kicked off, requiring precise timing. In order to make the appointed hour of the Tokyo Bay flyover, LeMay's bombers had begun lifting off their Marianas fields at 2:00 a.m.

Yet despite exquisite planning and timing, not even Douglas MacArthur could control the main variable: the weather. On the day before, Navy meteorologists had predicted conditions over Tokyo would be "average to undesirable." Original plans for B-29s called for an aerial parade stacked between 8,000 and 14,000 feet but that would have put the Superforts in "the soup." Upon arrival after a six-and-a-half-hour flight, aircrews began forming up, and descended to about 3,000 feet. Once assembled the aerial armada eased into a huge clockwise circle, prepared to make two or even three orbits of Tokyo Bay depending on fuel status.

Meanwhile, 349 of Halsey's tailhookers dealt with the same conditions and averaged 1,500 feet over the bay.[10]

It is unlikely that many airmen had time to count the ships anchored within Tokyo Bay's 579 square miles. But those who stole a glance at the panorama might have seen ten battleships (two British), one light and three escort carriers (two British), 14 cruisers (four British Commonwealth), 61 destroyers (11

Commonwealth) and destroyer escorts, 12 submarines, 31 mine craft, and a full menu of transports, cargo ships, auxiliaries including hospital ships, various landing craft, and tugs.

Crammed beneath low-lying clouds, the densely packed formations narrowly averted multiple collisions. Lieutenant Malcolm Cagle, whose *Yorktown* Hellcat squadron had fought the biggest combat of August 15, considered it "a thrill and an honor to participate in such an historic occasion" but described "a full throttle, off-throttle formation with no real order or organization." Years later he confessed that he was seldom so scared as in the victory flyover.[11]

A *Ticonderoga* pilot, Lieutenant (jg) George Wood, had similar sentiments. "I definitely remember the flight. It was hairy! Low ceiling, intermittent rain and planes of various speeds in huge formations all over the sky from ocean to overcast. Wow!"[12]

The British Pacific Fleet was included in the airshow lineup with HMS *Indefatigable* scheduled to provide 24 aircraft. But her contribution was scrubbed when only one of her two crash barriers remained operational. That morning a Hellcat pilot from USS *Shangri-La*, anxious to get aboard, ignored a waveoff – the cardinal sin in carrier aviation – missed all the arresting wires, and demolished the first barrier, writing off three Seafires in the process.

Deck hands reported that when the errant pilot unwrapped himself from the mangled aluminum and saw the result of his decision he exclaimed, "Gee, I'm sorry!" Reputedly he had ditched before and didn't want to repeat the experience.[13]

Among the 18 Royal Navy ships present was HMS *Whelp*, a 1,700-ton destroyer. The executive officer – the first lieutenant in British terms – was tall, lanky Lieutenant Philip Mountbatten, the 24-year-old son of Prince Andrew of Greece and Princess Alice of Battenberg, by whom he was nephew to Admiral Louis Mountbatten of Southeast Asia Command. By that summer Philip had engaged in a six-year correspondence with Princess Elizabeth of Britain, whom he would marry in 1947. On August 27 *Whelp* had the honor of leading the Allied ships into Sagami Bay, preceding the battleships USS *Missouri*, *Iowa*, *New Jersey*, and HMS *Duke of York*.

Shangri-La launched 126 sorties on September 2, including 46 on CAP, and 68 "other." But more significantly, three of the ship's missing fliers returned to the fold. Lieutenant (jg) Howard Dixon (VF-85, June 3), Ensign J.H. Chapman (VBF-85, August 13), and Lieutenant (jg) John Dunn (VBF-85, August 15) were liberated in Atsugi. That afternoon they were flown back to the "*Shang*" for an exuberant reunion in VBF-85's ready room.[14]

Notable among those absent was Major General Claire L. Chennault, recent commander of the CBI's Fourteenth Air Force. Chennault had made a career of bucking the system, leaving the Air Corps in 1937 as an unpromotable 44-year-old captain. Hired by Chiang to improve the Chinese Air Force, Chennault had fought Japan far longer than any U.S. contemporaries and had risen to prominence with his American Volunteer Group. In 1941–42 the Flying Tigers provided an all-too-rare boost to the nation's morale when Tokyo's rising tide seemed unstoppable.

Despite accomplishing much over the past three years, the Fourteenth remained a relatively low priority in the global scheme of things. Chennault, with his creased, craggy face and Louisiana accent, did not suit the well-heeled Washington set, who arranged to prevent his attendance aboard the *Missouri*. On August 1, Chennault had been succeeded by Major General Charles B. Stone, III, a long-service support and administrative officer.

As Chennault briefly recalled in his memoir, he learned of the surrender while transiting the Nile Delta en route to Britain before the transatlantic leg home.

However, a fellow southerner represented his former boss and mentor. Colonel Robert L. Scott had been Chennault's choice to stand up the 23rd Fighter Group in July 1942 immediately after the AVG was disbanded. Then 34, though a West Pointer, Scott was considered by some as too old for combat, but he possessed an enormous amount of experience – nearly 5,000 flight hours, unheard of for a fighter pilot. As he later confessed, he told numerous lies ("and not little white ones") to get to the war.

A loquacious Georgian, Scott turned his tenure with the 23rd into a 1943 best seller, *God is My Copilot*, which became a movie. By the time he had finished his public relations duties, he had incurred a red-faced session with the Air Forces chief, General Henry Arnold, who berated the literary lion for offering to strafe mine union boss John L. Lewis who repeatedly broke a wartime no-strike pledge. Scott reflected, "I think that's when General Arnold began looking for a way to send me back to combat where I could get killed."[15]

Finally, in 1945, Scott arranged with a Navy colleague to send thousands of aerial rockets to China, returning to Chennault with a tactical demonstration team. There was a growing need for aerial rockets: carrier squadrons expended 22,226 on targets in July and August, nearly 400 per day.[16]

With the surrender imminent, Scott and his 1942 wingman, now Major Dallas Clinger, flew to Okinawa to provide a CBI presence for the surrender, and to honor Claire Chennault.

On August 28 Scott wrote his hometown Boy Scout troop, "I guess I've seen an interesting time in this war, but good Americans are buried on lots of strange islands and places. I saw 9,000 white crosses yesterday marking graves on Okinawa – we are the lucky ones – they paid for this entry into an enemy land."[17]

Scott flew 1,000 miles overnight from Kadena to position himself in Atsugi for the morning of September 2. Circling on the periphery of the huge Army-Navy aerial armada, he gunned his Mustang's engine three times, saluting the airman who was not there. "Then I slipped a corner of a Confederate battle flag out the crack between the bubble canopy and the windshield and watched it flutter and erode away in the 300mph slipstream. I thought the spent threads that sifted down upon the surrender scene were the best tribute I could think of for the Old Man."[18]

Meanwhile, several Superfortress crews broke formation (and regulations) in some low-level sight-seeing. Upon return to the Marianas the miscreants learned that MacArthur's hard-nosed chief of staff expressed the supreme commander's displeasure. Nobody paid any attention.

Celebrating in his own way, Major General LeMay – a captain a mere five years earlier – had flown a C-54 transport to Yokohama to attend the surrender, then fired up the Skymaster for a low-level look at some of the cities XXI

Bomber Command had seared. It was as close to a victory lap as Curtis LeMay ever took.

That same day another ceremony was held 2,300 miles away. A Vietnamese Communist-born Nguyễn Sinh Cung presided over a gathering at Ba Đình Square in Hanoi, named for the anti-French uprising of 1886. Over the previous five years he had been more commonly known as Ho Chi Minh, having lived abroad from 1911 to 1941, including China, Russia, Europe, and reportedly a year in America. Before a throng of thousands, as first president of what became North Vietnam, Ho read the Proclamation of Independence of the Democratic Republic of Vietnam, leading to nine years of conflict with France's postwar governments. Ironically, in view of later events, the proclamation began, "All men are created equal; they are endowed by their Creator with certain inalienable rights; among these are life, liberty, and the pursuit of happiness."[19]

SEPTEMBER 3 AND BEYOND

After the excitement of Japan's formal surrender on the 2nd, the next day edged into something resembling peace. At 5:30 p.m. Third Fleet crews learned that there would be no more "gun watches" except when at sea. All weapons were secured while in port, and ammunition removed from ready access. Some old hands remarked that they had never seen five-inch mounts locked in place.

In the U.S.A., people found an enormous variety of ways to celebrate. On VJ Day Lieutenant Tilman E. Pool was a 21-year-old Hellcat ace en route to his next assignment. He recalled:

On June 6, 1945, the *Hornet* had a severely damaged bow in a typhoon and was sent back to Alameda with the air group on board. Air Group 17 was broken up, pilots given new assignments and thirty days rehab leave before reporting to new stations. I was driving from Houston to my new duty station in Pensacola and received news of VJ while in Lake Charles, Louisiana. That was before the I-10, and the Cajuns in every small town were celebrating big time. They blocked the streets, tried to get us out of the car and celebrate with them. Booze flowed freely and they opened all gas stations (remember gasoline was strictly rationed at that time).

Finally made it to Pensacola where the Navy found it had too many pilots, too many Navy bases, and started a great downsizing. Much confusion, but much relief we would not have to invade Japan.[20]

Beverly Jean Barrett was a princess on the Pendleton, Oregon, Round-Up court in September 1945. A 25-year-old green-eyed brunette, she rode a large sorrel horse called Jimmy who enjoyed ice cream cones and the occasional hamburger. During the week-long rodeo, she and her friends became acquainted with some naval aviators who attended the event with all the innovative enthusiasm of Frederick Wakeman's wartime novel, *Shore Leave*.

Beverly explained, "The '45 event was the first full-scale rodeo since the war, and a lot of boys were home from the service. It was and is the major event in Umatilla County every year, and my family had been involved since it began in 1910."

On the first day – Wednesday, September 12 – the queen and court rode into the arena, waving to the crowd in the grandstand, and went to the box seats. Beverly recalled, "We were just sitting down when I heard a sudden, loud noise. I turned around just in time to see a fighter plane swooping down into the arena and pulling up on the other side. There were American flags all around the top row, so I don't know how the pilot missed any of the poles. He was *very* low."

That was just the beginning. The miscreant aviator was about 50 air miles off track from NAS Pasco, Washington, across the Columbia River. Pasco was home to part of a light carrier air group and Composite Squadron 82, which had completed a combat tour aboard the escort carrier *Anzio* (CVE-57) in March. Lieutenant Commander F.A. Green's unit, with FM-2 Wildcats and TBM-3 Avengers, was recycling for another deployment when the war ended. But flying continued with instrument practice and rocket firing.

Aside from end-of-war exuberance, the Navy fliers probably relished the opportunity to upstage their khaki counterparts. Pendleton Army Airfield was home of the B-25 group that provided the Doolittle Raiders in 1942 and continued as an operational training and maintenance facility. Shortly after Pearl Harbor, then-Major Curtis LeMay briefly flew from Pendleton.

The blue intruders made themselves known to Umatilla County. Wildcats buzzed tractors in fields and cars on highways – allegedly running an Oregon State trooper off the road. Local legend related the tale of an Avenger that executed a mock torpedo attack against fishing boats on the reservoir south of town – with bomb bay doors open. Finally enough was enough. Some high-decibel phone calls were made, and Pasco grounded the errant tailhookers.

Nobody complained – the Navy men were stranded for the duration of Round-Up. Beverly Barrett explained, "They were definitely ready to party. They sort of attached themselves to us, though the court had escorts as well as a chaperone. I had already met Jack Tillman when he was a flight cadet. I had seen him in his dress uniform, leaning against a light pole, and I remember thinking, 'Hmmm... how did I miss *that*?'"

Tillman had already encountered the Pasco fliers downtown, where they carried a 20mm ammunition case filled with ice and beer. Beverly continued:

> One evening the Round-Up court was at the country club for an event. The fliers from Pasco were there in dress blues, because some of them had met other local girls. It got to be late and we decided to go to dinner, and I got up to leave. Then somebody asked, "Where's Mack?"
>
> Mack was a short, stocky young man. I never did know the full names of any of the fliers because they came and went

so much. But we all knew Mack. Finally somebody found him out behind the club house, asleep under a tree with the club's big Saint Bernard. Mack had drunk about 12 Alexander cocktails and apparently crawled through the sprinklers on the green, because his blues were ruined from water and grass stains.

I've often wondered if Mack or any of those other fliers remember that night. But I certainly do![21]

While cowboys and cajuns celebrated in the U.S., Allied warships made port at their four-year destination: Japan itself.

Among the British ships visiting Nagasaki was the year-old light cruiser *Swiftsure*. The sailors went ashore, largely unknowing about the radiation potential, and interacted with the citizens. A schoolboy recalled:

The word came, they were on their way. What would they be like? They came down the road toward us in jeeps and trucks. We had images of demons with horns sprouting from their heads. We peeked out, trying to get a glimpse of them. We were disappointed, no horns at all. Friends who had bumped into them on the street brought back chocolates. "They're good people," they said. But it couldn't be true. "They must be liars," we said.[22]

Some local girls were more willing to make friends and crowded around white-clad sailors from the cruiser, giggling among themselves behind cupped hands.[23]

An American sailor reported a similar reception in Yokosuka. Allowed off the destroyer *Franks* (DD-554), Quartermaster Michael Bak and some friends – prohibited from going armed – walked the long pier to the naval base. They were met by "a bunch of young Japanese kids, boys and girls, looking for handouts... They couldn't talk in English, just looking for something that we could give them. A short distance behind them... were the parents."

Bak and his burly shipmate Eugene Reardon, a professional wrestler, hitched a ride with some soldiers engaged in black market free enterprise in Tokyo. The GIs provided information on how to catch a return train and, with time to spare, the sailors took in the sights of the capital, such as they were. They met "an elderly Japanese gentleman" who spoke decent English and passed the time of day with him. When they parted "He seemed to want to talk about how happy he was that nobody was going to get hurt anymore. The biggest thing I remember was the fact that it was just desolate and bombed out. We saw nothing but ruins, and how people lived in that ruin is beyond me. Why didn't they end the war a lot sooner?"[24]

Despite the peace, career paths continued. One example was USS *Hancock*, which received a new skipper within days of the surrender. Captain Daniel V. Gallery was a rarity – a plainspoken officer who advanced despite his independence. A year previously he had brought off one of the major coups of the war. Commanding an antisubmarine task group in the Atlantic, in June 1944 he and his team had captured the German *U-505* and towed it to port.

"Cap'n Dan" narrowly missed his opportunity to fight Japan but retained his trademark confidence in his men. He wrote, "When I took command I addressed the crew at the evening movie and told them that since the war was now over, there was no further need for secrecy, and I would cut them in on all operation schedules as soon as I found out about them."

The next day, "I had a problem dumped in my lap." The Navy Department sent an "AllNav" listing the order in which ships would rotate home, and *Hancock* was near the bottom. She had been in the Pacific more than a year, from Formosa to the Philippines to Okinawa and Japan itself. She had lost 201 shipmates and taken a kamikaze. But many other ships had longer service. Gallery and his executive officer considered temporarily keeping the news from all but senior chief petty officers to head off impulsive sailors. Finally Gallery decided to keep his pledge to the crew.

When the CO delivered the blow that night, "for a few moments a flake of dandruff falling anywhere on the hangar deck would have made an audible thud. After a pregnant pause, scattered applause started and swelled into a nice hand. It wasn't any ovation and there were no cheers or whistling. But that crew knew now they could depend on the skipper to tell them the bad news as well as the good."

"*Hanna*" eventually returned to the West Coast in late October.[25]

HOME IS THE SAILOR... AND SOLDIER... AND MARINE

Japan's surrender marked a slash on the world's calendar, although it did not, as events have shown, neatly delineate war on one side and peace on the other. However, in the summer and fall of 1945 the huge majority of Allied servicemen wanted just one thing: out.

An anonymous GI penned a bit of doggerel that made its way around the world. "Those who want to be a hero, they number almost zero. Those who want to be civilians, geez! They number in the millions."

U.S. public opinion shared that sentiment, letting Congress know in crystal-clear terms. Conscription dropped to 50,000 men per month, below the level for planned replacements. Washington's goal was to bring troops home from Europe by February 1946 and from the Pacific two months later.[26]

However, for many people – perhaps most – at noon yesterday was not fast enough. But few realized the enormous logistics and complexities of "bringing the boys home." As one analyst noted, "It had taken four years to get the estimated 7.6 million troops overseas and it was going to take more than four months to get them home. Beset by homesickness and boredom, the GIs were prey to manipulations by politicians in Washington and agitators within their ranks."

According to a study of the subject, "During the five months from VJ Day into January 1946, thousands took to the streets at bases around the world, protesting delays. Soldiers carried placards mocking their commanders and defied orders in a way that would have been unthinkable six months earlier... the action of many soldiers easily qualified for the charge of mutiny."[27]

However, to its credit the U.S. Government probably did as much as humanly possible. From May to October more than 3 million troops returned, accelerating to an astonishing 1 million in December.

Magic Carpet Rides

With broad vision, two years before VJ Day, Army Chief of Staff George C. Marshall anticipated the need to return millions of servicemen to their homes. He raised the subject as early as 1943, and after D-Day in June 1944 some planners thought that VE Day might dawn by year's end. But whenever the timeframe, some essential factors forced themselves upon joint staffs.

First was the need for large-capacity staging areas and processing facilities, not only in Europe but in the much broader expanse of the Pacific. Internal concerns within the U.S. included receiving ports and railroads capable of absorbing huge numbers of personnel and delivering them to "separation centers" in every state.

Paramount was shipping, as the vast majority of returnees had to travel by sea. The U.S. Navy was only marginally available at the time, with millions of tons of vessels committed to the two-phase invasion of Japan in November 1945 and March 1946. Therefore, heavy reliance was placed upon Army and Merchant Marine ships with some augmentation by Coast Guard vessels.

Tasked with finding enough hulls to meet the demand, the War Shipping Administration (WSA) came through. Shortly after VE Day it identified nearly 550 vessels capable of carrying useful numbers of personnel.

In the actual event, absent Operation *Downfall*, the Navy suddenly afforded a huge bonus for Operation *Magic Carpet*. Ten aircraft carriers, six battleships, and 26 cruisers were hastily modified to accept cheek-by-jowl accommodations for troops who willingly endured long days and nights at sea, returning to "Uncle Sugar."[28]

Within two months of Emperor Hirohito's surrender announcement, more than 700 ships of all types were available, notably Liberty and Victory cargo ships. Foreign vessels obtained for the project included origins as diverse as Panama and Italy.

The record for returning troops home belonged to the veteran aircraft carrier *Saratoga* (CV-3), which embarked some 29,000 grateful veterans, as fleet carriers were among the fastest ships afloat. But for maximum capacity, living space was likened to cramming 12 pounds into a ten-pound bag. The new carrier *Lake Champlain* (CV-39), only commissioned in June, was altered to accept 3,300 bunks. On her first *Magic Carpet* mission she set a transatlantic record of 32 knots, only surpassed by the liner *United States* in 1952.

The millions of personnel returned from war zones were not limited to American servicemen. The Army and WSA allocated 29 troop ships to transport nearly 500,000 European war brides. On the other side of the globe, it was estimated that 12,000 Australian women married American servicemen as well.

Magic Carpet was an immense success. At the time of VE Day in May 1945 more than 3 million soldiers were stationed in Europe alone. By year's end, seven months later, the Army counted fewer than 700,000 troops.

The Navy also experienced a huge reduction: from 3.3 million personnel in 1945 to fewer than 500,000 at the end of 1946.

Overall, *Magic Carpet* spanned the year following the climax in Tokyo Bay. On average, between September 1945 and September 1946 the operation landed 22,000 men and women at a U.S. port every day for 13 months. As noted by the National WWII Museum, "The sum total of which provides the mathematical framework behind the staggering post-war baby boom nine months later."[29]

Some returning veterans received unexpected good news. First Lieutenant Benjamin Drew of Detroit was known as the Eighth Air Force Mustang ace who shot down two German jets in one mission.

Transferred to the Pacific, he flew P-47s from Iwo Jima and found himself in charge of a group of pilots returning to the U.S.

The ensuing train trek to demobilization involved full access to the dining car, which was used far less by diners than drinkers. As Drew explained, the returning pilots jumped, rather than fell, off the wagon. When they stepped on dry land in Portland, Oregon, their first order of business was to rent a hotel suite and have "one whale of a party for forty-eight hours." Memory of the time was fuzzy, but included "lots of booze, lots of women, and lots of hangovers."

Portland boasted a large personnel transfer center to handle the waves of returning servicemen. Most of Drew's hangover remained the morning he reported for out-processing. As reported by his co-biographer:

It was a walloping hangover, the kind the Germans call a *katzenjammer*, so Ben was not pleased when the first clerk he had to deal with, asked why he wasn't wearing his captain's bars. Ben could not believe the question. He made the clerk go through his record. It turned out his promotion papers had been chasing after him for seven months. The hangover was forgotten. The back pay alone made the new rank a good deal. He signed his name in a dozen places on originals and carbon copies. When the clerk handed him the fat envelope with all his records, Ben asked him for a set of captain bars. The corporal said, "Oh, we don't give out the insignia. Just stop by any Army-Navy store for a set. There's one down the street."

That's how I wound up pinning on my own captain's bars in a grubby little store in Portland. It was almost as bad as getting my Distinguished Flying Cross thrown over the wall of a privy. Not that it made any difference. I was really proud of that promotion. Relieved too. Second to first lieutenant is no big deal; practically automatic. Making captain meant that that 104th article of war (for a Stateside buzz job) was finally out of my record. I bought enough bars to go on my shoulders and collars so I could wear my new rank on the long train trip to Chicago.[30]

Some returning veterans had a tremendous financial future ahead. One was a senior member of General Albert Wedemeyer's CBI staff, George H. Olmsted, who ran clandestine operations while managing the enormous task of disposing of millions of dollars of equipment and supplies. A distinguished-looking West Pointer, Olmsted rose to captain of cadets, became a boxing champion, and stood second in the class of 1922. But in the postwar downturn he left the service and spent 19 years making a fortune in the Midwest.

Recalled to duty as a major in 1942, Olmsted deftly handled the complexities of Lend-Lease to most U.S. Allies, and upon arriving in China in 1944 he was promoted to brigadier general. He oversaw the disposition of millions of dollars of U.S. property and negotiated a sale to Chiang's government rather than abandon equipment and supplies in place. Reputedly Truman lauded the program as "the best liquidation of surplus U.S. equipment anywhere in the world."

According to family lore, when Olmsted returned home he took with him the one man he trusted completely: his sergeant chauffeur. Benefiting from his erstwhile commanding officer's success in finance and insurance, the former non-commissioned officer retired a millionaire and then some.

Recalled Commander James L. Jackson who had led the minesweepers in Tokyo Bay:

> Everybody was a hero when they came back. I was on terminal leave so I wore my uniform for three months because I didn't have any other clothes in particular. All I was interested in was getting myself married and getting a job. I was thirty-two years old and I didn't even know what I was going to do... I wasn't interested in talking about the war, that was in the past, I had a future to worry about. But nothing in my life matured me more than the navy.

Jackson died in his native Georgia in 2007, age 93.[31]

One of the most perceptive comments came from *Essex*'s senior chaplain, Victor H. Morgan. With more life experience than nearly everyone aboard – he had been an artillery officer in World War I – he cautioned and inspired his shipmates about what lay ahead:

> Yes, we are on the way back. Back to wives, sweethearts, children, parents, and friends. Back to the ways of peace. Yet we can never go back, only forward. We will not find conditions just as we left them. The buildings, the land, the trees will still be there, but we cannot expect to find people unchanged. Those with whom we worked and played, many will not be there, others will have developed new friends, new interests, different habits. Even we ourselves will not be quite the same. Men who have had to face the probability of death day after day, week after week, will always look at life through different eyes. The normal man will have a keener appreciation of the values that contribute to life. He will appreciate many kindly, true, and beautiful influences we had, before the war, taken for granted. The near-neurotics will try to make the world give them a living, will more and more tend to live in the past, nursing their grievances, pathetic creatures who won a war and lost their souls.
>
> Shipmates, we cannot go back, only forward. All of us having a lot of living yet to do. We can make the years ahead great in accomplishment, rich, satisfaction. We had what it takes to win a tough war, we cannot fail to win our personal victory when we return to the ways of peace.
>
> May you all be blessed with that inner strength and peace which the world can neither give nor take away.[32]

*   *   *

As many as 150 Japanese soldiers and sailors became "holdouts," remaining in the field for months, years, or decades after the war. Whether from ignorance, suspicion, or extreme sense of duty, they survived in the Philippines, New Guinea, Indonesia, the Marianas, Palaus, and Iwo Jima, sometimes by avoiding all contact but sometimes by theft and robbery. The last two known bitter-enders were coaxed from hiding in 1974, but Singapore's *The Sunday Times* newspaper mentioned two more who surrendered with Communist forces in Malaya in 1989.[33]

The best-known holdout was Lieutenant Hiroo Onoda, an intelligence officer who fled into the Philippine jungle with a few others. Over the years his comrades deserted or were killed, leaving him alone from 1972.

Two years later Onoda encountered "a hippie boy" from Japan seeking the holdout, and was persuaded that the war had ended 29 years earlier. He duly surrendered to his former commanding officer, ceding his sword, a rifle with 500 rounds, and hand grenades. Alternating between Japan and his family in Brazil, Onoda died in Tokyo in 2014, aged 91.[34]

7

Downstream From VJ Day

The postwar influence

Months before the Tokyo surrender was signed, British Prime Minister Winston Churchill defined the postwar world. Immediately after VE Day, in correspondence with Truman, he referred to a Soviet "iron curtain" and repeated the phrase during the Potsdam Conference shortly before losing re-election. Then on August 16, recently voted out of office, Churchill emphasized the East-West reality when he stated, "it is not impossible that tragedy on a prodigious scale is unfolding itself behind the iron curtain which at the moment divides Europe in twain." Though defeated at the polls, he retained enormous influence and continued to have an impact on public opinion.[1]

The European Advisory Commission (EAC), established among the Western Allies in Moscow in 1943, anticipated the defeat of Germany and the need to prosecute Nazi crimes. On August 8, 1945, the EAC issued the Charter of the International Military Tribunal, better known as the Nuremberg Charter.

The charter identified three types of offenses: crimes against peace, war crimes, and crimes against humanity. Precedent rested heavily upon the Geneva Conventions of 1929, the most recent international agreement regarding conduct of war. The original EAC signatories were the U.S., Britain, Russia, and France, though 20 other Allied nations had ratified the charter.

Critics, though few, described Nuremberg as "victor's justice," in which the winners prosecuted the losers. From a practical aspect, little else could be expected, given the post-VE Day turmoil in Europe where the Court of International Justice at The Hague, Netherlands, had disbanded upon the 1940 German invasion. Nevertheless, some comments on the selective nature of the tribunal were evident, notably Luftwaffe chief Hermann Göring who, upon entering the court, reportedly looked around and asked, "Where are the Soviet defendants?"

The International Military Tribunal for the Far East was established in Tokyo in April 1946. Participants were the U.S., China, Britain, Australia, New Zealand, Canada, India, France, the Netherlands, and the Philippines – all objects of Japanese aggression. The Tokyo Trial was largely based on procedures established under the Nuremberg Charter covering detention of the accused, rules of evidence, and examination.

Oddly enough, Fleet Admiral Chester Nimitz was drawn into the Nuremberg trial of Grand Admiral Karl Dönitz, commander of the German Navy and Adolf Hitler's short-term successor as Führer. Dönitz was charged with violation of the Rules of Prize Warfare, an international agreement covering seizure of hostile vessels dating from 1899, well before submarines entered combat. Because the U-boat arm had operated on a sink-on-sight basis without surfacing to challenge an enemy ship, Dönitz faced charges for his navy's conduct. Nimitz, himself a submariner, replied to a defense request by submitting a statement that his Pacific Fleet subs also conducted unrestricted warfare, as 20th-century reality permitted no practical option. Consequently, Dönitz was not charged with unrestricted submarine warfare against neutral vessels in designated areas.[2]

Against the geo-strategic backdrop, the specter of war touched its icy hand around the globe. In one example among millions, the families of the four *Yorktown* pilots killed on August 15 received the dreadful telegrams four to six weeks later, between September 19 and 24. Seldom had "the last man syndrome" been better illustrated – or more heartbreakingly received.[3]

REVISIONISM AND THE BOMBS

For 30 years after VJ Day the argument persisted: the A-bombs averted a horrific invasion, saving millions, or the A-bombs were a war crime against a nation about to surrender.

In those three decades the debate existed in an information vacuum. Not until the late 1970s were partial wartime intelligence decrypts released, and they should have ended further argument, though they did not. By summer 1945 U.S. and British code breakers were working on an industrial scale, reading a million or more Japanese military and diplomatic messages per month. Between them the U.S. Army and Navy maintained six radio intercept stations in Washington, Hawaii, Australia, and the Philippines. Britain's work was done in Ceylon (now Sri Lanka) and at Bletchley Park outside London. The decrypts provided valuable insight to President Truman and his advisors, clearly showing that, despite decades of postwar assumptions and misrepresentation, Japan was not "ready to surrender."

Truman knew that Tokyo had approached Moscow seeking intercession with the Western Allies for better terms, however unrealistic that prospect, even lacking knowledge of Russia's impending invasion of Manchuria.

Richard B. Frank, author of the definitive study, wrote that "right to the very end, the Japanese pursued twin goals: not only preservation of the imperial system, but also preservation of the old order in Japan that had launched a war of aggression that killed 17 million."[4]

Furthermore, British historian Sir Max Hastings concluded, "Those who seek to argue that Japan was ready to surrender before Hiroshima are peddlers of fantasies. The Tokyo leadership was indeed eager for peace, but on terms rightly unacceptable to the Allied powers."[5]

The "Magic" intelligence – U.S. decrypts of enemy radio traffic – took a ponderous route from darkness into the light. A heavily edited version was released in 1978, showing Tokyo's request for Moscow's intercession with the other Allies. However, the redactions seemed to leave room for doubt among those seeking to blame Washington for being too fast on the nuclear trigger. The complete Magic documents were released in 1995, showing that the U.S. was not only reading Tokyo's electronic mail, but that of 30 other nations as well.[6]

Revisionist theory held that Truman's hidden reason for authorizing the A-bombs was to intimidate the Soviets, anticipating postwar tensions. His wartime actions indicate otherwise.

Although the European war ended in May, Truman allowed Lend-Lease to continue almost until the end of September. America had already provided nearly $11 billion in funds and materiel to Moscow, but the post-VE Day contributions further supported Russian efforts in the Far East. That largess included more than 30 naval vessels and landing craft certain to be used in Soviet amphibious operations against the Kurils, Korea, and elsewhere. Therefore, because Washington continued supporting Moscow's offensive actions toward Japan, the two bombs are unlikely to have been deployed as a way of cowing Stalin.

Project Hula – U.S. transfer of naval vessels to the Soviets – had been underway for five months, via a joint base at Cold Bay in the Aleutians. Originally the plan provided for 250 ships and small craft to be delivered between April and December 1945. However, Hula was pared to 180 frigates, minesweepers, and submarine chasers, including four floating workshops and 30 infantry landing craft (LCIs). The first Russians arrived in March, beginning orientation on Yankee ships and systems. The program ended on September 5, the day the Soviets sealed their conquest of the Kurils, with 149 transfers. The LCIs were especially helpful, as the Red Navy had nothing comparable for the Kurils operation. Five were lost to Japanese artillery during the campaign.[7]

A related controversy focused on projected American and Allied casualties in conquering the Home Islands. The numbers were vastly different, depending on how they were estimated and the agendas involved, but, ultimately, they approached three quarters of a million at the upper end. Extrapolating Okinawa's casualties was one method, with losses to all causes pushing 40 percent. MacArthur's staff, notoriously sycophantic, chose to interpret Pacific Theater intelligence in the "best" possible light or dismissed radio intercepts reporting greater Japanese defenses as enemy deceptions.

Thus MacArthur's *Olympic* estimate: 94,250 killed or wounded and 12,600 attributed to illness or accidents, a total of 106,850.

However, about the same time, the Sixth Army medical office estimated nearly 395,000 casualties among Army and Marine forces committed to the conquest of Kyushu. Extrapolating the 4,900 naval casualties at Okinawa as potentially ten times greater off Japan, a reasoned total for *Olympic* ran as 490,000 killed, missing, and wounded.[8]

An impartial indicator is that after VE Day the War Department, which usually procured medals for all services, ordered 370,000 Purple Hearts beyond those in stock to be awarded to wounded personnel or the families of the slain. That supply lasted into the Vietnam War.[9]

And Operation *Coronet* on Honshu was yet to come.

EXIT: WHAT BECAME OF THEM?

The leaders who starred in the August 1945 drama alternately exited stage right or retained the spotlight. The only one with genuine staying power was Stalin, finishing ahead of Truman. Later Churchill pulled off a return engagement, upstaging his sometime colleague Attlee. MacArthur's star faded in the pale wintry light of Korea. Mountbatten far outlasted Nimitz and Halsey among the naval senior officers, to die by assassination.

Hirohito
Emperor Hirohito escaped accountability for his role in the Asia-Pacific War, as the Americans needed his postwar compliance, if not outright support. Though reckoned Japan's 124th emperor, he denied his previous divine status at the insistence of the occupying powers. Under diminishing Allied control from 1949, a newly independent Japanese nation was established in 1952.

Hirohito died at age 88 in 1989. The debate still continues whether he was an unaccountable figurehead or, according to the wartime constitution, he was actually supreme commander of the army and navy.

Also likely to remain uncertain is Hirohito's reason for deciding in favor of surrender. His rescript cited the atom bombs, but apparently he was never asked specifically what tipped the scale for him.

Whatever the emperor's complicity, many of his subjects faced postwar prosecution as war criminals. In 1946 28 Japanese defendants were charged with Class A offenses (crimes against peace), mostly high-ranking military officers and government officials. They stood trial by the International Military Tribunal Far East, the "Tokyo Trial." Two died during the trial; seven were hanged; and 16 were sentenced to life imprisonment.

Forty-two military and civilian leaders were liable as Class A criminals but all had been released by the end of 1948. Another 5,700 Japanese were indicted for Class B (conventional war crimes) and Class C (crimes against humanity). Of that number, nearly 1,000 (17%) were initially condemned to death; 475 (8%) received life sentences; 2,944 (52%) received shorter prison terms; 1,018 (17%) were acquitted; and 279 were either not brought to trial or never sentenced. The number of initial Japanese death sentences handed out by country is the following: Holland 236, Great Britain 223, Australia 153, China 149, U.S.A. 140, France 26, and the Philippines 17.[10]

Harry S. Truman

Following VJ Day, Truman looked more than three years downstream to fill out his unexpected term as president. He was confronted with the Cold War, including the need to supply Berlin by air in 1948 amid a Soviet blockade.

The commander-in-chief supported integration of the War Department and Navy Department into a unified Department of Defense, a bitter D.C. fight that left professional blood on Washington's polished hallways. Truman the former artilleryman blatantly sided with the Army and the nascent Air Force against the Navy, resulting in resignation of the Secretary of the Navy and the Chief of Naval Operations in 1949. Since then, only one other member of the Joint Chiefs of Staff has laid his stars on the table for any reason.

Internationally, Truman enacted the Marshall Plan to provide aid and economic recovery to the war-torn nations of Europe. But he overrode Secretary of State George C. Marshall in immediately recognizing the provisional government of Israel in May 1948.

Truman confounded the pundits by winning election for himself that November, teamed with Kentucky Senator Alben Barkley. Two years later Truman survived an assassination attempt by Puerto Rican nationalists, emerging unharmed.

However, by then Truman's attention was forced upon the Korean peninsula. His administration had been caught unprepared for the Communist onslaught, having foolishly stated that Korea lay beyond D.C.'s concern. Subsequently Truman clashed with his theater commander, General Douglas MacArthur, and fired him for insubordination in 1951. Much later Truman said, "I fired him because he wouldn't respect the authority of the President. I didn't fire him because he was a dumb son of a bitch, although he was, but that's not against the law for generals. If it was, half to three-quarters of them would be in jail."[11]

Truman declined to run for a second full term, and was succeeded by recently retired General of the Army Dwight D. Eisenhower in 1952. Truman retired to Independence, Missouri, with his wife Bess.

The 33rd president died in Kansas City in 1972, aged 88.

Chester Nimitz

Fleet Admiral Chester Nimitz was spared the chilling responsibility of landing Douglas MacArthur's forces in Japan. Then, having commanded the transpacific offensive leading to Tokyo Bay, soon Nimitz faced a vastly different responsibility.

At year's end Nimitz succeeded Ernest King as Chief of Naval Operations, immediately confronting the enormous task of downsizing the world's greatest fleet. Over the next two years Nimitz managed reduction of the U.S. Navy from 3.4 million personnel with 6,700 ships and vessels to 530,000 personnel with barely 800 ships just 18 months later. (Manning numbers excluded the Marine Corps and Coast Guard.)[12]

Probably Nimitz's most far-reaching decision was support of nuclear propulsion, leading to the world's first atomic-powered submarine, USS *Nautilus* (SSN-571) commissioned in 1954.

Following retirement in December 1947, Nimitz accepted United Nations assignments and became a regent for the University of California.

Chester Wilhelm Nimitz died in San Francisco in 1966, aged 80.

William Halsey

Halsey rode the Third Fleet battleship *South Dakota* to San Diego's Navy Day observance at the end of October 1945, and a month later he reported to the Secretary of the Navy's office for "special duty," however defined. At that point there was little for a spare four-star admiral to do, but his public reputation propelled him to the ultimate status when he was elevated to five-star rank at year's end. Thus, he became the fourth and last fleet admiral in U.S. Navy history.

Subsequently Halsey made an 11-nation Latin American goodwill tour (wholly outside his previous realm) before leaving active duty in March 1947 but continuing on full pay. By statute, five-star flag officers did not actually retire, so the honorific followed them into private life. Halsey spent several years with International Telephone and Telegraph Company in New York, lending his name and fame to IT&T with socializing and public appearances. He was also nominal head of an effort to preserve his 1942 flagship, USS *Enterprise*, but the Navy declined to cooperate.

In 1947, the year he left the Navy, Halsey published a splashy memoir, *Admiral Halsey's Story*, coauthored with journalist Joseph Bryan, III, who had served in the Army, Navy, and Air Force. Halsey spent much of the text defending his controversial record at Leyte Gulf, "Halsey's Hurricane," and the unnecessary air strikes on Kure. Because he escaped accountability for the attendant losses, historians still argue whether he deserved his fifth star, but to deny him seemed politically impossible.

William Frederick Halsey, Jr., died in 1959, aged 76, and is buried in Arlington National Cemetery.

Douglas MacArthur

General of the Army Douglas MacArthur probably accomplished more as the supremo in Japan than he had during the war. He feared the potentially disastrous results if Hirohito were indicted as a war criminal, and coordinated Allied and Japanese scripts portraying the emperor as a symbol of Japan rather than taking an active role. For decades after, surviving Allied POWs and families of prisoners who died in captivity voiced bitter resentment over MacArthur's lenient "big picture" policy regarding many Japanese offenders.

MacArthur ceded control of Japan to an emerging new government in 1949 but almost immediately faced a grave crisis. North Korea launched a surprise invasion of the South in June 1950, forcing MacArthur to assume control of a nominally United Nations command. Though 15 allied nations contributed, the defense of the Republic of Korea rested largely upon the United States. MacArthur's reversal of the Communist flood tide pushed almost to the China border that winter, but he ignored indications of massive Chinese forces. The result was an unresolvable conflict with President Truman, leading to MacArthur's dismissal in April 1951.

Douglas MacArthur died in Washington, D.C., in 1964, aged 84.

Curtis LeMay

General Curtis Emerson LeMay's postwar military career lasted not quite 20 years, featuring assignments of startling contrast. In 1948, as chief of the U.S. Air Force in Europe, he oversaw the lengthy Berlin Airlift, delivering food and supplies to West Berlin deep within the Soviet zone. His competence and persistence finally forced Moscow to stand down after nearly a year, achieving a peaceful victory for airpower.

Subsequently LeMay, now with four stars, took over the benighted Strategic Air Command (SAC). His predecessor, formerly MacArthur's leading airman George C. Kenney, had allowed SAC to deteriorate to little more than a four-engine flying club. When LeMay arrived at SAC's Omaha, Nebraska, headquarters he said he encountered a lone guard armed with a ham sandwich.

Facing a growing Soviet threat, LeMay resolved to turn his command into the world's foremost practitioner of deterrence. The philosophy was expressed in the motto, "Peace is our profession."

LeMay resurrected his wartime policies of strict accountability, extremely high professional standards, and "looking out for the troops." His improvements in pay, housing, and family support produced results: growing morale and retention of aircrews and maintenance men.

Meanwhile, LeMay oversaw the transition to an all-jet force, both with bombers and aerial tankers. He was likely to show up anywhere, anytime, flying a B-47, B-52, or a KC-135. Through it all, SAC developed its own unique ethic, essentially a force within the Air Force, preparing for Armageddon.

Inevitably, LeMay clashed with his civilian superiors. As Air Force chief of staff he was that Beltway rarity: an apolitical four-star. His bluntness earned him the enmity of Secretary of Defense Robert Strange McNamara and President Lyndon Johnson, especially in opposing the administration's "guns and butter" approach to Vietnam. LeMay, the ultimate Cold Warrior, could not abide halfway measures, and he urged Washington to commit to victory in Southeast Asia or to pull out. His tenure ended in February 1965, ten years before America's eventual defeat in Vietnam.

Throughout his career LeMay had taught subordinates to state their opinions and provide evidence to support them. If their recommendations were denied, the professional response was to salute smartly and carry on – or retire. In 1968, the watershed year of the Vietnam debacle, LeMay spoke from retirement by running on Alabama Governor George Wallace's third-party ticket. The American Independent Party carried five states that November, one of the most significant third-party records in U.S. politics.

LeMay died at an Air Force retirement home in 1990, aged 83.

Winston Churchill

Turned out of office in 1945, Churchill headed the Conservative minority in Parliament and returned to Number Ten Downing Street in 1951, remaining another four years. His tenure returned Britain's emphasis from domestic to foreign policy including arenas as varied as the Cold War, the Mau Mau uprising in Kenya, and the prolonged anticommunist campaign in Malaya.

In 1953 Churchill suffered his second stroke in four years, but despite lingering effects he remained prime minister until retiring two years later, aged 80.

In private life Churchill continued writing, and his six-volume history, *The Second World War*, completed in 1953, received the Nobel Prize for literature. He also compiled his four-volume *History of the English-Speaking Peoples* between 1956 and 1958. Additional publications included anthologies of his speeches and a booklet explaining his other hobby: *Painting as a Pastime*.

Winston Spencer Churchill's wartime partner became President Dwight Eisenhower who conferred honorary American leadership upon him in 1963. The man whom Clement Attlee called "the greatest citizen of the world in our time" passed away during his 90th year in 1965.[13]

Clement Attlee

As head of government between 1945 and 1951, Clement Richard Attlee steered Labour increasingly leftward toward broader socialism. The philosophical difference with the individually oriented Conservatives assured continuing clashes, but the electorate clearly welcomed policies more favorable toward health care, welfare, wages, and government ownership or control of utilities and industry.

Attlee's 1920s work on Indian independence resurfaced immediately in the wake of VJ Day. The program evolved from self-government to full autonomy in 1947. Meanwhile, international strife captured London's attention, especially in Palestine and "the Jewish question" that led to Israel's independence in 1948. Simultaneously, British interests in Africa received closer scrutiny, eventually leading to decolonization that produced violent consequences in Rhodesia and South Africa.

Attlee barely won re-election in 1950 when Labour's pledge of sweeping changes collided with fiscal and political reality. Rationing continued for almost a decade after the war, and in 1951 Attlee faced a leadership crisis partly over funding Britain's commitment to the United Nations effort in Korea. He called for an unscheduled election, expecting to regain the seats lost the year before, but the plan backfired. Attlee was forced out, returning to opposition leader for the last four years of his career.

He died in 1967 at age 84.

Louis Mountbatten

Mountbatten's postwar career was intimately involved with the end of imperial rule of India. Clement Attlee appointed Mountbatten the last Viceroy of India and interim governor-general. "Dickie" Mountbatten remained through the 1947–48 transition period to independence, then returned to the navy. His wife, wealthy socialite Edwina Ashley, had a string of lovers, most notably Jawaharlal Nehru, later the nation's first prime minister. Mountbatten tolerated the situation for the duration of their marriage, until she died in 1960.

Subsequently Mountbatten served as First Sea Lord, the Royal Navy's senior position, and Chief of the Defence Staff. He retired from the Royal Navy in 1965 after half a century of service, including his time as viceroy and governor-general of India.

Frequently Mountbatten summered in the Irish Republic, enjoying sailing and fishing on his 30-foot boat. In 1979 he was targeted by the Irish Republican Army, which planted a bomb aboard his boat, moored near the border with Northern Ireland. The explosion killed Mountbatten and three others, including his grandson and a local boy.

Mountbatten perished at 79 after leading one of the most extraordinary lives of the 20th century.

Joseph Stalin

The Soviet dictator enjoyed the fruits of his people's sanguinary, hard-won victory. He tightened Moscow's grip on the Baltic republics – Estonia, Latvia, and Lithuania – and deported tens of thousands of resisters. Moreover, by 1953 Stalin's regime had imprisoned 5.3 million people – three percent of the population – in a network of prisons, isolated "settlements," and work colonies.[14]

Soviet sympathizers in the Manhattan Project had kept Moscow informed of Allied A-bomb progress, and Stalin played dead-pan with Truman at Potsdam when the president alluded to an awesome new weapon. Thereafter, Russia surged a scientific and technical program to produce its first nuclear bomb in 1949. At the same time Stalin nearly doubled the size of the Red Army between 1949 and 1953.[15]

In May 1950 Stalin endorsed Pyongyang's conquest of the South, and the Korean War began the next month. Previously he had supported revolutionary movements in Yugoslavia – already nominally Communist – and Greece.

Stalin's health failed in his last three years, dying at 74 in March 1953. His Western obituaries mostly were neutral to laudatory. Truman described him as "a decent fellow" and "a prisoner of the Politburo." The enormously partisan *New York Times*, which had flat-out lied about Stalin's genocidal tyranny in the 1930s, omitted all mention of his crimes against the Russian people.[16]

Aleksandr Vasilevsky

The conqueror of Manchuria was amply rewarded for his *August Storm*. Within days of his victory, Marshal Aleksandr Vasilevsky became a two-time Hero of the Soviet Union and received honors from 11 nations including Great Britain and the United States. He was retained as chief of staff of the Soviet Forces in the Far East, then was recalled to Moscow as defense minister in 1949. He still held that post upon Stalin's death in March 1953, then entered a declining spiral from which there was no recovery.

Relieved as defense minister, Vasilevsky slid down a rung on Moscow's ladder as Nikolai Bulganin's deputy. Three years later Vasilevsky was appointed minister for military science, essentially a space-keeping position for someone of his seniority. But the assignment only lasted a year before Premier Nikita Khrushchev ordered the marshal's retirement in 1956. The new regime tossed Vasilevsky an honorific as inspector general of the ministry of defense in 1959.

Vasilevsky published a memoir in 1973 and died in December 1977, aged 82.

Chiang Kai-shek

In the immediate postwar period Chiang leveraged his huge military manpower advantage in Indochina to compel the French and Communist forces to reach a short-lived agreement of cooperation. Subsequently, in early 1946 he negotiated removal of French holdings in China while he agreed to withdrawal from Vietnamese territory. He complied with that pact beginning in the spring.

Chiang became President of the Republic of China in 1948, only remaining until the Kuomintang suffered a series of defeats at the hands of Mao Tse-tung's Communists. Following the Nationalists' expulsion from the mainland in 1949 to Formosa (now Taiwan), Chiang regained the presidency in March 1950, shortly before the Korean War began. Chiang's forces took no part in the United Nations action against North Korea. However, on the international stage, Nationalist China retained its seat on the U.N. Security Council until displaced by Communist China in 1971.

Chiang Kai-shek died in 1975 at the age of 87.

Chiang's son Chiang Ching-kuo succeeded him as party ruler. Subsequently the younger Chiang served as premier (head of government) of the Republic of China, Taiwan's official name, from 1972 to 1978, then as president and head of state, until he died in 1988.

Mao Tse-tung

Following Japan's defeat Mao wore multiple hats, often simultaneously. His consolidation of power included Chairman of the Chinese Communist Party (1943–76), Chairman of the Central People's Government (1949–54), Chairman of the People's Republic of China (1954–59), and Chairman of the Central Military Commission (1954–76). As such, Mao represented the ultimate authority in the People's Republic of China (PRC).

Through 1949 the Communists inflicted crippling losses on Chiang's Nationalists, both by siege and by maneuver. Following Chiang's withdrawal to Formosa and Communist establishment of the People's Republic of China, Mao pursued a ruthless policy of extermination and imprisonment of remaining opponents, with at least 700,000 killed to 1952.

Though Stalin had doubted China's ability to organize and maintain so large a Communist state, Mao and his supporters drew on the Soviet model. Also, Mao poured immense human and materiel resources into North Korea following Kim Il-sung's invasion of the South in 1950. Over the next three years Mao's support of Pyongyang cost some 140,000 Chinese lives, ending in an armistice in July 1953.

Still following Moscow's example, China's first five-year plan began in 1953, relying heavily on Moscow for technical knowledge and even entire factories.

Mao's policies, however well intended, produced enormous misery. The Great Leap Forward (1958–62) resulted in massive famine, while the Cultural Revolution (1966–76) scoured remaining traditionalist thought from the nation. Meanwhile, Beijing-Moscow relations suffered under doctrinal and practical pressures, including occasional military clashes.

Despots' death tolls are so immense that they seem to defy comprehension. Throughout his tenure, 1949 to 1976, Mao's policies probably resulted in at least 42 million deaths. Other estimates run to more than 110 million. In contrast, Adolf Hitler's genocidal holocaust was 14 million compared to Joseph Stalin's 13 million internal deaths, exclusive of warfare.[17]

Mao's appearance on the world stage regained the spotlight when he hosted U.S. President Richard M. Nixon in 1972. The timing was significant: near the end of the Vietnam War, it was indicative of further distancing China from Russia. Three years later the trip led to Washington's recognition of the PRC as China's government rather than the 30-year status quo with Taiwan.

Mao Tse-tung died in 1976, aged 81.

Ho Chi Minh

For one of the longest-serving postwar heads of state, Ho Chi Minh remains a unique enigma. Neither his date nor place of birth seems known for certain, and apparently he used between 50 and 200 aliases.

In any case, returning from nearly 30 years in exile in 1941, Ho was Prime Minister of North Vietnam from 1945 to 1955, doubling as President from 1945 to his death in 1969. The entire period was marked by multinational conflict, most immediately with Nationalist Chinese forces accepting Japan's surrender, return of the French, and ultimately the long war with America from 1964 onward.

Aside from foreign opposition, Ho and the Communists ruthlessly suppressed other domestic movements, even going to the extent of cooperating with the French to achieve that aim. A Paris anarchist-socialist, Daniel Guerin, quoted Ho as saying in 1946, "All those who do not follow the line which I have laid down will be broken."[18]

Following France's expulsion from Indochina in 1954, Vietnam was divided north and south at the 17th parallel, the area later famously (and inaccurately) termed the Demilitarized Zone.

Internally, Ho's regime enforced land reform with political "purification" and widespread executions – as many as 13,000 or more.[19]

From 1956 onward, Hanoi sharpened its focus at unification of the nation by conquest. The Communist campaign began in earnest in 1961, augmented by the indigenous Viet Cong movement in the South.

Ho died in September 1969, aged 79. His lifetime goal was achieved with American abandonment of the Republic of Vietnam in 1975, and Saigon was renamed Ho Chi Minh City. In 1998 *Time* magazine named him one of the 100 most influential people of the 20th century.

LIVING WITH PEACE

The immediate postwar period had two priorities: bringing the troops home and paying for the war.

In October the Treasury Department launched the 11th Victory Loan, a fund-raising drive with a goal of $11 billion. The Navy Office of Information established the "Victory Squadron" to work hand in glove with the Treasury. Leading the unit was a long-term Pacific veteran, Lieutenant Commander Willard E. Eder, a Wyoming ace with victories from 1942 to 1945. He selected 23 other pilots – all combat veterans – plus 19 enlisted men to operate 15 Navy, Marine, and enemy aircraft on a nationwide barnstorming tour. As he described it, the squadron was ordered – not merely authorized but ordered – to fly low and party its way across postwar America, mixing with taxpayers who would then purchase war bonds.

At each appearance "The Navy's Flying Might" launched Hellcats, Corsairs, Avengers, Helldivers, and the Marines' brand-new Tigercats in a mock attack on an "enemy" target. The tame Zero was popular until a pilot stood it on its nose, ending that portion of the program. Meanwhile, attendees thrilled to the sight and sound of high-performance aircraft roaring low overhead in a presentation of a carrier air group at work.

The aviators thoroughly enjoyed themselves. One pilot received word that his baby had just been born and toasted the boy's arrival with a glass of milk. A squadron mate said, "It was the only non-alcoholic drink I saw him take on the whole tour."

When the Victory Squadron stood down at the Miami Air Races in January, Eder's crew had performed for 680,000 people in 22 states who dug deep and purchased $18 million of bonds in barely two months.[20]

Postwar America entered a cyclone of adjustment, prosperity, and growth. More babies were born in 1946 than ever; 3.4 million or 20 percent more than the year before. That was six births per minute among 50 million born in the next 15 years.

The postwar economic boom was driven by 25 million new jobs. Tax returns rocketed from 14.7 million in 1940 to 50 million in six years.[21]

Simultaneously, a housing crisis required congressional attention, granting the president extraordinary powers through 1947, presumably because the shortage could not be overcome sooner. But actually, a million housing starts were filed in 1946 – three times the 1945 figure or 2,800 per day. In the first full year of peace a six-room home in the suburbs ran little more than $5,000 with a $550 down payment and monthly 25-year mortgage of $30.[22]

The GI Bill was passed in June 1944 as the Servicemen's Readjustment Act. Pushed by the American Legion, the bill afforded immediate benefits for nearly all World War II veterans including high school and college tuition plus living expenses for those who had served at least 90 days and had been honorably discharged. The bill was a major factor in enabling veterans to re-enter civilian life, especially in catching up with lost years of education.

However well intended, the GI Bill had its limits: black veterans were subjected to southern Democrats' "Jim Crow" discrimination, and the Merchant Marine (which suffered 8,600 wartime fatalities) was omitted due to a prewar congressional definition. Surviving merchant mariners were only accommodated in 2007.

Amid the universal sentiment "Bring the boys home," the girls were already occupied. Servicemen who expected to find profitable employment as civilians unwittingly displaced home-front workers. Nearly 19 million women had jobs during the war. But two years later the proportion of working women fell from 36 to 28 percent, the prewar figure.

Yet among enormous growth, America and the West demonstrated both brilliance and folly in the wake of VJ Day. Demobilization gutted the armed forces. Said General Albert Wedemeyer, "America fought the war like a football game, after which the winner leaves the field and celebrates."[23]

Wedemeyer's perception was irrefutable. The theater he knew best – Asia – was left open to the new threat, and American forces paid the interest on that debt in a three-year endurance contest on the Korean peninsula.

Meanwhile, contradicting the mantra that democracy cannot be enforced at gunpoint, the Allies did just that – in Italy, Germany, and Japan. Though Germany would remain divided until 1990, the economic powerhouses in Bonn and Tokyo generated renewals of astonishing speed and stamina.

When former D-Day supremo Dwight Eisenhower left the Oval Office in 1961, he turned over to the wartime generation. The next seven presidents were younger World War II veterans, six being Navy men: PT boat skipper John Kennedy, bogus hero Lyndon Johnson, supply officer Richard Nixon, navigator Gerald Ford, Annapolis graduate Jimmy Carter, former cavalryman Ronald Reagan, and naval aviator George H.W. Bush.

Beside the presidents and politicians, "real people" continued making their own contributions. The cruiser *Montpelier* had been among the first ships to call at Hiroshima, where sailors wandered amid the radioactive rubble. Some incurred radiation poisoning that would not be apparent for years.

Eighteen years after VJ Day, *Montpelier* gunner James J. Fahey found himself a literary lion with publication of his surreptitious diary, a 1963 best seller. He sent the royalties to a Catholic priest, Father Michael, for construction of a church in southern India, and in 1967 some 100,000 worshipers cheered the American benefactor at the dedication of Our Lady of Dolors. Then Fahey resumed his trade as a trash collector and truck driver in Waltham, Massachusetts, retiring in 1979. He died in 1991, aged 73.

Pulitzer Prize-winning author Stephen Hunter wrote a penetrating 1998 assessment in reviewing *Saving Private Ryan*: "This movie is about a generation that put its heart on the shelf, dialed its minds down into a small, cold, tunnel, and fought with its brains."

Among those Hunter referenced were veterans of *Ticonderoga*'s fighter-bomber squadron. In 1988 VBF-87 issued a booklet titled *September Song*, condensing what VJ Day meant to them. In the foreword, W.E. "Johnny" Johnson wrote:

For VBF-87 the days of combat duty grew short with the first atomic bomb, and they ended with the signing of the peace treaty on September 2, 1945, in Tokyo Bay. That was forty-three years ago. For us the autumn weather has turned the leaves to flame and we have reached the September of our lives. We now are in "those golden days" when we look back at the greatest adventure of our lives – and the great and enduring friendships that grew out of it.

This is our September Song – a celebration of life and friendship in those golden days we were promised so long ago.[24]

THE GREATEST GENERATION?

Since the 1980s the World War II generation of Americans has been called "the greatest" so often that the phrase has become unthinking, reflexive. It is not true by any objective standard compared to the enormous achievement of the Republic's founders, even with the combined challenges of the Great Depression and the greatest conflict in history. Furthermore, the previous generation of Americans – the one that fought "The War to End All Wars" in 1917–18 – dealt with economic hardship as adults rather than as children or adolescents and sent millions of its sons and daughters off to fight in the next conflagration.

As Marine Corps Medal of Honor aviator and South Dakota Governor Joe Foss insisted, "We weren't the greatest. We just did what we had to do."[25]

Nonetheless, the "War Two" generation gained eye-watering achievements. It threw off the potentially crippling effects of the Depression; pulled together as seldom before and never since; outdid the rest of the world in every category save human reproduction; and spurred a postwar economic boom with technical and cultural innovation that is still felt seven decades later.

And yet the "greatest" generation spawned enormous contradictions. Technically, it sent its heroes rocketing into Earth orbit en route to the moon, and culturally it squandered more than 50,000 of its children in the ten-year morass of Southeast Asia. Vietnam's political-cultural fault lines remain evident today.

Contrary to much rheumy-eyed sentimentality, the victors of VJ Day did not save America from fascist oppression. Ultimately the Allies outnumbered the Axis perhaps eight to one, and out-produced Berlin, Rome, and Tokyo by something approaching infinity. For an objective assessment, consider that the U.S. coexisted with the Soviet menace for 70 years, including nearly 50 years facing nuclear incineration. The Axis powers had neither the numbers, ability, nor the willingness to invade and conquer North America. To believe otherwise is maudlin folly.

But what the VJ generation of Americans, Britons, and others did achieve was genuine, and grander. They shed their peacetime roles and ambitions, donned uniforms and work clothes, and set their minds to a long, open-ended slugfest against tough, competent, often courageous enemies. In so doing, the VJ generation returned dozens of nations to their rightful owners, leaving them to determine their own courses, however wise or fallacious.

That remains the lingering heritage of VJ Day.

Acknowledgments

RANKS AS OF 1945

(* denotes deceased as of 2021)
Lieutenant Malcolm E. Cagle, USN, VF-88, USS *Yorktown* *
Corporal Edwin D. Carlson, U.S. Army *
First Lieutenant Dino Cerutti, 8th Fighter Group, Okinawa
Major John D. Cooper, III Amphibious Corps *
Lieutenant Commander William N. Leonard, USN, Task Force 38 *
Ensign Donald M. McPherson, VF-83, USS *Essex*
Lieutenant Tilman E. Pool, VF-17, USS *Hornet* *
Colonel Robert L. Scott, Fourteenth Air Force, China and Okinawa *
Ensign Doniphan B. Shelton, USS *St. Louis* *
Private Zoeth Skinner, 194th Tank Battalion, Philippines *
First Lieutenant Robert M. Stevens, 348th Fighter Group,
    Okinawa *
Lieutenant (jg) George D. Wood, VBF-87, USS *Ticonderoga* *

CONTRIBUTORS

(* denotes deceased as of 2021)
Terry Aitken, Senior Curator, National Museum of the Air
    Force (Ret)
Mary Ames Booker, Battleship North Carolina
John Wayne Carlson
Barbara Collins

Robert J. Cressman
Michael Fink
Richard B. Frank
Jon Guttman
Dr. Richard P. Hallion, Historian Emeritus of the U.S. Air Force
Mark Herber
Bob Kattenheim, USS Shangri-La Association
Peter Lindsay
Lex McAulay
George Mellinger
Commander Peter B. Mersky, USNR (Ret)
Larry Miller
George H. Olmsted III *
Dr. Frank J. Olynyk (special thanks)
Marilynn Pantera
Robert R. Powell
Scott Price, Chief Historian of the U.S. Coast Guard
David Reid
Matt Robbins
Henry Sakaida *
James Sawruk
Dr. M.G. Sheftall
Paul Stillwell
Osamu Tagaya
John L. Tillman
Anthony Tully

Endnotes

INTRODUCTION

1. "Potsdam Declaration." Atomicarchive.com. http://www
.atomicarchive.com/Docs/Hiroshima/Potsdam.shtml. Accessed
August 15, 2019.

CHAPTER 1 WAR OR PEACE?

1. Hajime Hoshi. *Handbook of Japanese Exhibits at World's Fair, St.
Louis*, 1904.
2. Mark Parillo. *The Japanese Merchant Marine in World War II*.
Annapolis: Naval Institute Press, 1993, p. 242.
3. "56 Years Ago." https://user.xmission.com/~tmathews/b29
/56years/56years-4508a.html. Accessed July 4, 2019.
4. David McCullough. *Truman*. New York: Simon & Schuster, 1992,
p. 436.
5. Thomas Fleming. *The New Dealer's War*. New York: Basic Books,
2001, p. 514.
6. "The Gwinn 'Angel' Scholarship." https://www.ussindianapolis
.com/gwinn-scholarship. Accessed July 30, 2020.
7. Lynn Vincent and Sara Vladic. "Survivor Accounts from the Worst Sea
Disaster in U.S. Naval History." https://www.history.com/news/uss
-Indianapolis-sinking-survivor-stories-sharks. Accessed July 30, 2020.
8. Ibid.
9. "OWI Pacific Psyop Six Decades Ago." http://www.psywarrior
.com/OWI60YrsLater2.html. Accessed August 15, 2019.
10. Szilard cover letter, July 4, 1945. http://www.dannen.com/decision
/45-07-04.html. Accessed July 6, 2019.

11. "Szilard Petition." Atomic Heritage Foundation. https://www.atomicheritage.org/key-documents/szilard-petition. Accessed July 6, 2019.

12. Richard B. Frank. "Why Truman dropped the Bomb." *The Weekly Standard*, August 8, 2005.

13. Vincent C. Jones. *The United States Army in World War II. Manhattan: The Army and the Atomic Bomb.* Washington, D.C.: Center of Military History, 1985, p. 534.

14. Adrian Weale. "Eye Witness to Hiroshima" in *The Norton Anthology of English Literature.* https://www.wwnorton.com/college/english/nael/20century/topic_2/atombomb.htm. Accessed July 4, 2019.

15. John Toland. *The Rising Sun, 1936–1945. Volume 2.* New York: Random House, 1970, pp. 970–971. Hereafter Toland. *The Rising Sun.*

16. "Atomic Bombings of Hiroshima and Nagasaki." http://www.atomicarchive.com/Docs/MED/med_chp10.shtml. "Hiroshima POWs." https://hiroshima-pows.org/chapter-7. Both accessed August 10, 2019.

17. Atomic Heritage Foundation. "Hiroshima and Nagasaki Bombing Timeline." https://www.atomicheritage.org/history/hiroshima-and-nagasaki-bombing-timeline. Accessed August 10, 2019.

18. "The Manhattan Project." U.S. Department of Energy. https://www.osti.gov/opennet/manhattan-project-history/Events/1945/trinity.htm. Accessed July 5, 2019.

19. "Press Release Alerting the Nation About the Atomic Bomb. August 6, 1945." https://teachingamericanhistory.org/library/document/press-release-alerting-the-nation-about-the-atomic-bomb/. Accessed July 5, 2019.

20. "Damage Surveys After the Bombing." City of Hiroshima Virtual Museum. http://www.pcf.city.hiroshima.jp/virtual/VirtualMuseum_e/exhibit_e/exh0307_e/exh03074_e.html. Accessed September 2, 2019.

21. René Francillon. *Japanese Aircraft of the Pacific War.* London: Putnam, 1970, p. 443.

22. "Nakajima Kikka Jet Interceptor." http://www.combinedfleet.com/Nakajima%20Kikka.htm. Accessed October 2, 2020.

23. "Kikka: The Special Attacker." *War Thunder.* https://www.reddit.com/r/Warthunder/comments/ebolrs/kikka_the_special_attacker/. Accessed October 2, 2020.

24. Edward Davidson. *Chronology of World War Two*. London: Cassell Military, 1999, p. 252.

25. Gavan Daws. *Prisoners of the Japanese*, in Richard B. Frank. *Downfall: The End of the Imperial Japanese Empire*. New York: Penguin Books, 1999, p. 285.

26. Ellen Bradbury and Sandra Blakeslee. "The Harrowing Story of the Nagasaki Bombing Mission." *Bulletin of Atomic Scientists*, August 4, 2015. https://thebulletin.org/2015/08/the-harrowing-story-of-the-nagasaki-bombing-mission/. Accessed August 24, 2020.

27. Katherine Hignett. "The Devastation of Nagasaki and the Luck of Kokura." *Newsweek*, August 9, 2018. https://www.newsweek.com/devastation-nagasaki-and-luck-kokura-tale-two-cities-1064991. Accessed August 2, 2019.

28. Wesley Frank Craven and James Lea Cate. *The Army Air Forces in World War II. Volume Five, The Pacific: Matterhorn to Nagasaki*. Washington, D.C.: Office of Air Force History, 1983, p. 720.

29. "Eighth Air Force Historical Society of Minnesota." https://sites.google.com/site/8thafhsmn/pictures/ray-l-tarte-jr-p-47-thunderbolt-pilot. Accessed August 1, 2019. Hereafter "Eighth Air Force Historical Society of Minnesota."

30. Toland. *The Rising Sun*, pp. 1000–1001.

31. "Eighth Air Force Historical Society of Minnesota."

32. Navy Nuclear Weapons Association. "Studs Turkel Interviews Paul Tibbets." https://navynucweps.com/History/terkel_interviews_tibbets.htm. Accessed August 10, 2020.

33. Atomic Heritage Foundation. "Target Committee Recommendations." https://www.atomicheritage.org/key-documents/target-committee-recommendations. Accessed August 12, 2020.

34. Kat Eschner. "How the Presidency Took Control of America's Nuclear Arsenal." *Smithsonian Magazine*. https://www.smithsonianmag.com/history/how-the-presidency-took-control-americas-nuclear-arsenal-180967747/. Accessed August 12, 2020.

35. Richard Lloyd Parry. "The Luckiest or Unluckiest Man in the World?" *The Times*, September 21, 2014.

36. "How I Survived Hiroshima – and then Nagasaki." *The Independent*, March 26, 2009. "Tsutomu Yamaguchi." *The Telegraph*, January 6, 2010.

37. "Landing Craft Depot Ship." http://www.combinedfleet.com/Kibitsu_t.htm. Accessed November 17, 2020.

38. Japanese ship losses. http://www.ibiblio.org/hyperwar/Japan/IJN /JANAC-Losses/index.html. Accessed November 27, 2020.

39. USS *Jallao* patrol report, September 9, 1945.

40. "Pacific Wrecks: USS *Bullhead* (SS-332)." https://www .pacificwrecks.com/subs/SS-332.html. Accessed July 16, 2019.

41. Cited by Mary Ames Booker in email, September 14, 2020.

42. *The Essex Buccaneer*, August–September 1945, courtesy Mark Herber.

43. "40mm/56 Bofors Medium Antiaircraft Gun." http://pwencycl .kgbudge.com/4/0/40mm_45_Bofors_AA_gun.htm.   Accessed June 15, 2020.

44. https://usnhistory.navylive.dodlive.mil/2019/03/18/theoerlikon -20-mm-the-right-tool-for-the-job. Accessed June 14, 2020.

45. *All Hands*, "Ships and Station," August 1945. https://www.ibiblio .org/hyperwar/USN/ref/AH-4508/AH-4508-12.html.   Accessed June 2020.

46. Navy Department Press Release of June 26, 1945. https://www .fold3.com/image/300872041. Accessed June 15, 2020.

47. Rear Admiral Doniphon Shelton (Ret) emails to author, December 2020.

48. *Nav Weps*. "Torpedoes of Japan." http://www.navweaps.com/ Weapons/WTJAP_WWII.php. Accessed November 20, 2020.

49. Lieutenant Clifton B. Cates, Jr. *War History of the USS Pennsylvania (BB 38)*. Ship's Welfare Fund, 1946.

50. Richard B. Frank. *Downfall: The End of the Imperial Japanese Empire*. New York: Penguin Books, 1999, pp. 117–118. Hereafter Frank. *Downfall*. "Operation Downfall: Allied Plans." http:// www.historyofwar.org/articles/wars_downfall4.html#:~:text= %28Sixth%20Army%20Field%20Order%20No.%2074%2C %20Troop%20List%2C,the%20United%20States%20premier %20obsession%20-%20motor%20cars.   Accessed January 2, 2020.

51. WWW Virtual Library: Logistics. http://www.logisticsworld.com /logistics/quotations.htm. Accessed February 8, 2020.

52. Richard Overy. *Why the Allies Won*. New York: Norton, 1996, p. 319.

53. Peter B. Mersky, "My Dad Made Models." *Naval Institute Proceedings*, June 1987.

54. Cooper to author, personal conversation, 1980.

55. Frank. *Downfall*, pp. 183–184.

56. Dr. Jerry D. Morelock. "Eisenhower Under Fire." 2014. https://
www.historynet.com/eisenhower-fire-1944-45.htm.   Accessed
September 1, 2019.

57. John T. Correll. "The Invasion That Didn't Happen." *Air Force*.
June 2009. https://www.airforcemag.com/article/0609invasion/.
Accessed August 10, 2020.

58. E.B. Potter. *Nimitz*. Annapolis: Naval Institute Press, 1976, p. 384.
https://www.amazon.com/Nimitz-B-Potter/dp/1591145805.

59. Dr. Richard P. Hallion. https://history.stackexchange.com/
questions/33637/how-many-suicide-attack-kamikaze-pilots
-died-and-how-many-of-them-successfully. Accessed August
10, 2020.

60. Toland. *The Rising Sun*, pp. 1011–1012.

61. "Adm. Nimitz Dead; Built Pacific Fleet That Fought Japan."
United Press International, February 21, 1966. https://archive
.nytimes.com/www.nytimes.com/learning/general/onthisday/
bday/0224.html. Accessed August 18, 2019.

62. Samuel Eliot Morison. *History of United States Naval Operations
in World War II. Volume XIV: Victory in the Pacific*. Edison:
Castle Books, 2001, p. 256. Hereafter Morison. *Victory in the
Pacific*.

63. "56 Years Ago." August 10, 1945. https://user.xmission.com/
~tmathews/b29/56years/56years-4508a.html. Accessed July 18, 2019.

64. Rear Admiral William N. Leonard, USN (Ret) letter to author,
1980.

65. William F. Halsey and J. Bryan III. *Admiral Halsey's Story*.
Whittlesey House 1947, p. 267. Hereafter Halsey and Bryan.
Admiral Halsey's Story.

66. Robert Sherrod. *History of Marine Corps Aviation in World War
II*. Washington, D.C.: Combat Forces Press, 1952, pp. 404–405.

67. Kit C. Carter and Robert Mueller. *U.S. Army Air Forces in World
War II Combat Chronology*. Washington, D.C.: Center for Air
Force History, 1991.

68. *The Lucky Bag Yearbook, Class of 1908*, p. 123. http://www
.e-yearbook.com/yearbooks/United_States_Naval_Academy
_Lucky_Bag_Yearbook/1908/Page_123.html. Accessed July 21,
2019.

69. http://www.navweaps.com/Weapons/WNUS_16-50_mk7.php.
Accessed July 22, 2019.

70. Morison. *Victory in the Pacific*, p. 313.

71. Halsey and Bryan. *Admiral Halsey's Story*, pp. 268–269.
72. "Chronological List of Japanese Naval and Merchant Losses." http://www.ibiblio.org/hyperwar/Japan/IJN/JANAC-Losses/index.html. Accessed November 26, 2020.
73. Toland. *The Rising Sun*, p. 1009.
74. Harry S. Truman. *Memoirs: 1945: Year of Decisions*. New York: Doubleday, 1955, p. 11.
75. Donald M. Goldstein and Katherine V. Dillon. *Fading Victory: The Diary of Admiral Matome Ugaki 1941–1945*. Annapolis: Naval Institute Press, 2008, p. 659.
76. Saburo Sakai and Martin Caidin. *Samurai!* New York: Simon & Schuster, 1957, p. 369. Hereafter Sakai and Caidin. *Samurai!*
77. Howard Cha-Eoan. "War of the Worlds." *Time* magazine, June 24, 2001. http://content.time.com/time/magazine/article/0,9171,134519,00.html. Accessed July 16, 2019.
78. Henry Stimson. "Memorandum of conversation with General Marshall, 'Objectives toward Japan and methods of concluding war with minimum casualties.'" Office of Secretary of War, July 1940–September 1945, S-1 records NARA. http://www.nuclearfiles.org/menu/library/correspondence/stimson-henry/corr_stimson_1945-05-29.htm. Accessed June 19, 2019.
79. Walter E. Grunden. "No Retaliation in Kind: Japanese Chemical Warfare Policy." https://link.springer.com/chapter/10.1007/978-3-319-51664-6_14. Accessed June 19, 2019.
80. Richard B. Frank. "Why Truman Dropped the Bomb." *The Weekly Standard*, August 8, 2005.
81. Halsey and Bryan. *Admiral Halsey's Story*, pp. 269–270.
82. Sakai and Caidin. *Samurai!*, pp. 347–348.
83. "World War II Database." https://ww2db.com/person_bio.php?person_id=341. Accessed July 25, 2019.
84. Toland. *The Rising Sun*, p. 1019.
85. Frank. *Downfall*, p. 317.
86. Ibid., p. 302.
87. J.A. Hitchcock. "The B-29 Raid that ended World War II." http://www.jahitchcock.com/mission/b29.htm. Accessed December 18, 2020.
88. "Warning Leaflets." Atomic Heritage Foundation. https://www.atomicheritage.org/key-documents/warning-leaflets. Accessed August 15, 2019.
89. Halsey and Bryan. *Admiral Halsey's Story*, p. 267.

90. Barrett Tillman. *TBF Avenger Units of World War 2*. Oxford, U.K.: Osprey, 1999, p. 26.

91. Carl Dobson et al. *Cleo J. Dobson: U.S. Navy Carrier Pilot of World War II, A Personal Account*. Privately published, 2018, pp. 98–99. Hereafter Dobson et al. *Cleo J. Dobson*.

92. Henry Sakaida. *Imperial Japanese Navy Aces 1937–1945*. U.K.: Osprey, 1998, p. 80. Hereafter Sakaida. *Imperial Japanese Navy*.

93. "The Solomons Campaign: Cactus Air Force and the Bismarck Sea." U.S. Naval Institute Blog, September 23, 2009. Accessed August 10, 2019.

94. Barrett Tillman. *Whirlwind: The Air War Against Japan*. New York: Simon & Schuster, 2010, pp. 187–188.

95. James H. Doolittle and Carroll V. Glines. *I Could Never Be So Lucky Again*. New York: Bantam, 1991, p. 444. Hereafter Doolittle and Glines. *I Could Never Be So Lucky Again*.

96. Lt. Col. Terrence Popravak, Jr. (Ret). "Pacific Northwest Lightning." https://www.142fw.ang.af.mil/News/Features/Display/Article /864363/pacific-northwest-lightning-portlands-p-38-lightning -flying-training-program-of/. Accessed February 21, 2020.

97. Ibid.

98. "56 Years Ago." https://user.xmission.com/~tmathews/b29 /56years/56years-4508a.html. Accessed July 5, 2019.

99. "Explanation of the ASR Points System." *Stars and Stripes*, June 17, 2011.

100. Benjamin Paul Hegi. *From Wright Field, Ohio, to Hokkaido, Japan. General Curtis E. LeMay's Letters to His Wife Helen, 1941–1945*. Denton: University of North Texas Libraries, 2015, pp. 384–385. Hereafter Hegi. *From Wright Field*.

101. Toland. *The Rising Sun*, p. 1031.

102. *Army Air Forces Statistical Digest – World War II*. Washington, D.C.: December 1945.

103. AAF Combat Chronology for August 14–15, 1945.

104. Ralph L. Swann. "A Unit History of the 315th Bomb Wing." Maxwell AFB: Air Command and Staff College, 1986, p. 73. Hereafter Swann. "315th Bomb Wing."

105. Ibid, p. 113.

106. Ibid, p. 113.

107. Barrett Tillman. "The Day the Shooting Stopped." *The Hook World War II Special*, August 1991, p. 100.

CHAPTER 2 *AUGUST STORM*

1. Thomas B. Allen and Norman Polmar. *Code Name Downfall: The Secret Plan to Invade Japan – and Why Truman Dropped the Bomb*. New York: Simon & Schuster, 1995, p. 197. Hereafter Allen and Polmar. *Code Name Downfall*.

2. Bruce Lee. *Marching Orders: The Untold Story of How the American Breaking of the Japanese Secret Codes Led to the Defeat of Nazi Germany and Japan*. New York: Crown Publishers, 1995.

3. For one of the most thorough analyses, see Yale historian Timothy Snyder. *Bloodlands: Europe Between Hitler and Stalin*. New York: Basic Books, 2010.

4. Sergei Radchenko. "Did Hiroshima Save Japan From Soviet Occupation?" *FP News*, August 15, 2015. https://foreignpolicy.com/2015/08/05/stalin_japan_hiroshima_occupation_hokkaido/. Accessed May 2019.

5. Edward Behr. *The Last Emperor*. New York: Bantam Books, 1987, p. 202.

6. *The Annals of the American Academy of Political and Social Science*. Vol. 152, pp. 278–292.

7. Robert L. Bolin, depositor, University of Nebraska-Lincoln. *Handbook on USSR Military Forces, Chapter VII: Logistics*. Washington, D.C.: War Department, 1946, VII-23.

8. Studer: https://www.historynet.com/studebaker-us6-the-lend-lease-deuce-and-a-half.htm. Accessed May 19, 2019.

9. Albert L. Weeks. *Russia's Life-Saver: Lend-Lease Aid to the U.S.S.R. in World War II*. Lanham, Maryland: Lexington Books, 2004, p. 1.

10. Allen and Polmar. *Code Name Downfall*, pp. 263–264.

11. Record of Operations Against Soviet Russia, Eastern Front (August 1945). Military History Section, Headquarters U.S. Army Forces Far East, April 6, 1954 (Based on Japanese Historical Monograph 154), p. 4.

12. Lilita I. Dzirkals. *Lightning War in Manchuria: Soviet Military Analysis of the 1945 Far East Campaign*. Santa Monica: RAND Corporation, 1976. Hereafter Dzirkals. *Lightning War in Manchuria*.

13. Dzirkals. *Lightning War in Manchuria*, pp. 52–56.

14. G.F. Krivosheev, ed. *Soviet Casualties and Combat Losses in the Twentieth Century*. London: Greenhill Books, 1997, pp. 160–161.

15. Dzirkals. *Lightning War in Manchuria*, p. 56.
16. "The Soviet Army Offensive: Manchuria 1945." https://www.globalsecurity.org/military/library/report/1986/RMF.htm. Accessed June 8, 2019.
17. David M. Glantz. *August Storm: The Soviet 1945 Strategic Offensive in Manchuria*. Leavenworth: Combat Studies Institute, February 1983, p. 79. Hereafter Glantz, *August Storm*.
18. Dimitry Loza, *Commanding the Red Army's Sherman Tanks*. University of Nebraska Press, 1996. Hereafter Loza. *Sherman Tanks*.
19. https://en.wikipedia.org/wiki/Hailar_District. Accessed May 4, 2019.
20. Loza. *Sherman Tanks*.
21. Glantz. *August Storm*, p. 81.
22. Mark Ealey. "An August Storm: The Soviet-Japan Endgame in the Pacific War." *The Asia-Pacific Journal*, February 2006. https://apjjf.org/-Mark-Ealey/1988/article.html. Accessed January 19, 2019.
23. "Survivor of Gegenmiao Massacre Continues Telling Tale." *The Mainichi*, August 11, 2017. https://mainichi.jp/english/articles/20170811/p2a/00m/0na/012000c. Accessed January 19, 2019.
24. The Pacific War Online Encyclopedia. "Hutou." https://pwencycl.kgbudge.com/H/u/Hutou.htm. Accessed June 8, 2019. See also Glantz, *August Storm*.
25. Details courtesy of Jon Guttman, August 20, 2020.
26. Details courtesy of George Mellinger, July 26, 2019.
27. Glantz. *August Storm*, p. 106.
28. Dzirkals. *Lightning War in Manchuria*, pp. 97–100.
29. Loza. *Sherman Tanks*.
30. "Russia Invaded Japanese Islands With U.S. Ships." https://warisboring.com/russia-invaded-japanese-islands-with-u-s-ships-after-japan-surrendered/. Accessed November 4, 2020.
31. Glantz, *August Storm*, p. 175.
32. G.F. Krivosheev. *Soviet Casualties and Combat Losses in the Twentieth Century*. London: Greenhill, 1997, pp. 161–163.
33. Saburo Hayashi and Alvin D. Coox. *Kogun: The Japanese Army in the Pacific War*. Virginia: Marine Corps Association, 1959, p. 175.
34. The Pacific War Online Encyclopedia. "Manchuria." http://pwencycl.kgbudge.com/M/a/Manchuria.htm. Accessed March 19, 2019.

35. "The Cold War Comes to Korea." encyclopedia.com. Accessed December 4, 2020.

36. Wyatt Olson. "Who Fired the Final Salvo of World War II?" *Stars and Stripes*, August 30, 2020.

CHAPTER 3 THE DAY THE SHOOTING STOPPED

1. https://www.newspapers.com/clip/55814610/fcc-monitors-radio-broadcast-saying/. Accessed August 14, 2020.

2. "Japan Surrenders, VJ Day August 14, 1945." https://www.youtube.com/watch?v=CZ85j6U2Fvs. Accessed July 20, 2019.

3. Contradictions remain about Davies' given name; he is listed both as James and John in official Air Force documents.

4. "315th Bomb Wing anthologies." https://www.315bw.org/wing5.html. Accessed July 3, 2020.

5. Robert F. Griffin. "One Last Mission." http://www.315bw.org/anthologies.html. Accessed July 3, 2019.

6. Swann. "315th Bomb Wing," p. 116.

7. "315th Bomb Wing anthologies." http://www.315bw.org/anthologies.html. Accessed June 18, 2019.

8. Major General Frank A. Armstrong, Jr., USAF (Ret). Unpublished manuscript, "Wake the Sleeping Giant." East Carolina Manuscript Collection. J.Y. Joyner Library, Greenville, N.C.

9. Harold F. Adkins. "315th Bomb Wing Anthologies." http://www.315bw.org/anthologies.html. Accessed June 18, 2010.

10. Clark G. Reynolds. *The Fast Carriers.* McGraw-Hill, 1968, p. 374.

11. Peter C. Smith. *Task Force 57: The British Pacific Fleet 1944–45.* London: William Kimber, 1969, p. 11.

12. Air Group Six report No. 53, August 15, 1945.

13. VBF-1 report No. 48, August 15, 1945.

14. VBF-6 report No. 103, August 15, 1945.

15. Air Group Six report No. 53, August 15, 1945.

16. Ibid.

17. Ibid.

18. VF-6 report No. 97, August 15, 1945.

19. VBF-6 report No. 105, August 15, 1945.

20. VF-31 action report No. 33, 15 August 1945.

21. Ibid.

22. VF-49 action report No. 68, August 15, 1945.

23. David Brown. *Carrier Operations in World War II. Volume I: The Royal Navy.* Annapolis: Naval Institute Press, 1974; David Brown. *The Seafire.* London: Ian Allan, Ltd., 1973.

24. Halsey and Bryan. *Admiral Halsey's Story,* pp. 270–271.

25. VBF-88 report No. 43, August 15, 1945.

26. "Operation Dumbo." CV-10.com. Accessed April 3, 2021.

27. John Wukovits. *Dogfight Over Tokyo.* New York: Da Capo, 2019, p. 234.

28. Yasuho Izawa and Tony Holmes. *J2M Raiden and N1K1/2 Shiden/Shiden-Kai Aces.* Oxford, U.K.: Osprey, 2016.

29. Roy D. Erickson. *Tail End Charlies: Navy Combat Fighter Pilots at War's End.* Pasadena: privately published, 1995.

30. Barrett Tillman. "The Day the Shooting Stopped." *The Hook,* August 1990.

31. Richard Newhafer. "I'll Remember." *Naval Aviation News,* December 1976.

32. USS *Cavalla* patrol report, September 12, 1945.

33. VBF-85 report No. 73, August 15, 1945.

34. Dobson et al. *Cleo J. Dobson,* pp. 99–100.

35. McPherson email to author, August 1, 2019.

36. DeMott diary, courtesy of USS *Shangri-La* Association.

37. Halsey and Bryan. *Admiral Halsey's Story,* p. 272.

38. USS *Stembel* war diary, August 15, 1945.

39. Halsey and Bryan. *Admiral Halsey's Story,* p. 273.

40. "Antiaircraft Action Summary." https://www.history.navy.mil/research/library/online-reading-room/title-list-alphabetically/a/antiaircraft-action-summary.html. Accessed June 7, 2020.

41. Halsey and Bryan. *Admiral Halsey's Story,* p. 271.

42. Henry Sakaida and Koji Takaki. *Genda's Blade: Japan's 343 Kokutai.* London: Ian Allan, 2003, p. 170. Hereafter Sakaida and Takaki. *Genda's Blade.*

43. "Imperial Rescript on Surrender." Wikipedia. Accessed July 26, 2019.

44. Sakaida and Takaki. *Genda's Blade.*

45. The Pacific War Online Encyclopedia. "Ugaki Matome." https://pwencycl.kgbudge.com/U/g/Ugaki_Matome.htm. Accessed July 26, 2019.

46. "Pacific Wrecks." https://pacificwrecks.com/aircraft/d4y/ugaki.html. Accessed July 26, 2019.

47. Timothy Lang Francis. "To Dispose of the Prisoners: The Japanese Executions of American Aircrew at Fukuoka, Japan, during 1945."

Pacific Historical Review, November 1997. Cited in http:// mansell.com/pow_resources/camplists/fukuoka/fuk_01_fukuoka /fukuoka_01/page06.htm. Accessed July 3, 2019.

48. "Shoham Grammarians: Fred Hockley 1934–1940." http://www .sohamgrammar.org.uk/fred_hockley_inmem.htm.   Accessed January 21, 2020.

49. M.G. Sheftall. *Blossoms in the Wind: Human Legacies of the Kamikaze*. New York: NAL Caliber, 2005, pp. 499–500.

50. "Exchange of messages between General MacArthur and Japanese General Headquarters." http://www.ibiblio.org/pha/policy/1945 /450815b.html. Accessed July 19, 2019.

51. John Dower. *Embracing Defeat: Japan in the Wake of World War II*. New York: Norton, 2000.

52. http://24thida.com/stories/compere_tom_letters/45-08%20OPT .pdf. Accessed June 23, 2020.

53. www.kilroywashere.org/003-Pages/Tillery-Paul/03-Harm-Tillery .html. Accessed June 23, 2020. Cited by permission of Barbara Collins.

54. "Japanese Officer Assists U.S. Marines in Final Days of World War II." https://flyingleathernecks.org/wwii/minoru-wada/; "Japanese Officer Led U.S. Air Strike Against His Own Troops." *Merriam Press*. https://www.merriam-press.com/ww2ejour/articles/iss_001 /is001_01.htm. Both accessed June 23, 2020.

55. Alan Hartmann. "Iwo Looked Beautiful." *Brief* magazine, VJ Issue, p. 6.

56. Cory Graff. *Strike and Return: American Airpower and the Fight for Iwo Jima*. North Branch: Specialty Press, 2006, p. 148. Hereafter Graff. *Strike and Return*.

57. Thomas M. Coffey. *Iron Eagle: The Turbulent Life of General Curtis LeMay*. New York: Random House, 1987, pp. 180–181.

58. Hegi. *From Wright Field*, pp. 385–386.

59. Stevens interview with author, 1983.

60. Paul Fussell. "Thank God for the Atom Bomb." *The New Republic*, August 1981.

61. "In Their Own Words." Veterans History Project. Accessed December 5, 2020.

62. "Victory Celebrations." State Library of Victoria. http://ergo .slv.vic.gov.au/explore-history/australia-wwii/home-wii/victory -celebrations. Accessed November 30, 2020.

63. "VP Day Jumper." Australian War Memorial. https://www.awm .gov.au/collection/C296674. Accessed November 30, 2020.

64. "VE and VJ Days." New Zealand History. https://www.sfgate
    .com/bayarea/article/Peace-Riots-left-trail-of-death-at-end-of
    -6445437.php. Accessed November 30, 2020.

65. https://www.aviationarchaeology.com/src/AFmacrMO.htm.
    Accessed December 7, 2020.

66. "Victory Reports Around the World." *Life.* August 20, 1945.

67. "Lady in the Dark – Last Kill." http://www.military.cz/usa/air/
    war/fighter/p61/p61_docum.htm. Accessed July 5, 2019.

68. *The Essex Buccaneer,* August–September 1945, courtesy Mark
    Herber.

CHAPTER 4 AROUND THE WORLD

1. Lawrence Verria and George Galdorisi. "The Story Behind the
   Famous Kiss." https://www.usni.org/magazines/naval-history
   -magazine/2012/july/story-behind-famous-kiss. Accessed July 20,
   2019.

2. "Interview with Greta Zimmer Friedman." Veterans History Project.
   http://memory.loc.gov/diglib/vhp/story/loc.natlib.afc2001001
   .42863/transcript?ID=sr0001. Accessed July 20, 2019.

3. "Truman announces Japanese surrender." https://www.c-span
   .org/video/?c4548205/truman-announces-japanese-surrender.
   Accessed July 14, 2019.

4. *Yank,* September 7, 1945.

5. Gary Kamiya. "SF Whitewash covered up 'peace riots' at end of WW
   II." https://www.sfgate.com/bayarea/article/S-F-whitewash-covered
   -up-peace-riots-at-6458585.php. Accessed December 5, 2020.

6. "POW and Civilian Camps Throughout Japanese Empire." www
   .mansell.com/pow-index.html. Accessed May 30, 2020.

7. Some war criminals could not be indicted for specific offenses
   because Western military law provided no penalty for cannibalism.
   https://historycollection.co/20-horrific-details-about-japanese-
   pow-camps-during-world-war-ii/16/. Accessed May 30, 2020.

8. "American POWs Still Waiting for an Apology 70 Years Later."
   Time, September 14, 2014. https://time.com/3334677/pow-world
   -war-two-usa-japan/. Accessed June 24, 2020.

9. For a detailed examination of *Bushido*'s evolution, see Damian
   Flanagan's three-part series in *The Japan Times.* https://www
   .japantimes.co.jp/culture/2016/07/23/books/bushido-samurai
   -code-goes-war/. Accessed June 24, 2020.

10. Linda Goetz Holmes. *Unjust Enrichment: How Japan's Companies Built Postwar Fortunes Using American POWs*. Mechanicsburg: Stackpole Books, 2001, p. xiv.

11. Ibid., pp. 121–122.

12. Oregon National Guard Museum history panel, 1978.

13. Lester I. Tenney. *My Hitch in Hell: The Bataan Death March*. Washington, D.C.: Brassey's, 1995, p. 141. *LA Times* obituary: https://www.latimes.com/local/obituaries/la-me-lester-tenney -20170227-story.html. Accessed June 24, 2020.

14. George MacDonell. "On this day in 1945, Japan released me from a POW Camp. Then U.S. Pilots saved my life." *Quillette*, August 15, 2020. https://quillette.com/2020/08/15/on-this-day-in-1945 -japan-released-me-from-a-pow-camp-then-us-pilots-saved-my -life/. Accessed September 9, 2020.

15. Ibid.

16. "Light and Darkness." Material derived from internee correspondence and U.S. State Department records. https://www.foitimes.com/ internment/compare.htm. Accessed October 22, 2020.

17. "Mary Previte's Speech at the Sixtieth Anniversary Celebration." https://web.archive.org/web/20070810174750/http://beijing.usem bassy-china.org.cn/081705e.html. Accessed October 22, 2020.

18. John Dower. *War Without Mercy: Race and Power in the Pacific War*. New York: Pantheon, 1986. Hereafter Dower. *War Without Mercy*.

19. Indonesia: WWII and the Struggle for Independence 1942–50. Library of Congress, 1992.

20. Elizabeth Van Kampen. "Memories of the Dutch East Indies." *The Asia-Pacific Journal*. January 2009. https://apjjf.org/-Elizabeth -Van-Kampen/3002/article.html. Accessed May 31, 2020.

21. *UK Forces War Records*. "Prisoners of War of the Japanese 1939– 1945." https://www.forces-war-records.co.uk/prisoners-of-war -of-the-japanese-1939-1945. Accessed June 26, 2020.

22. "Air Drops to Newly Liberated POWs and Liberation Procedures." http://www.atomicarchive.com/Docs/MED/med_chp10.shtml. Accessed May 30, 2020.

23. Dwight R. Rider. *Hog Wild, 1945*. Morgan Hill: Bookstand Publishing, 2012, pp. 200–202.

24. "Nuclearfiles.org." http://www.nuclearfiles.org/menu/library /correspondence/cavert-samuel/corr_cavert_1945-08-09.htm. Accessed July 26, 2019.

25. *Stars and Stripes,* August 5, 2015. "When the President said yes to the bomb." https://www.stripes.com/news/special-reports/world-war-ii-the-final-chapter/wwii-victory-in-japan/when-the-president-said-yes-to-the-bomb-truman-s-diaries-reveal-no-hesitation-some-regret-1.360308. Accessed July 26, 2019.

26. https://news.gallup.com/vault/191897/gallup-vault-americans-mindset-hiroshima.aspx. Accessed May 17, 2020.

27. James Kunetka. *The General and the Genius: Groves and Oppenheimer, the Unlikely Partnership that Built the Atom Bomb.* Washington, D.C.: Regnery History, 2015, p. 369–370.

28. Jennet Conant. *109 East Palace: Robert Oppenheimer and the Secret City of Los Alamos.* New York: Simon & Schuster, 2005, p. 329.

CHAPTER 5 UNEASY PEACE

1. Halsey and Bryan. *Admiral Halsey's Story,* p. 267.

2. Stephen Harding. "The Last to Die." *Air & Space Magazine,* November 2008. Hereafter Harding. "The Last to Die."

3. Henry Sakaida. *Winged Samurai: Saburo Sakai and the Zero Fighter Aces.* Mesa: Champlin Museum Press, 1985, p. 134.

4. Swann. "315th Bomb Wing."

5. Harding. "The Last to Die."

6. Ibid.

7. Sakaida. *Imperial Japanese Navy,* p. 80.

8. https://pacificwrecks.com/aircraft/b-32/42-108544.html. Accessed October 18, 2020.

9. "B-32-20-CF Hobo Queen II." Pacific Wrecks. https://pacificwrecks.com/aircraft/b-32/42-108532.html. Accessed October 18, 2020.

10. William Manchester. *American Caesar: Douglas MacArthur 1880–1964.* New York: Little, Brown Co., 1978, p. 441. Hereafter Manchester. *American Caesar.*

11. Jay Stout. *Air Apaches: The True Story of the 345th Bomb Group and its Low, Fast and Deadly Missions in World War II.* New York: Stackpole, 2019, p. 341. Hereafter Stout. *Air Apaches.*

12. "The 345th's Final Show." https://airwarworldwar2.wordpress.com/2015/08/19/the-345ths-final-show/. Accessed July 27, 2019.

13. Manchester. *American Caesar,* p. 442.

14. "Prelude to Occupation." *Yank,* September 28, 1945, p. 4.

15. Stout. *Air Apaches*, pp. 342–343.

16. https://airwarworldwar2.wordpress.com/2015/08/19/the-345ths -final-show/. Accessed July 27, 2019.

17. Samuel Eliot Morison. *History of U.S. Naval Operations in World War II. Volume XIII: Liberation of the Philippines 1944–1945.* New York: Little, Brown, 1959, pp. 300–301. Hereafter Morison. *History of U.S. Naval Operations in World War II.* Other accounts of the incident vary in details. See Chris Knupp. "The Last Naval Battle of World War 2." Navy General Board. https://media.defense .gov/2017/Mar/31/2001724974/-1/-1/0/B_0096_RODMAN_ WAR_OF_THEIR_OWN.PDF?fbclid=IwARojoNR-JOOgoKo M7ANgH5JPxWixlACCWv3_HDTLb2jXttibJNfwlhKYKno. Accessed July 29, 2020. Swentzel's Navy Cross citation: https:// valor.militarytimes.com/hero/21002. Accessed July 29, 2020.

18. James J. Fahey. *Pacific War Diary 1942–1945: The Secret Diary of an American Sailor.* Boston: Houghton Mifflin Company, 1963.

19. *Wasp* CV-18 war diary, August 1945.

20. Halsey and Bryan. *Admiral Halsey's Story*, p. 277.

21. Correspondence with Captain Seth Searcy and Vice Admiral Malcolm Cagle, 1977.

22. Graff. *Strike and Return*, p. 149.

23. Email to author, August 1, 2019.

24. Morison. *History of U.S. Naval Operations in World War II*, p. 362.

25. "U.S. Technical Mission to Japan. Target Report: Japanese Mines." January 11, 1946.

26. "Japan Mines." NavWeps. http://www.navweaps.com/Weapons/ WAMJAP_Mines.php. Accessed October 22, 2020.

27. "Oral history of James Leland Jackson." *Digital Library of Georgia.* https://dlg.usg.edu/record/geh_vhpohr_223. Accessed October 24, 2020.

28. Commander Mine Squadron 104 report, September 6, 1945.

29. Linda Miller and Cora Holt. *Window to the Future: Air Force Communications Command 1938–1988.* AFCC, Scott AFB, Illinois, 1988, pp. 32–33. http://www.afcommatc.org/uploads/3/4 /3/0/34302180/afchrono_1938-1988_windowtofuture_sm.pdf. Accessed November 1, 2020.

30. https://www.asisbiz.com/Il2/USAAF-History-WWII-1945.html. Accessed February 28, 2020.

31. "Prelude to Occupation." *Reports of General MacArthur.* Library of Congress, 1994. https://history.army.mil/books/wwii

/MacArthur%20Reports/MacArthur%20V1%20Sup/ch1.htm. Accessed March 4, 2020.

32. Henry I. Shaw, Jr. *The United States Marines in the Occupation of Japan*. Washington, D.C.: 1969. http://www.ibiblio.org/hyperwar /USMC/HRP-Occupation/index.html. Accessed June 15, 2020.

33. "Memorandum for members of the Third Fleet Landing Force." http://web.archive.org/web/20091027084106/http://www .geocities.com/bb01usa/otherpics/landingmemo.jpg.   Accessed December 4, 2020.

34. "Securing   the   Surrender."   http://www.npshistory.com/ publications/wapa/npswapa/extContent/usmc/pcn-190-003143 -00/sec1.htm. Accessed December 5, 2020.

35. "Pacific   Wrecks: Rekata   Bay."   https://pacificwrecks.com/ provinces/solomons_rekata.html. Accessed November 3, 2020.

36. https://www.navycs.com/charts/1942-military-pay-chart.html. Accessed August 6, 2020.

37. Hegi. *From Wright Field*, p. 392.

38. Harry S. Truman. *Memoirs: 1945, Year of Decisions*. New York: Signet Books, 1965, p. 497. Hereafter Truman. *Memoirs*.

39. Paul Stillwell. "The Battleship Missouri and the Trumans." Naval Institute *Proceedings*, September 2010.

40. Truman. *Memoirs*, p. 498. https://archive.org/stream/yearofdecis ionsvo30151mbp/yearofdecisionsvo30151mbp_djvu.txt. Accessed August 15, 2019.

41. http://11thairborne.com/index.html. Accessed December 1, 2020.

42. Richard B. Frank. *MacArthur*. Palgrave's Great Generals Series. New York: St. Martin's Press, 2007, p. 121.

43. H.W. Brands. *The General vs the President: MacArthur and Truman at the Brink of Nuclear War*. New York: Anchor Books, 2017, p. 11.

44. Thomas O'Toole. "Mountbatten Predicted Pearl Harbor." *The Washington Post*. Accessed August 15, 2019.

45. Barbara Tuchman. *Stilwell and the American Experience in China: 1911–1945*. New York: Random House, 1970, p. 62.

46. "Mao Zedong," *Encyclopedia Britannica*. https://www.britannica .com/biography/Mao-Zedong. Accessed July 24, 2020.

47. Richard B. Frank to author, citing Rana Miller fatalities, August 24, 2020.

48. Meirion Harries. *Soldiers of the Sun: Rise and Fall of the Imperial Japanese Army*. New York: Random House, 1994, p. 235.

49. https://history.army.mil/books/wwii/MacArthur%20Reports/
MacArthur%20V1/ch14.htm. Accessed December 2, 2020.

CHAPTER 6 TOKYO BAY

1. Charles R. Smith. "Securing the Surrender." Marine in World War
II Commemorative Series. https://www.nps.gov/parkhistory/
online_books/npswapa/extContent/usmc/pcn-190-003143-00/
sec1b.htm. Accessed December 5, 2020.

2. United States Naval Academy Lucky Bag of 1920, p. 206. Accessed
January 26, 2020.

3. "Reminiscences of the Surrender of Japan and the End of World
War II." Admiral Stuart S. Murray, U.S. Navy (Ret). Battleship
Missouri Memorial. https://ussmissouri.org/learn-the-history/
surrender/admiral-murrays-account. Accessed January 29, 2020.

4. Ibid.

5. Ibid.

6. Doolittle and Glines. *I Could Never Be So Lucky Again*, p. 424.

7. Halsey and Bryan. *Admiral Halsey's Story*, p. 282.

8. Michael Kelly. "He was 40 Feet from General MacArthur." *Omaha
World-Herald*, September 2, 2015.

9. "The Man Who Signed on the Wrong Line." Acres of Snow.
https://acresofsnow.ca/the-man-who-signed-on-the-wrong-line/.
Accessed December 8, 2020.

10. Cory Graff. "Final Mission: Staging Japan's Surrender." *Air & Space*,
September 2020. https://www.airspacemag.com/airspacemag/
surrender-spectacle-180975607/. Accessed September 5, 2020.

11. Cagle letter to author, May 1977.

12. Wood letter to author, March 1977.

13. Teddy Key. *The Friendly Squadron: No. 1772 Squadron 1944–45*.
https://www.faaa.org.uk/resources/Sammy_Samuelson.pdf.
Accessed August 10, 2020.

14. "History of Bomber-Fighting Squadron 85." http://vbf-85
.com/History%20of%20Bomber%20Fighting%20Squadron
%20Eighty%20Five.pdf. Accessed January 3, 2021.

15. Barrett Tillman. "Colonel Robert L. Scott: God's Pilot." *Aviation
History*, September 2018. https://www.historynet.com/col-robert
-l-scott-gods-pilot.htm.

16. Naval Aviation Combat Statistics – World War II. Washington,
D.C.: December 1945, p. 35.

17. Scott letter to Boy Scout Troop 23 in Macon, Georgia. Courtesy of Marilynn Pantera, May 2020.

18. Robert L. Scott. *Boring a Hole in the Sky*. New York: Random House, 1961, p. 210.

19. "History Matters." Proclamation of Independence of the Democratic Republic of Vietnam. http://historymatters.gmu.edu /d/5139/. Accessed July 16, 2019.

20. Email to author, August 1, 2019.

21. Author's mother, 1975.

22. "British Occupation Forces Japan 1945." Youtube video. https:// www.youtube.com/watch?v=nqz0Wo1yOVQ. Accessed April 6, 2020.

23. Ibid.

24. Michael Bak, Jr. "As I Recall." *Naval History*, August 2020, p. 3.

25. Daniel V. Gallery. *Eight Bells*. New York: Warner Paperback, 1968, p. 195.

26. R. Alton Lee. "The Army 'Mutiny' of 1946." *The Journal of American History*, Vol. 53, No. 3 (December 1966), p. 557. Hereafter Lee. "The Army 'Mutiny.'"

27. Sam Perkins. "Why WWII Soldiers Mutinied After VJ-Day." history.com. Accessed November 5, 2020.

28. Lee. "The Army 'Mutiny,'" p. 557.

29. "Home Alive by '45: Operation Magic Carpet." National WWII Museum, October 2, 2020. https://www.nationalww2museum.org /war/articles/operation-magic-carpet-1945. Accessed December 16, 2020.

30. Robert R. Powell with Urban L. Drew, *Ben Drew, The Katzenjammer Ace*. iUniverse, 2001.

31. "Oral history of James Leland Jackson." Digital Library of Georgia. https://dlg.usg.edu/record/geh_vhpohr_223. Accessed October 24, 2020.

32. *Essex Buccaneer*, August–September 1945.

33. "The Real Japanese Surrender." *The Sunday Times*, September 4, 2005. https://wayback.archive-it.org/all/20080119210334/http:/ /staff.science.nus.edu.sg/~sivasothi/blog/pdf/jap_surrender-sto 4sep2005.pdf. Accessed April 3, 2021.

34. Nikola Budanovic, "Legendary Japanese Holdout." https://www .thevintagenews.com/2018/03/23/hiroo-onoda/. Accessed April 3, 2021.

CHAPTER 7 DOWNSTREAM FROM VJ DAY

1. "Debate on the address." House of Commons debate, August 16, 1945, vol. 413. https://api.parliament.uk/historic-hansard /commons/1945/aug/16/debate-on-the-address#column_84. Accessed February 6, 2020.
2. E.B. Potter. *Nimitz*. Annapolis: Naval Institute Press, 1976, pp. 422–423.
3. John Wukovits. *Dogfight Over Tokyo*. New York: Da Capo, 2019, p. 234.
4. Richard B. Frank. "Why Truman Dropped the Bomb." *Washington Examiner*, August 8, 2005. https://www.washingtonexaminer.com /weekly-standard/why-truman-dropped-the-bomb.   Hereafter Frank. "Why Truman Dropped the Bomb."
5. Max Hastings. *Retribution: The Battle for Japan, 1944–45*. New York: Knopf, 2008, p. 513.
6. Frank. "Why Truman Dropped the Bomb."
7. Richard A. Russell. *Project Hula: Secret Soviet-American Cooperation in the War Against Japan*. "The U.S. Navy in the Modern World Series." Washington, D.C.: Naval Historical Center, 1997.
8. Norman Polmar and Thomas B. Allen. "Invasion Most Costly." *Naval Institute Proceedings*, August 1995.
9. Michael Chimaobi Kalu. "Purple Heart Stockpile." *War History Online*.   https://www.warhistoryonline.com/instant-articles/ purple-heart-stockpile-wwii-medal.html. Accessed February 8, 2020.
10. Dower. *War Without Mercy*, p. 447.
11. "Historical Notes, Giving Them More Hell." *Time* magazine, December 3, 1973.
12. "U.S. Navy Active Ship Force Levels 1945–1950." https://www .history.navy.mil/research/histories/ship-histories/us-ship-force -levels.html. Accessed August 17, 2019.
13. "Clement Attlee's Noble Tribute to Winston Churchill." https:// richardlangworth.com/clement-attlee-tribute-winston-churchill. Accessed September 1, 2019.
14. Oleg V. Khlevniuk. *Stalin: New Biography of a Dictator*. London: Yale University Press, 2019, p. 268.
15. Ibid., p. 297.
16. Jeremy Friedman. "The Ambiguity of Stalin." The Imaginative Conservative.   https://theimaginativeconservative.org/2019/04/

ambiguity-stalin-jeremy-friedman-kotkin-khlevniuk-rubenstein
.html. Accessed August 20, 2019.

17. "Mao – Greatest Mass Murderer in History?" https://www
.globalsecurity.org/military/world/china/mao-murder.htm. "The
Deadliest Dictators in History." https://www.worldatlas.com
/articles/the-deadliest-dictator-regimes-in-history.html.   Both
accessed July 24, 2020.

18. https://en.wikipedia.org/wiki/Ho_Chi_Minh#Becoming_
president_and_Vietnam_War. Accessed July 24, 2020.

19. Vietnam Studies Group, November 2017.

20. Barrett Tillman. "The Best Deal: The Navy's Victory Squadron."
The Hook, Winter 1987, pp. 34–41.

21. https://www.irs.gov/pub/irs-soi/16-05intax.pdf.   Accessed
December 6, 2020.

22. https://www.desert.com/1992/1/22/18963518/u-s-housing-starts
-plummet-to-lowest-level-since-1945-br. Accessed December 6,
2020.

23. Robert D. Heinl, USMC (Ret). "The Inchon Landing: A Case
Study in Amphibious Planning." *Naval War College Review,*
Spring 1998.

24. "The Last Days of World War II." *Deseret News,* August 13, 1993.
https://www.deseretnews.com/article/304855/THE-LAST-DAYS
-OF-WORLD-WAR-II.html. Accessed January 26, 2020.

25. Foss interviews with author 1990 and 2001.

Bibliography

OFFICIAL SOURCES

Carrier Air Group 1
Carrier Air Group 6
Light Carrier Air Group 31
Light Carrier Air Group 49
Carrier Air Group 85
Carrier Air Group 88
USS *Belleau Wood* (CVL-24)
USS *Benner* (DD-807)
USS *Bennington* (CV-20)
USS *Borie* (DD-704)
USS *Cavalla* (SS-244)
USS *Hancock* (CV-19)
USS *Jallao* (SS-368)
USS *San Jacinto* (CVL-30)
USS *Shangri-La* (CV-38)
USS *Yorktown* (CV-10)
Mine Squadron 104

Air Branch, Office of Naval Intelligence. *Naval Aviation Combat Statistics – World War II*. Washington, D.C.: Navy Department, June 1946.
Carter, Kit C., and Robert Mueller. *U.S. Army Air Forces in World War II: Combat Chronology 1941–1945*. Washington, D.C.: Center for Air Force History, 1991.

Craven, Wesley Frank, and James Lea Cate. *The Army Air Forces in World War II. Volume Five. The Pacific: Matterhorn to Nagasaki, June 1944 to August 1945*. Washington, D.C.: Office of Air Force History, 1983.

Cressman, Robert J. *The Official Chronology of the U.S. Navy in World War II*. Washington, D.C.: Naval Historical Center, 1999.

Hansell, Haywood S. *The Strategic Air War Against Germany and Japan: A Memoir*. Washington, D.C.: Office of Air Force History, 1986.

Jones, Vincent C. *The United States Army in World War 2, Special Studies. Manhattan: The Army and the Atomic Bomb*. Washington, D.C.: Center of Military History, 1985.

Russell, Richard A. *Project Hula: Secret Soviet-American Cooperation in the War Against Japan*. Washington, D.C.: Naval Historical Center, 1997.

Swann, Ralph L. "A Unit History of the 315th Bomb Wing." Maxwell AFB: Air Command and Staff College, 1986.

Yank, the Army Weekly. Alaska Edition. September 28, 1945. http://www.indianamilitary.org/YANK/1945-09-28%20Yank%20Magazine.pdf

ARTICLES AND PAPERS

Armstrong, Frank A., Lieutenant General. "Wake the Sleeping Giant." Unpublished manuscript held by the East Carolina Manuscript Collection, Joyner Library, Greenville, N.C.

Bradbury, Ellen, and Sandra Blakeslee. "The Harrowing Story of the Nagasaki Bombing Mission." *Bulletin of Atomic Scientists*, August 4, 2015.

Correll, John T. "The Invasion That Didn't Happen." *Air Force*, June 2009.

DeMott, Richard, diary. Courtesy of USS *Shangri-La* (CV-38) Association.

Ealey, Mark. "An August Storm: The Soviet-Japan Endgame in the Pacific War." *The Asia-Pacific Journal*, February 2006. Retrieved January 19, 2019. https://apjjf.org/-Mark-Ealey/1988/article.html

Fussell, Paul. "Thank God for the Atom Bomb." *The New Republic*, August 1981. https://www.uio.no/studier/emner/hf/iakh/

HIS1300MET/v12/undervisningsmateriale/Fussel%20-%20thank
%20god%20for%20the%20atom%20bomb.pdf

GlobalSecurity.org. "The Soviet Army Offensive: Manchuria 1945." 1986.
https://www.globalsecurity.org/military/library/report/1986/RMF.htm

Graff, Corey. "Final Mission: Staging Japan's Surrender." *Air & Space*,
September 2020.

Griffin, Robert F. "One Last Mission." in Larry Miller (ed.) 315th
Bomb Wing Anthologies. http://www.315bw.org/anthologies.html

Grunden, Walter E. "No Retaliation in Kind: Japanese Chemical
Warfare Policy." https://link.springer.com/chapter/10.1007/978-3
-319-51664-6_14

Harding, Stephen. "The Last to Die." *Air & Space Magazine*,
November 2008.

Newhafer, Richard L. "I'll Remember." *Naval Aviation News*,
December 1976.

Stillwell, Paul. "The Battleship Missouri and the Trumans." Naval
Institute *Proceedings*, September 2010.

Thompson, Warren E. "Bite of the Black Widow." History Net.
https://www.historynet.com/bite-of-the-black-widow-northrops-p
-61-night-fighter.htm

Tillman, Barrett. "The Day the Shooting Stopped." *The Hook, World
War II Special*, August 1990.

Verria, Lawrence and George Galdorisi. "The Story Behind the
Famous Kiss." https://www.usni.org/magazines/naval-history
-magazine/2012/july/story-behind-famous-kiss

BOOKS

Allen, Thomas B., and Norman Polmar. *Code Name Downfall: The
Secret Plan to Invade Japan – and Why Truman Dropped the Bomb*.
New York: Simon & Schuster, 1995.

Behr, Edward. *The Last Emperor*. New York: Bantam Books, 1987.

Blair, Clay. *Silent Victory: The U.S. Submarine War Against Japan*.
Volume 2. New York: J.B. Lippincott Company, 1975.

Bolin, Robert L., depositor, University of Nebraska-Lincoln. War
Department, Washington, D.C.: 1946. *Handbook on USSR Military
Forces, Chapter VII: Logistics*. VII-23. http://digitalcommons.unl
.edu/cgi/viewcontent.cgi?article=1027&context=dodmilintel

Brown, David. *Carrier Operations in World War II. Volume I: The Royal Navy*. Annapolis: Naval Institute Press, 1974.

Brown, David. *The Seafire*. London: Ian Allan, Ltd. 1973.

Coffey, Thomas M. *Iron Eagle: The Turbulent Life of General Curtis LeMay*. New York: Crown, 1986.

Conant, Jennet. *109 East Palace: Robert Oppenheimer and the Secret City of Los Alamos*. New York: Simon & Schuster, 2005.

Cressey, George B. "The Geographic Regions of China." *The Annals of the American Academy of Political and Social Science*. Vol. 152, November 1930.

Dobson, Carl, with Dorothy Dobson Zoellner and Nancy D. Napier. *Cleo J. Dobson: U.S. Navy Carrier Pilot of World War II, a Personal Account*. Privately published, 2018.

Doolittle, James H., and Carroll V. Glines. *I Could Never Be So Lucky Again*. New York: Bantam, 1991.

Dower, John W. *War Without Mercy: Race and Power in the Pacific War*. New York: Pantheon, 1986.

Dower, John W. *Embracing Defeat: Japan in the Wake of World War II*. New York: Norton, 2000.

Dzirkals, Lilita I. *Lightning War in Manchuria: Soviet Military Analysis of the 1945 Far East Campaign*. Santa Monica: RAND Corporation, 1976.

Erickson, Roy D. *Tail End Charlies: Navy Combat Fighter Pilots at War's End*. Pasadena: privately published, 1995.

Fahey, James J. *Pacific War Diary 1942–1945: The Secret Diary of an American Sailor*. Boston: Houghton Mifflin Company, 1963.

Fleming, Thomas. *The New Dealers' War. F.D.R. and the War Within World War II*. New York: Basic Books, 2001.

Francillon, René. *Japanese Aircraft of the Pacific War*. London, U.K.: Putnam, 1970.

Frank, Richard B. *Downfall: The End of the Imperial Japanese Empire*. New York: Penguin Books, 1999.

Frank, Richard B. *MacArthur. Palgrave's Great Generals Series*. New York: St. Martin's Press, 2007.

Gallery, Daniel V. *Eight Bells*. New York: Warner Paperback, 1968.

Gardiner, Juliet. *Wartime: Britain 1939–1945*. London: Headline Publishing, 2005.

Glantz, David M. *August Storm: The Soviet 1945 Strategic Offensive in Manchuria*. Leavenworth: Combat Studies Institute, February 1983.

Glantz, David M. *The Soviet Strategic Offensive in Manchuria*. London: Frank Cass, 2001.

Goldstein, Donald M., and Katherine V. Dillon. *Fading Victory: The Diary of Admiral Matome Ugaki 1941–1945*. Annapolis: Naval Institute Press, 2008.

Graff, Cory. *Strike and Return: American Airpower and the Fight for Iwo Jima*. North Branch: Specialty Press, 2006.

Halsey, William F., with J. Bryan, III. *Admiral Halsey's Story*. New York: Whittlesey House, 1947.

Harding, Stephen. *Last to Die: A Defeated Empire, a Forgotten Mission, and the Last American Killed in World War II*. New York: Da Capo Press, 2015.

Harries, Meirion. *Soldiers of the Sun: Rise and Fall of the Imperial Japanese Army*. New York: Random House, 1994.

Hastings, Max. *Retribution: The Battle for Japan, 1944–45*. New York: Knopf, 2008.

Hata, Ikuhiko, Yasuho Izawa and Christopher Shores. *Japanese Naval Air Force Fighter Units and Their Aces 1932–1945*. London: Grub Street, 2011.

Hayashi, Saburo, and Alvin D. Coox. *Kogun: The Japanese Army in the Pacific War*. Virginia: Marine Corps Association, 1959.

Hegi, Benjamin Paul. *From Wright Field, Ohio, to Hokkaido, Japan. General Curtis E. LeMay's Letters to His Wife Helen, 1941–1945*. Denton: University of North Texas Libraries, 2015.

Inoguchi, Rikihei, with Tadashi Nakajima and Roger Pineau. *The Divine Wind: Japan's Suicide Squadrons in WWII*. New York: Ballantine Books, 1968.

Izawa, Yasuho, and Tony Holmes. *J2M Raiden and N1K1/2 Shiden/Shiden-Kai Aces*. Oxford, U.K.: Osprey, 2016.

Krivosheev, G.F. (editor). *Soviet Casualties and Combat Losses in the Twentieth Century*. London: Greenhill, 1997.

Kunetka, James. *The General and the Genius: Groves and Oppenheimer, the Unlikely Partnership that Built the Atom Bomb*. Washington, D.C.: Regnery History, 2015.

Loza, Dimitry (James F. Gebhardt, editor). *Commanding the Red Army's Sherman Tanks*. University of Nebraska Press, 1996.

Manchester, William. *American Caesar: Douglas MacArthur 1880–1964*. New York: Little, Brown Co., 1978.

McCullough, David. *Truman*. New York: Simon & Schuster, 1992.

Morison, Samuel Eliot. *History of United States Naval Operations in World War II. Volume XIV: Victory in the Pacific.* Edison: Castle Books, 2001.

Olynyk, Frank. *USAAF (Pacific Theater) Credits for Destruction of Enemy Aircraft in Air-to-Air Combat.* Privately published, 1985.

Olynyk, Frank. *USN Credits for Destruction of Enemy Aircraft in Air-to-Air Combat.* Privately published, 1982.

Overy, Richard. *Why the Allies Won.* New York: Norton, 1996.

Parillo, Mark. *The Japanese Merchant Marine in World War II.* Annapolis: Naval Institute Press, 1993.

Potter, E.B. *Nimitz.* Annapolis: Naval Institute Press, 1976.

Reynolds, Clark G. *The Fast Carriers: The Forging of an Air Navy.* New York: McGraw-Hill, 1968.

Rider, Dwight R. *Hog Wild, 1945.* Morgan Hill: Bookstand Publishing, 2012.

Sakaida, Henry, and Koji Takaki. *Genda's Blade: Japan's 343 Kokutai.* London, U.K.: Ian Allan Publishing, 2003.

Sakaida, Henry. *Imperial Japanese Navy Aces 1937–45.* Oxford, U.K.: Osprey, 1998.

Sakaida, Henry. *Winged Samurai: Saburo Sakai and the Zero Fighter Aces.* Mesa: Champlin Fighter Museum Press, 1985.

Scott, Robert L. *Boring a Hole in the Sky.* New York: Random House, 1961.

Sheftall, M.G. *Blossoms in the Wind: Human Legacies of the Kamikaze.* New York: NAL Caliber, 2005.

Sherrod, Robert. *History of Marine Corps Aviation in World War II.* Washington, D.C.: Combat Forces Press, 1952.

Smith, Peter C. *Task Force 57: The British Pacific Fleet, 1944–45.* Manchester, U.K.: Crecy Publishing, 1969.

Tagaya, Osamu. *Mitsubishi Type 1 Rikko "Betty" Units of World War 2.* Oxford, U.K.: Osprey, 2001.

Tenney, Lester I. *My Hitch in Hell: The Bataan Death March.* Washington, D.C.: Brassey's, 1995.

Tillman, Barrett. *Corsair: The F4U in World War II and Korea.* Annapolis: Naval Institute Press, 1979.

Tillman, Barrett. *Hellcat: The F6F in World War II.* Annapolis: Naval Institute Press, 1979.

Tillman, Barrett. *TBF Avenger Units of World War 2.* Oxford, U.K.: Osprey, 1999.

Tillman, Barrett. *Whirlwind: The Air War Against Japan*. New York: Simon & Schuster, 2010.

Toland, John. *The Rising Sun: The Decline and Fall of the Japanese Empire, 1936–1945, Volume 2*. New York: Random House, 1970.

Truman, Harry S. *Memoirs: 1945: Year of Decisions*. New York: Signet Books, 1965.

Tuchman, Barbara. *Stilwell and the American Experience in China: 1911–1945*. New York: Random House, 1970.

U.S. Army. *Record of Operations Against Soviet Russia, Eastern Front (August 1945)*. Historical Monograph 154, Military History Section, Headquarters U.S. Army Forces Far East, April 6, 1954.

Weeks, Albert L. *Russia's Life-Saver: Lend-Lease Aid to the U.S.S.R. in World War II*. Lanham, Maryland: Lexington Books, 2004.

Wukovits, John. *Dogfight Over Tokyo: The Final Air Battle of the Pacific and the Last Four Men to Die in World War II*. New York: Da Capo Press, 2019.

Index